THE DEVIL'S
OWN LUCK

THE DEVIL'S OWN LUCK

From Pegasus Bridge to The Baltic

by

DENIS EDWARDS

Pen & Sword
MILITARY

First published in Great Britain in 1999
and reprinted in this format in 2001, 2009, 2016 and 2021 by
PEN & SWORD MILITARY
An imprint of
Pen & Sword Books Ltd
47 Church Street
Barnsley, South Yorkshire
S70 2AS

ISBN 978 0 85052 869 5

A CIP catalogue record for this book is
available from the British Library

Typeset in 11/13 pt Sabon by
Phoenix Typesetting, Auldgirth, Dumfriesshire

Printed and bound in the UK on FSC accredited paper by 4edge Ltd, Essex,
SS5 4AD

Pen & Sword Books Ltd incorporates the Imprints of Aviation, Atlas,
Family History, Fiction, Maritime, Military, Discovery, Politics, History,
Archaeology, Select, Wharncliffe Local History, Wharncliffe True Crime,
Military Classics, Wharncliffe Transport, Leo Cooper, The Praetorian
Press, Remember When, Seaforth Publishing and Frontline Publishing.

For a complete list of Pen & Sword titles please contact
PEN & SWORD BOOKS LIMITED
47 Church Street, Barnsley, South Yorkshire, S70 2AS, England
E-mail: enquiries@pen-and-sword.co.uk
Website: www.pen-and-sword.co.uk

CONTENTS

ACKNOWLEDGEMENTS

My 'Normandy Diary' was crudely written in September, 1944, immediately after we returned to England and were sent home for a not over-generous spell of much-needed Leave.

After numerous re-types, enough Publishers Rejections to paper a fair-sized room and more than 50 years without success I gave up the idea of ever seeing my story in print, but so many people asked to borrow the few copies of my manuscript that I produced an A4-size 50-page edited version which my colleagues and I were able to sell to visitors to our local D-Day Aviation Museum at Shoreham-by-Sea municipal airport as fast as I could run them up. We sold to visitors from almost every part of the world and many wrote later expressing surprise that my story had never been published! One such purchaser was Sid Green, a successful businessman living in semi-retirement in Portugal who had flown his private aircraft to our airport and liked my story so much that, with time on his hands, he offered to help me with a completely fresh re-write. For his considerable help, input and encouragement I offer my very grateful thanks.

I have also received much help from many of the forty known surviving members of the original 180-man Coup de Main force (for whom I act as correspondent).

My thanks to my former Company Commanders, Major John Howard, DSO, and Colonel John Tillett (Retd.) for words of wisdom against any tendency towards overblown rhetoric. (Colonel Tillett, as Regimental Curator, kindly allowed me access to Regimental archives.)

Among the others my thanks also go to Bob Ambrose (for use of his story as a PoW) and Harry Clark (for his account of our Rhine landing); Frank Bourlet; John Burns, MM; Stan Evans, CdeG; Bill Gray; the late John Lathbury; the late 'Pete' Musty and the late Ted Noble; Tom (and Joan) Packwood; Wally Parr; Colonel 'Todd' Sweeney, MC; Fred Weaver; and Colonel David Wood, MBE. From our Airborne Engineers Captain N.R.K.Neilson; and our volunteer Medical Officer Major John 'Doc' Vaughan. From the Glider Pilots Geoff Barkway, DFM; Peter Boyle; Roy Howard, DFM; Alan Richards, DFM (for the use of his Normandy and Rhine landing plans); Tony Shorter and especially Jim Wallwork, DFM and RAF Glider Pilot Stan Jarvis who piloted me into battle. Without their skill we could never have achieved our objectives.

My thanks also to Lieutenant-Colonel D.A.Armitage (Curator, Museum of Army Flying at Middle Wallop for free use of archive photographs and plans); Gerard Mailland (France – for donated photographs); Marc Jacquinot (France – for helpful local research); Tony Neal (for Rhine landing research); Major Freddy Scott (for German route plan); Dr Tony Leake (for early post-war Normandy photographs); and Dr Mel Turland (for more recent Normandy photographs). With so much help, if I have missed anyone out, my sincere apologies.

Denis Edwards

THE DEVIL'S OWN LUCK

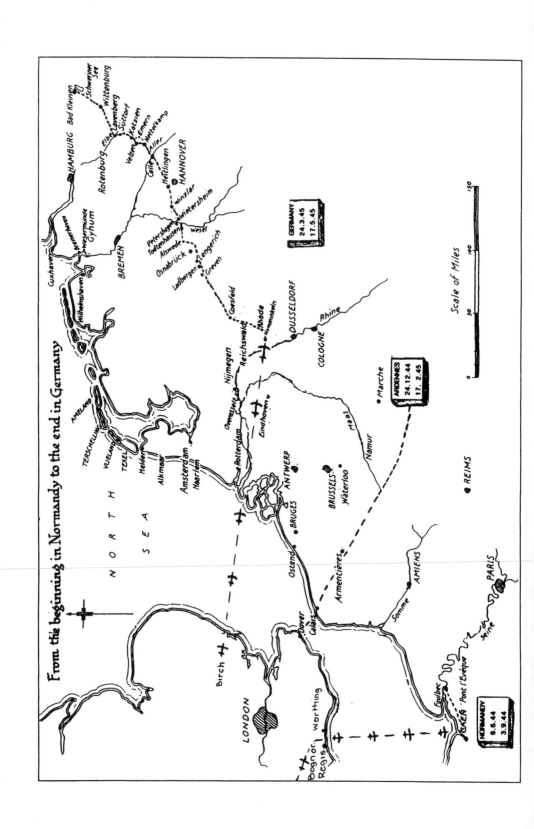

From the beginning in Normandy to the end in Germany

NORTH SEA

Scale of Miles
0   50   100   150

NORMANDY
6.6.44
3.9.44

ARDENNES
24.12.44
17.2.45

GERMANY
24.3.45
17.5.45

Part 1

THE HAND OF DESTINY

Chapter 1

EARLY DAYS

My Army career was anything but the result of a long-held wish to take up soldiering. With only very minor adjustments to the story of my early life, I could just as easily have ended up in the Merchant Navy, the Royal Navy or even the Royal Air Force, but fate decreed that I was to be a soldier in the Army.

I was born in Sundridge, near Sevenoaks in Kent, and, despite some confusion about the matter, I believe that the event occurred on 15 July, 1924. It may sound odd to say "I believe" that to be my birth date, but if there was any doubt about the matter the responsibility is that of my parents.

Both my mother and my father were interesting personalities, albeit unconventional people by the standards of those days. I have to admit that in my entire life I have never met another person whose parents were so casual about the birth of their first son; I celebrated my birthday on 22 July until I was thirteen years old.

Soon after my thirteenth birthday I had a notion that I would like to be a cabin boy on the P&O line and I wrote to London to apply for a position. I received a reply, but the letter requested sight of my birth certificate. Neither my mother nor my father could recall having ever possessed such a document, but when eventually I obtained the certificate, it was then, and only then, that I knew my true date of birth.

My parents had either noted the day of the week, but had then misremembered how many weeks had passed since my arrival, therefore making an error of one week in the date, or they had accurately registered the date but had later forgotten what they

3

had registered. Since the certificate said 15 July, and since my parents were never able to shed any further light on the matter, I opted to accept the date on the certificate as being my true birth date.

This kind of eccentricity was quite typical of my parents, who, while being in every way respectable, and respected, were both decidedly non-conformist – my mother more so than my father, I think. They were never outlandish or bizarre, but their priorities and standards were not in line with those that were considered the norm by more typically conservative members of their social class.

They had both been married previously, and this, although not unheard of, was unusual in those times. They each had a daughter by their first marriages, my half-sisters, and I had two younger brothers, Ian and Terry. I also had an adopted brother, Mick, who was a year older. He was adopted because a Harley Street specialist had told my mother that she could not have more children, but after the adoption I arrived, followed by my two brothers at annual intervals. Whenever birthdays were mentioned, my mother liked to remind me that I came into the world as an ugly wrinkled bundle covered with black, blue and red blotches, and that her reaction was to exclaim, "My God, it isn't human – take it away!" Although it was difficult to detect much in the way of maternal instinct about her, this is not to say that she was cold, or lacking in love for us, but simply that she was rather hopeless at being a typical mother.

Prue, my mother's daughter by her first marriage, lived with us and I thought of her simply as my sister. My father's daughter, however, was Thelma Edwards, and I hardly knew her at all. She became the wife of Douglas Bader, who, despite having lost his legs in a flying accident, went on to become a war hero, but we had little contact with them and I met them only once, in 1935 or 1936. I must have been a horrible little brat at the time, as I remember sitting on our front lawn and being amused to see the poor fellow struggling up the steps to our front door.

Irish born, my mother was artistic and full of character. Her own mother died in childbirth, the daughter of a wealthy Irish brewing family, who disowned her. My mother's father, my grand-father, was a young officer serving in the Black and Tans, who became eventually a knighted General. He recognized his daughter, however, became her legal guardian and shipped her to England, where she spent her early years in the care of the family of her father's retired batman.

It was probable that my mother was something of an embarrassment to my grandfather's military career and he sent her to a succession of continental convent schools, from two of which she was expelled. On at least two other occasions she ran away from her convent school and managed to reach England – much to the annoyance of her father. She spoke fluent French and German, and later she worked for a while as an interpreter for the Government. She also spent some time driving an ambulance in London during the First World War. At the end of that war she became a member of a dancing and singing troupe – the Benson Girls – and spent some time on the stage. She joined the Suffragettes, managing to get arrested several times, but escaping imprisonment or other serious consequences because of her youth. She died in 1993 at the age of ninety-nine.

After joining the Artillery in 1901, my father served for some years as an artillery officer. During the 'Great War' – as the First World War was commonly known before the Second World War started in 1939 – he fought in the Dardenelles, and later on the Western front, where he was engaged in artillery spotting from balloons. His willingness to go aloft in all weather conditions earned him the unenviable nickname of 'rubber guts'. Attacks on his balloon by enemy aircraft were frequent and on several occasions it was necessary to haul him down quickly before his bullet-ridden balloon came plunging to the ground unaided.

It was the impression made on my father by this rather disagreeable contact with German aircraft that made him determined to become a flier himself. Accordingly he transferred to the Royal Flying Corps, rapidly rising to the rank of Lieutenant-Colonel in the RFC before the end of the War.

When the German air ace von Richthofen, known as 'The Red Baron', was at last shot down in 1918, he fell in allied territory. The senior RFC officer in the sector into which the German ace crashed happened to be my father, and it was his responsibility to supervise the burial. He gave instructions that the propeller from the Baron's aircraft should be used to mark the grave. But the news spread rapidly and within a very short time the propeller had fallen victim to the penknives of countless souvenir hunters. Realizing the importance of this grave, however, my father had carefully noted its location on his map. After the war a German general came to London to meet my parents and to offer them an invitation from notable German flying personalities, including Hermann Goering, to go to Berlin as the guests of the German flying fraternity. The invitation was accepted and my father was able to give to his hosts the precise location of von Richthofen's grave, as a result of which the body was exhumed and taken to Germany for re-burial with the appropriate military honours.

Towards the end of the war, and for a short time after the Armistice, my father was a staff officer at the Air Ministry, and after retiring from the service in 1919 he became Deputy Director Air Transport Department of Civil Aviation at the Air Ministry. His immediate superior at the Ministry, and his very good friend, was Major General Sir Sefton Brancker, who also became my godfather. As a small boy I saw Brancker on rare occasions as a visitor to our home, but unfortunately he died in the R101 airship disaster in October, 1930.

At the end of the Great War my father held the Croix de Guerre, the Légion d'Honneur and the CMG, although in our family it was always said that the CMG was awarded to him for having taught the then Prince of Wales to fly an aeroplane.

Upon returning to civilian life after spending over twenty years in the military, my father put his money into business. At the Air Ministry his work had been concerned with setting up airfields and so, perhaps not surprisingly, he involved himself in a commercial venture with similar objectives. He was financed by one of his friends, Handley Page, of the aircraft manufacturing company that bore that name, to establish a chain of airfields across the Indian sub-continent.

In 1928 the family had moved from Sundridge to Downe Hall in Kent. Downe Hall was, and indeed still is, a very large house with extensive grounds and various outbuildings, including stables and its own electricity generating plant, and a garage block with a

6

bachelor flat above it. Our chauffeur, Pope, lived in the flat – until his unnatural interest in young boys was discovered, when he was dismissed. As well as a chauffeur, my parents employed a nanny, a butler, a cook, a housekeeper and several maids, who all lived in, while in addition there were three full-time gardeners who lived in the village.

The huge house even had a ballroom, where my mother and her many theatrical friends acted parts from various plays, which our nanny would sometimes allow us to watch, to our great delight.

While we were living at Downe Hall, my father developed plans of his own to set up a number of airfields throughout the British Isles. This latter venture was to be based at Hanworth Hall, and he set about taking the necessary steps to acquire it as the head-quarters of the new enterprise.

The Hall had been empty for years, guarded by a caretaker and three ferocious Alsatian dogs. Upon enquiring as to the fate that the dogs could expect after completion of the purchase, my mother learned that they were to be put down. She would have none of it and insisted on rescuing the dogs, taking them home to join her collection of various animals, which included three monkeys and at least twenty cats of various types.

The arrival of the dogs caused panedemonium among the servants, as the creatures were so vicious that tradesmen even stopped delivering to the house. My father was obliged to rig up a bell system that could be operated from the gates at the top of the drive, so that the trades people could draw attention to their arrival.

I was a toddler at this time, and on one occasion I wandered away and it was some time before I was missed. The servants scoured the grounds for me, eventually finding me in a stable loose box lying in the straw with a litter of puppies while their mother slept nearby. Despite the fact that I had come to no harm at all, the servants would not approach the dogs and called my mother to come to my rescue.

Most unfortunately for the Edwards family the new enterprise conceived by my father never really got under way. The big 'Crash' put paid to his plans, so that finally he lost just about everything.

This was a fate shared, of course, by hundreds of thousands of other entrepreneurs of that era. He even commuted his pension to keep some part of the business going, but it was to no avail. Regrettably, he finished up a great deal poorer than when he started.

After this misfortune we were never well off, but nor were we ever starving or desperate, because, luckily for us, my parents were an optimistic couple who knew that they must simply pick themselves up and start all over again. They had the strength of character to shrug off a disaster even of this magnitude, although it was not a strength born of religious conviction. In fact, neither of them had any time for the Christian religion, sometimes expressing a very strong sympathy for the old Celtic beliefs from the countries of their ancestors (Wales in my father's case, Ireland in the case of my mother). I remember both of them being incensed at the Church's attitude to the abdication of King Edward VIII. They were, however, inclined to be fatalistic, and so, instead of brooding or wanting to know why this thing had happened to them, they simply adjusted and got on with their lives.

As for myself, I had no real appreciation of the financial catastrophe that had overtaken us, and certainly had no idea of its future implications. Nonetheless, it affected my long-term prospects very profoundly, as may be imagined. Since my father was now no longer able to afford the lifestyle that he had previously enjoyed, the future for me and for my brothers could never be as he might have hoped. But we were a happy family and we thrived, albeit in a much-restricted manner as compared to former times.

Because my mother was a clever and accomplished artist, while my father was very practical and good with his hands, it came about that the two of them set up a small business, bearing the grand title of 'The Red Diamond Manufacturing Company', making lamps as a cottage industry. Father would make the stands and bases for lamps, and the frames for the lampshades, while mother painted the vellum and assembled the completed lampshades. The results had a quality and appearance that were the equal of anything you could buy in the finest stores. Indeed, it was to such stores as Harrods that the completed lamps were finally sent for sale, and it was this which kept the wolf from our door in those difficult days.

Alas, my father's financial misfortunes made it necessary for us to move house again in 1932, this time to "Danehurst" at Nutfield Marsh, near Redhill in Surrey. Although "Danehurst" was a very substantial house, with five bedrooms and three reception rooms, after the vastness of Downe Hall it seemed to me, as a young child, to be little more than a glorified rabbit hutch. Nevertheless, we settled in and, for the most part, adapted quickly to our reduced circumstances, although my mother found it difficult to live without servants around her. She would often proclaim that she had never cooked a meal in her life, nor had she ever been reduced to doing housework, so somehow she managed to find an elderly couple, Mr and Mrs Allen, who lived in and did most of the chores.

The Allens were not with us for very long, however, which was probably just as well, since Mr Allen was an ardent supporter of Sir Oswald Mosley and the British Fascists. When my parents were away, which was quite often, he would put on his Fascist uniform and spend hours marching me and my brothers up and down the back garden and teaching us to make the Fascist salute. Had my father discovered this he would have been furious, but the Allens soon moved on, taking what remained of the family silver with them – in lieu of unpaid wages I strongly suspect.

At Nutfield Marsh, among the local slag heaps and ponds left by the fuller's earth industry, I learned fieldcraft, battling with catapult and bow-and-arrow in the tussles between the lads from the marsh and those from Nutfield village. I learned to move stealthily through the tall reeds and rushes of the marsh, and I do not believe that I could have become so successful as a sniper without this youthful experience.

Finally, in 1936, we moved to Meadvale, near Redhill, which was to be my home until I joined up, and from where the fate that propelled me into the Army began to take shape.

It would have been perfectly natural for me and my brothers to have gone to one of the great public schools, but I was totally unaware of such considerations, and the unconventional way in which we were brought up meant that we had no expectations in this regard. In the same way, for a family such as ours, it would

9

have been quite normal for one or more of my father's sons to be commissioned as officers in one or other of the Armed Services. Needless to say, my own eventual military career owed nothing at all to any such expectation or tradition.

While the path that led to a "respectable" profession, through public school and university, or to a commission in the armed forces, was now closed to us, I was unaware of ever having lost anything important. I can say truthfully that even when I was old enough to appreciate how much had been lost, I never suffered any sense of deprivation, nor did I feel any resentment at the way fate had changed my life. My brothers shared my lack of dismay at our curtailed educational prospects, and we were, I think it fair to say, a remarkably well-balanced and sensible family.

With no possibility of a private education, even at a minor public school, my brothers and I received a basic education such as was available from the state system. This meant that I could look forward to a rudimentary schooling in the three 'Rs' and that I would be expected to leave school at fourteen to find work and to learn a trade. There were ways in which brighter children could stay at school for much longer, and even go to university, but I was not considered to be particularly bright; in any case I hated school.

As a result my education was destined to end when I attained the age of fourteen. This seems incredibly young by today's standards, but was quite normal for the majority of youngsters in those times, and indeed until after the end of the Second World War.

I feel obliged to say that the end of my formal education caused me no great concern or sadness. I had not enjoyed my last years at a Church of England school, where bullying by sadistic male teachers seemed to be the norm and the cane was in daily use.

I remember in particular my maths teacher, whose response to any failing on the part of a pupil, whether in behaviour or mathematical comprehension, was horrific. He would take the offender's ear-lobe between the nails of his thumb and forefinger, dragging the poor wretch to the front of the class, there to be reviled as an idiot and a dullard in front of his classmates. I would frequently play truant rather than face this sadistic character, and I soon found myself in conflict with kindly old Mr Rose, the school attendance officer. He listened sympathetically to my problem and, recognizing in me a certain rebellious spirit, he enrolled me into the local branch of the Young Communist League!

The official Communist position before the invasion of the Soviet Union was one of more or less full support for the Nazis. The party line held that the War was a direct result of the machinations of decadent and wicked capitalist powers aimed at destabilizing and overthrowing the German people's National Socialist revolution. When I eventually joined the Army I lied about my age and on my first home leave the local Communist Party Secretary threatened to expose my deceit, such was his disgust at my eagerness to join up to fight against Joe Stalin's German friends.

My mother, however, was on good terms with senior figures in the police force and she succeeded in making a small mountain of that particular molehill, with the result that I was interviewed by the Special Branch about my Communist connections. I simply told them the truth, answering all their questions completely honestly, and one result of this was that the local Party Secretary was leaned on heavily by the police and I had no more complaints from him.

At school I still had no ambition to join the Army. In fact, I had a long-held desire to join the Navy, and accordingly I became a sea cadet. I was suddenly and rudely cured of this ambition when we were sent up to HMS *Ganges* to do some sea training. The petty officers who were detailed to look after us were not very happy, as their colleagues had all gone on leave and training us was an unpopular additional duty. They vented their spleen on their unwanted charges – myself and a few dozen other young lads. They gave us a very hard time, especially when we were out to sea in the whalers learning how to row and to sail. They cursed and berated us, predicting an awful death by drowning if we didn't shape up and handle the boat properly. Somehow the glamour of the Navy faded away rapidly after that experience.

On Reigate Heath there were a couple of stud farms, one owned by Earl Beattie and the other belonging to J.V. Rank, the flour millionaire. Schoolboys such as I was could earn a couple of shillings now and then by helping with some of the dirty work around the stables and in this way I acquired an interest in and love of horses. I revelled in the idea of working with them, and so, at the end of my schooling, soon after my fourteenth birthday, I applied for a job with a riding stable that had opened nearby in Reigate.

The stables belonged to two brothers, Dennis and Buddy Hulme, whose wealthy father worked in the City. They were both quite young – still in their early twenties I think – and their father had bought the stables for them. To my delight they offered me a job as their sole assistant at a salary of ten shillings a week – fifty pence in today's money.

Work at the stables was interesting but quite demanding. I would arrive at around half past five in the morning, and by the time the brothers arrived at around half past eight I had fed, watered and groomed all eight horses and was ready for the first customers.

When war broke out I was still working at the stables in Reigate. I still have a clear recollection of that fateful Sunday, 3 September, 1939 when war was declared. During the morning the Hulme brothers, had turned on their wireless set and we heard the sombre tones of Mr Chamberlain making the fateful announcement. We all cheered loudly, little realizing the eventual consequences, the losses and the hardships that we would all suffer before it was over.

Characteristically, my father volunteered immediately and, although too old to fly as a pilot, he joined the RAF nonetheless, becoming a Wing Commander before the war ended, "flying a desk" as the saying goes. He moved out to be near his work, and never again returned to the family home.

As for myself, still without any desire to join the Army, I was nonetheless a very early volunteer for the Home Guard, and I would attend parades in the evenings after work, making my day even longer. Armed with pitchforks and broom handles, we carried out exercises on the North Downs, practising how we might protect the community from German paratroops if they should dare to land, a notion which invites derision now, but one which we all took very seriously. None of us had the slightest idea what a German paratrooper was like and I am sure that we all assumed that such an enemy would be impressed, if not exactly terrified, to be confronted by a collection of young boys and old men brandishing pitchforks and broom handles.

My Home Guard experience did have some interesting aspects, however, as for some of this time up on the North Downs we had a 'front-row' view of some of the most intense aerial activity in the Battle of Britain, positioned as we were on the southern approaches to London.

Quite soon after war started two army officers arrived at the riding stables on official business. They described themselves as being from 'Army Remount'. They acquired all our horses, paying forty pounds each for them. I have never since heard of this Army Remount unit, and I have never met anyone else who knows who or what they were. The Hulme brothers, however, were keen to get involved in the war, and now, with no horses and no business, they enlisted. I don't know where they went, or what service they joined, and I never again heard news of them, but before fading out of my life for ever they were conscientious enough to find alternative employment for me, which I thought was very decent of them.

The local dairy covering the Redhill and Reigate areas had seventy-five horses and I was introduced to the dairy as being a good lad and handy with horses. The stables at the dairy were managed by an old retired jockey, whose stable lad had just joined up, leaving the dairy with something of a staffing problem, so my introduction was timely.

The dairy paid me the princely sum of twelve shillings a week as I recall, but the work was even more demanding than that at the riding stables. The milk roundsmen liked to start their day early, some of them starting at about half past five in the morning, which meant that my day had to start two and a half hours beforehand, at three o'clock. I would have to work very hard and quickly during those first few hours, and I would not get away for breakfast until about nine o'clock.

My home was a mile or so away from the dairy, and I used to cycle in to work on my bike – a Bowen Special, for which I paid twenty pounds – a fortune for me at the time, being roughly ten months' wages, which I paid by modest monthly instalments. It had an alloy frame and I was immensely proud of it. I would cycle to

13

work, then cycle home for breakfast, after which I would go back to the dairy at eleven o'clock, home again for lunch, then back in time for the first horses coming back from the rounds. Normally I didn't finish until six in the evening, and so it was a long and arduous working day for a lad of my age.

Jim Tickner was the blacksmith who took care of all the smithying for the Dairy, as well as for a similar number of horses from the Co-op dairy. Jim had just lost his assistant – another volunteer for active service I believe – and he persuaded me to start working for him, instead of for the dairy. The new working day started at half past seven in the morning and ended at about six at night, and, best of all, there was no work at all on Sundays! The incentive he offered, apart from the shorter working day, was an extra shilling per week! One matter he impressed on me forcefully was that I must never attempt to ride any of the horses – words that would shape my entire life thereafter.

In fact, my fate was now close to being sealed. The Co-op had one special horse, a magnificent animal, a high-stepper which pulled a special carriage and which was taken to all the carnivals, processions and fêtes in the district. They were all intensely proud of this animal, and rightly so as it was probably the best horse the Co-op had anywhere in the South of England. On Monday, 24 March, 1941, this fine animal came in for shoeing and late in the evening I had to take it back to the Co-op yard.

It had started to rain and I was late finishing work. On Monday evenings I would usually go to the cinema with my friends, and there I was, still with that wretched horse to take back to the Co-op yard. The thought came to me, "What the heck, I'm going to be late, and it's raining", and so, once out of sight and confident that I would be observed, I jumped on its back and I rode it. There was no saddle or bridle, just a halter over its head and a rope.

I don't remember exactly what happened when the Canadian trucks came past us. The Canadian troops had just arrived and their trucks were to be seen everywhere in the district, driving on either the left or right hand side of the road – they showed no special preference. Whatever it may have been that startled the horse, it took off at a gallop. Unable to restrain it, I clung on as it galloped towards the Co-op dairy gates. Having no saddle, I was slowly slipping off, and at the gates I was unable to cling on a moment longer and I was dumped heavily and unceremoniously in the driveway as the animal sped into the cobbled yard, the cobblestones glistening shiny wet in the evening rain.

In horror I saw the beautiful animal slip on the wet cobblestones and do a complete somersault in the middle of the yard. As it staggered to its feet, I could see that its head and nose were cut and bleeding, its knees were grazed and the poor creature looked a most terrible mess.

Dazed, and stunned, I watched as the Co-op manager, the head groom and the roundsmen fussed about the horse, none of them taking the slightest notice of me. The full horror of my irresponsibility and the possible consequences began to dawn on me, and so, unobserved, I made a discreet exit and headed for home.

That night was a fearful experience for me as I relived the disastrous events of the previous day a hundred times over in my thoughts. I don't think that I slept very much, or even at all, worrying about what might be the consequences of my foolhardy actions.

At dawn, before anyone else was up, I rose and went down to the railway station in Redhill where I jumped on the early morning milk train to Guildford. Arriving at Guildford I found my way to the Army recruiting office, where I walked straight in and said, "I want to join the Army". It was 25 March, 1941.

Chapter 2

TRAINING

I have often thought how easy it would have been for a German spy to join the British Army in 1941. Having declared my wish to join up, everything I said to the recruiting sergeant was accepted without question; no identity documents were demanded nor were any embarrassing questions asked. I was sixteen and a half, but I gave my age as eighteen and a half, and the only question the sergeant asked me was how soon I wanted to join up, to which I replied, "Now".

The sergeant, I am sure, guessed that I was younger, but the Army needed men, and my heart was beating fiercely with apprehension as I watched him write out a travel warrant. He told me that there was a train leaving shortly for Dursley in Gloucestershire, where I would report for duty with the 70th Young Soldiers Battalion of the Oxfordshire and Buckinghamshire Light Infantry.

I wrote a note to my mother soon after arriving at the barracks in Dursley, simply telling her that I had joined the Army and asking her to convey my apologies to Mr Tickner for letting him down. Of course I knew that my mother was not the kind of person who would be frantic with worry and that she would take a 'what will be will be' view of events.

Soon after my arrival at Dursley we were taken to a camp near a small village in Cornwall, between Falmouth and Truro, where our training started.

Through the summer months we lived under canvas, rapidly becoming used to Army life. We were all youngsters, seventeen being the probable average age, and for me it was a tremendous adventure; I had no regrets at all at having joined up.

As winter approached we left the camp to relocate at Seaton Barracks in Plymouth. From there we had our first taste of real service when we were sent out to local airfield on defence duty, to man some slit trenches equipped with old Lewis guns. After two or three days we would be relieved by another team and return to barracks at Plymouth. It was not very exciting stuff, but airfield defences had to be manned and a group of young soldiers like us, not yet ready for anything more demanding, fitted the bill very well. This life continued until the end of 1941 when the Battalion was transferred to Northern Ireland.

I enjoyed my stay in Northern Ireland, there being none of the unpleasantness that has arisen there in more recent times. Wherever we went, in the towns or in the country, the people were always very kind and charming, and I have nothing but fond memories of them.

The only real problem with being stationed on the other side of the Irish Sea was the difficulty of getting home on leave. Naturally, therefore, there was great excitement when a notice was posted on the Battalion notice board calling for volunteers to transfer to the 2nd Battalion of the Oxfordshire and Buckinghamshire Light Infantry. Apparently this was something to do with the Airborne forces, about which we knew very little, but it sounded interesting. The greatest part of the attraction, however, was the location, which our enquiries revealed to be at Bulford, on Salisbury Plain, and therefore much closer to our homes. Almost everyone volunteered.

To join the Airborne forces there was a requirement for a good standard of vision, and I knew that my eyesight was slightly below par. To overcome this obstacle, I plotted with a pal of mine, persuading him to get into the queue ahead of me, to memorize the critical line from the eyesight chart and let me know it before I went in. The scheme worked perfectly, and when I was invited to read the chart, I told the doctor that I could only read down to the line that read "QEVFRT" – or whatever it was. "That's fine – that's all you're supposed to read," said the MO, and I was in.

* * *

17

Late in 1942 the 2nd Oxf and Bucks, with the 1st Royal Ulster Rifles, the 2nd Staffordshires and the King's Own Scottish Borderers were the four glider Battalions of the 1st Airborne Division. It was decided at this time that 1st Airborne was to go to the Middle East, but due to a shortage of gliders the 2nd Oxf and Bucks and the Royal Ulster Rifles were left behind at Bulford Camp on Salisbury Plain and became the first units of 6th Airborne Division. Very soon afterwards the parachute battalions arrived, and then the 12th Devons were added, who made up the third battalion of our 6th Airlanding Brigade. It felt very good to be wearing the red beret and to know that we were in at the very beginning of what would become 6th Airborne Division.

A dismal introduction to our new posting came when a sergeant greeted us with the terrifying news that a Hotspur glider had just crashed with the loss of all on board. He was clearly delighted to see the arrival of replacements for the lost men and for some reason he seemed to expect us to be equally happy to be making good the losses caused by the accident.

The regime at Bulford camp was tough, consisting of hard work, long marches and poor food. I was assigned initially to the Recce Platoon of 'S' Company and I have good memories of those times. The platoon consisted of a private soldier driving a motorcycle combination, with a sergeant on the pillion and an officer in the side-car, as well as a despatch rider on a second solo motorcycle, and six or seven of us riding airborne folding pedal cycles. On exercises five or six of the pedal cyclists would hitch their toggle ropes to the back of the combination while the other two would place one hand on the shoulder of the despatch rider. In this way we moved from place to place at a speed which caused considerable surprise when we were seen to leave one location and then pop up in another in a much shorter time than anyone expected.

I ran into a small personal problem soon after arriving at Bulford when I asked to be excused from Church Parades. I resented the way these parades were used for military ceremonial purposes: spit and polish, ranks lined up for inspection and so forth. I claimed to be an atheist, which was probably an exaggeration, but I was certainly not a committed Christian. In response to my request, the platoon sergeant would march me to the Platoon

Commander, who marched me to the Company Commander, who marched me to the Battalion Commander. He in turn handed me over to his Regimental Sergeant Major, who, furious that I had disrupted *his* spit and polish parade, marched me to the entrance of the church. There he told me that if he looked out during the service and saw that I had moved by as much as a single inch I would be hauled off to the Guard Room so fast that my feet wouldn't touch the ground.

I kept this up for some weeks, until, because I hadn't capitulated, I faced a succession of trumped-up charges that kept me busy doing dirty jobs around the camp, and my weekend passes were cancelled. On Sundays I was sent to the cookhouse to peel a mountain of spuds or clean blackened pots and pans so that, as the Cook Sergeant regularly said, he could use them as a shaving mirror.

When I still failed to respond in the required way, they eventually gave up and I was excused from all future church parades.

I transferred from 'S' Company Recce platoon into 'D' Company after a while and life became even tougher.

In 'D' Company we had the hardest of taskmasters in Major John Howard as Company Commander. He was proud of having come up from the ranks to achieve his position, having once been an Oxford City Police sergeant, and he took his responsibilities very seriously indeed. His Company had to be the best at everything, be it sport, marches, field exercises or physical and endurance training. Whenever we returned from a ten- or fourteen-day period of leave, he would want us back into shape immediately. We knew that he and his Company Officers and NCOs would wake us at the crack of dawn and take us through a series of strenuous physical exercises followed by a long run or march.

Sometimes, without warning, we would be roughly roused from our beds at around midnight, loaded into lorries and driven several miles out into Salisbury Plain. With little idea of our precise whereabouts we were dropped off in Sections and told to find our way back to camp, avoiding patrols that were sent out to catch us. To get back to the camp we would have to cross the Artillery Firing Ranges, which would be in use, with live shells, from dawn onwards!

19

Alternatively, in what were called Initiative Tests, we would be taken even further afield, dropped off in ones and twos, without money or food, and told that the local population had been advised to report any sightings of suspected enemy paratroops. Farmers tended to let fly with both barrels of their shotguns if they found us helping ourselves from their vegetable fields!

We learned about street fighting by being taken to bombed-out areas of south coast and midland cities for training among the ruined buildings, where live ammunition and hand grenades would be used, and damaged buildings would be further demolished if we missed concealed trip-wires and booby traps! Falling masonry was the biggest hazard and we all had several near misses.

Studland Bay in Dorset was the scene of many of our 'Live Exercises' where we would make mock attacks on enemy positions using live bullets, grenades and mortar bombs. After the war I frequently took holidays in the West country, but always gave Studland Bay a miss as I felt that it probably contained so many unexploded grenades and bombs that it was unlikely that they were all safely cleared!

The summer of 1943 was one of the hottest for several years. In May or June that year someone decided that it would be good for the morale of the Bristol armaments factory workers to send the Battalion to Ilfracombe. The factory workers tended take their annual two-week holiday in the West country resorts such as Ilfracombe in North Devon and the idea was to show them that with the Airborne Forces they were getting value for their money.

That was all well and good, but conveying an entire Battalion of some 750 men could be an expensive business. Our masters solved the problem by ordering us to march the 120 miles from Salisbury Plain to North Devon in full battle order, which included not only carrying our heavy packs and rifles but also our light machine guns, mortars and other heavy equipment.

This we achieved by almost continuous marching at a rate of around thirty miles a day, thus taking four days to complete the journey. The last leg of this marathon march included Porlock Hill which, after three days of foot slogging, seemed to us to be the steepest, and longest, hill in the whole world!

Once settled in at Ilfracombe we undertook long hours of

drilling, physical exercises, fieldcraft and swimming while wearing full equipment.

In addition, and presumably to show off our fitness to the civilian holiday makers, we were required to scale a steep cliff – I believe it was called Lantern or Lighthouse Hill – which seemed to rise several hundred feet from the sea.

Our officers selected the steepest cliff face, which we were required to climb without the aid of ropes or any form of safety equipment. Those who lost their footing simply fell into the sea below. Several were injured, but presumably boosting the morale of the civilian workers was considered more important than a few broken limbs.

It was while we were at Ilfracombe that I first saw one of my comrades being shot and killed.

We were taken out to one of the restricted beachside areas – I believe it was at Coombe Martin – to experience being shot at by our officers and senior NCOs using live ammunition, hand grenades and mortars.

Our Section was sheltering beneath a large sand dune. During a quiet spell one young lad crawled to the top to see what was happening at the moment that the Company Sergeant Major fired a burst from his Sten into the top of the dune, hitting the lad in the head. He crashed back among us with a look of surprise upon his bloody and lifeless face. If an inquiry took place I was never called upon to give evidence. It was probably put down to a casualty during training.

At the end of that very hot summer we returned to Bulford Camp, again making the journey on foot. Our Company Commander, ever competitive, determined that 'D' Company would be the first to arrive. While the other Companies therefore enjoyed the benefit of a ten- to twelve-minute roadside rest every hour or so, 'D' Company was allowed only about five or six minutes and so arrived back at Bulford half a day before the rest of the battalion.

While 'D' Company invariably appeared to be best at everything, we were probably no better or worse than the lads in the other Companies. However, our extraordinarily zealous Company Commander insisted that his Company had to win at everything.

This virtually ensured that when a Company from the gliderborne Airlanding Brigade – with a choice from twelve infantry companies from Oxf and Bucks, Devons and Royal Ulster Rifles – was required for a special mission 'D' Company stood out as the natural choice for the job. In fact, if 'D' Company had an advantage over the other companies in the Brigade, it was simply because it was led by the most determined and dedicated Company Commander.

Despite all the hardships, life was not entirely disagreeable. The tension of a gruelling week of training was alleviated by a trip into Salisbury at weekends, where we would drink the pubs dry and engage in pitched battles with the Americans, who also converged on Salisbury for rest and recreation. The local people must have dreaded our forays into the city and we were surely seen as a bunch of hooligans as we fell upon the city, our jam jars strung around our necks and ready to cause mayhem. The pubs rarely had glasses in those days and it was common practice to use a jam jar as a glass. We would carry a jam jar stuffed under our tunics and tied around our necks by a long string. Without such a makeshift 'glass' you simply could not get a drink. When the jam jar was in use, it would be secured to the wrist, as even jam jars were in short supply and you would have been foolish to allow it out of your sight.

Apart from the rough and tumble of our weekends, some of the training could also be interesting. We were always seeking ways to relieve the monotony and the hardship of the intensely tough training. The favourite method as far as I was concerned was to volunteer for 'live loads', which meant being a live passenger for glider pilot training. Many of the other lads were scared stiff of going up in a glider with a trainee pilot, and so the competition for doing this 'live load' work was not too serious.

As a result of frequent volunteering for live loads, I became well acquainted with most aspects of the Airspeed Horsa – the glider which was eventually to transport me into Normandy, and again, a while later, into Germany itself.

More than 3500 Horsas were built, and even the Americans used them at one time, to meet a shortage of their own equivalent aircraft, the Waco. Being a glider, and needing to carry a heavy load – thirty men or the equivalent in freight – it needed to be as light as possible. Of a fragile fabric-covered wood construction, posing some dangers for its pilots and passengers, it could easily be smashed to splinters if impeded by trees or other obstacles during landing. Its fragility meant that it was disposable, not needing to come back intact after being used in earnest, although some did. Fragile as it was, many were damaged in training, but luckily none that I trained in ever came to grief.

Unusually for those times, the Horsa had a tricycle under-carriage – i.e. a nose wheel instead of the more usual tail wheel – and the main undercarriage wheels could be jettisoned on take-off if required, so that the aircraft would then rely on a skid rather than wheels for landing purposes. This made perfect sense, as a conventional wheeled undercarriage was additional weight, and it could easily be torn off in a landing that crossed a ditch for example, while a simple skid could well be successful in bridging such irregularities in the terrain.

The Horsa pilot training was carried out at various places, Brize Norton being a favourite place, and for 'live load' volunteers it involved being billeted on the airfield. There were numerous advantages to these trips – the first being the food. A breakfast of ham and eggs was just a daydream at Bulford, but at Brize Norton or one of the other places we visited such fare was more or less the norm.

The locals too appreciated us and treated us very generously, although if we had spent every weekend in their towns, engaging in fist-fights with Americans as we did in Salisbury, they may have taken a different view of us. As things were, however, the airborne landings in Sicily had just taken place and if you wore a red beret then there was always someone ready to buy you a drink.

I was fortunate in possessing quite a reasonable singing voice and one of the other lads was a fair piano player, so we would regale our hosts with our version of the latest Nelson Eddy song at the time and this always went down very well. As I was 'Eddie' to the other lads anyway, they nicknamed me 'Eddie Nelson.'

After an evening of carousing and singing in this way, we would have some difficulty in getting up the next morning, but we would always manage eventually to stagger into the canteen for a delicious bacon and egg sandwich before reporting for duty at the airfield. This involved strapping ourselves into a Horsa glider, for no other reason than to give the trainee pilot confidence and experience in carrying live personnel. I was never in the least apprehensive during these flights, being not infrequently still suffering from the effects of the night before, and I would often sleep soundly during the numerous flights that I undertook.

Good food was, apart from the 'live load' occasions, very hard to find, but I did have the benefit of a first class meal, albeit an uncomfortable one, on the one occasion when I visited my aunt and her husband who lived in Salisbury. It was, however, a most embarrassing occasion for me, and one that I never repeated.

My father's sister, Gladys Edwards, was married to Dr Gerald Thornton, and, as I was stationed close to Salisbury, my father urged me to make contact with them. I was an uncouth eighteen-year-old lad, quite unlike the kind of young man my father's sister might have hoped her brother would raise.

A butler, fully attired in the appropriate garb, greeted me at the door, ushered me into a lounge and announced me to a number of complete strangers, my fellow dinner guests, who were sipping sherry from crystal glasses. I was acutely uncomfortable.

In the dining room my discomfort was even more acute. I was seated at a highly polished dinner table, confronted by a baffling array of knives, forks and spoons, with no idea how to proceed. I watched the other guests intently, hoping to be able to work out which implements to use. The food was lavish and made me wonder how such a spread could be possible in times of severe rationing, but such was my discomfort that I really didn't care. I only hoped to get out of the place as soon as was decently possible.

Later my Uncle Gerald did have a quiet word with me, but only to chide me for being one of the offending servicemen who regularly made unruly forays into the city to fight Americans and generally make nuisances of themselves.

My visit to the Thorntons' house was never repeated; I received no further invitation, and if I had, I am sure I would have found an excuse to decline.

Apart from flying training, we were continuously undergoing every other type of training for the skills that we should need when, eventually, we had to face a real enemy, so fieldcraft and rifle shooting were constantly practised. Although there was no fixed time allotted to our period of training as a glider-borne assault force, by the end of 1943 we all knew that we had learned enough to have become pretty good at it, and we were constantly wondering when we would go into action.

There were frequent rumours that this might happen soon, and the news constantly reminded us that the Russians were pushing hard for the Allies to open a second front in the West, to take the pressure away from them.

We could never have suspected that, to ensure a successful bridgehead for that second front, 'D' Company would be selected to carry out a daring and terrifyingly dangerous mission, a mission for which we were to receive the most intensive training.

Chapter 3

INTO THE FRAY

It was in the middle of May, 1944, when we were loaded into trucks, with the covering tarpaulins all tied down to conceal us from public view, as a security measure. We were transported to Exeter where we were briefed that we were to undertake an exercise to attack a pair of bridges with a view to capturing them intact.

One of the bridges was over the River Exe, while the second crossed the Exeter canal just a short distance from it. Unknown to anyone, with the exception of Major John Howard, the two bridges at Countess Weir, Exeter, being very similar in appearance and positioning to two bridges near Caen in Normandy, had become an important part of the plans being secretly discussed for the invasion of Normandy. To us this was just another exercise of course, and we had no notion that our objectives bore any relation to anything else. We would never have guessed that we were due to play a key part in the imminent invasion of the European mainland.

The Countess Weir bridges were defended by extremely conscientious Polish paratroops who were not ready or willing to surrender anything to anyone, and there were some fierce and physical exchanges with them as they fought ferociously, as if for the honour of Poland! For three days and nights we continued with the exercise, being driven to within varying distances of the bridges in trucks, to simulate glider landings, and then trying to wrest control of the bridges from those very uncooperative Poles.

Just a few weeks later, at the end of May, we were again loaded into trucks and we were driven to an airfield 'somewhere in southern England'. We were instructed to remain concealed at all times while en route, and when we arrived at our destination none of us knew where we were or why we were there. Within a short time we would learn that our exercise at Countess Weir had been a dress rehearsal. Now the stage was set and the curtain was about to go up.

It was 4 June, 1944, and something was definitely about to happen, but what?

For some time we had been cooped up in the camp, one of the many high-security tented camps behind guarded barbed-wire fences in Southern England and, in our case, near an airfield. We had been transported from Bulford Camp on Salisbury Plain in covered lorries, and when we arrived at our new location I had no idea where we were. Years later I was to learn that it was Tarrant Rushton in Dorset, which, like many of the temporary wartime airfields, no longer exists.

A day or so after our arrival we were ordered from our Section tents, told to 'Fall In' and marched to an inner guarded and wired-off enclosure in the heart of the camp. A notice at the entrance read 'SECRET – KEEP OUT UNLESS ON DUTY'

We entered a large tent and received a briefing from Major Howard. Later, by platoons, each consisting of about twenty-eight men, we went to smaller tents for more detailed briefings from our Platoon Commanders.

The initial briefing had given us the general outline of the special mission that lay ahead of us. The invasion forces of the Allied armies were at last about to land along the Normandy beaches. As soon as weather conditions permitted – and favourable weather was expected within the next two days – they would start rescuing continental Europe from the grip of Hitler's Germany.

The British 6th Airborne Division had been allocated the task of landing from the sky on to the left flank of the British seaborne forces. Two American Airborne Divisions would be carrying out a similar landing on the right flank of their seaborne armies.

The seaborne forces were to land, capture and secure the ground along the coastline to form a bridgehead. It would be expanded,

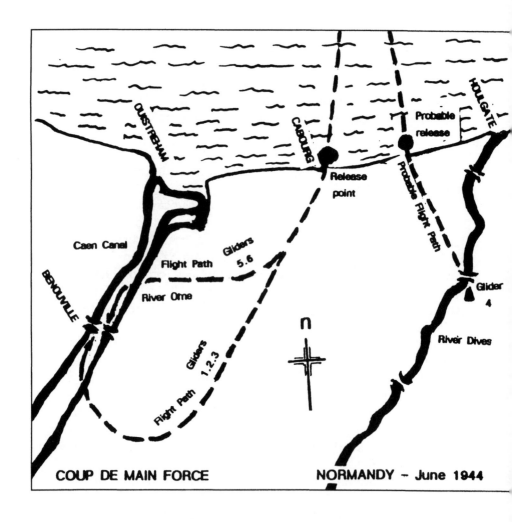

OUISTREHAM

CABOURG

HOULGATE

Probable
release

Release
point

Probable Flight Path

Caen Canal

Flight Path

Gliders
5.6

BENOUVILLE

River Orne

Gliders
1.2.3

Flight Path

n

Glider
4

River Dives

COUP DE MAIN FORCE   **NORMANDY – June 1944**

move inland for several miles, then pivot in an anti-clockwise direction and thrust eastwards on a wide front.

Our Division had to capture and hold a large area on the left flank and prevent any attempt by the enemy to rush reinforcements along the coast from the east, where their main forces were located. It was mainly low-lying ground a short distance inland, much of it heavily wooded and with a large area – the valley of the River Dives – flooded by the Germans as a counter-invasion measure. On the western boundary of our Divisional area the Caen Canal ran from the coast at Ouistreham down to Caen, eight miles

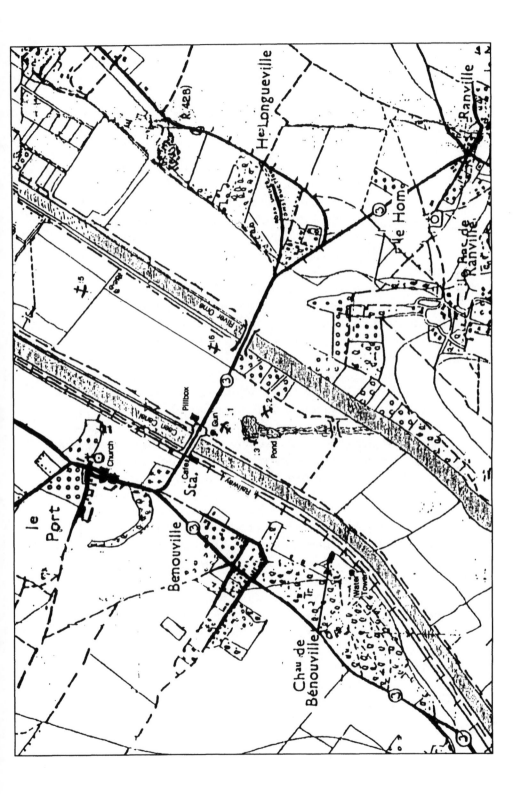

inland, and parallel with it, 500 yards or so to its eastern side, was the River Orne. At a point about four miles inland, just on the eastern edge of the small village of Bénouville, both waterways are crossed by bridges, the road through Bénouville running eastwards by way of the two bridges.

It was the special task of 'D' Company (with two additional platoons from 'B' Company) of the 2nd Battalion Oxfordshire and Buckinghamshire Light Infantry (of the gliderborne 6th Airlanding Infantry Brigade) to gain both bridges intact, to enable the British Army to thrust eastwards with their tanks and other heavy vehicles. It was known through local French partisan sources that both bridges had been prepared for demolition and our specific task was to capture these bridges before they could be demolished.

The invasion plan required that several bridges were to be destroyed, to hinder the enemy, while others, such as those allocated to us, were to be captured intact to facilitate the Allied advance. Once the Germans realized where the invasion was really taking place they would wish to rush reinforcements from the east and, by denying them access over the bridges, they would be forced into a detour down to Caen. While we were capturing our two bridges, several Parachute Battalions would destroy five bridges over the River Dives, some eight miles to the east, and generally harass the Germans to the east of our inland Airborne bridgehead. These operations would delay the enemy and buy the Allies the valuable time they needed to establish a firm bridgehead along the beaches during the first few vital days. Our party had been named 'The Coup de Main Force'[1]* by the Allied Commanders.

Various ways of carrying out a surprise attack for the capture of the bridges had been considered. Originally paratroops were to be used, but this idea was dropped due to the windy conditions that often prevailed in coastal regions, as there was a risk of the paratroops being scattered over a wide area. Subsequent events proved this to be a sound assumption as our back-up paratroops who were dropped to reinforce us shortly after we landed were badly scattered, many of them landing several miles from their intended dropping zones.

*See Notes p.234

It was finally decided that the most effective method would be to use a compact force carried in six gliders – three to land by each bridge. They were to be crash-landed at night-time in a small strip of rough land between the canal and river.

Each glider was to be fitted with identical equipment and its passengers would include five Royal Engineers to deal with the demolition charges on the bridges. Because it was considered necessary to carry five Engineers in every glider it meant that our infantry platoons – normally of twenty-eight men – would have to be reduced to twenty-three since the maximum glider load was twenty-eight plus two glider pilots. The Airborne Engineers and the glider pilots were fully trained to fight alongside the infantry.

Each one of the gliders had to be prepared to land in any sequence, and each team had to be ready to carry out any one of the six tasks in connection with the capture of the bridges. In any other circumstances we might have spent weeks learning our various tasks and practising them. Now we had no time left and we needed to learn and understand our individual responsibilities in just a day. The intense concentration helped to keep us from contemplating the implications of the awesome task that lay ahead of us.

Studying the different tasks of each platoon occupied us for several hours. We now understood the significance of the exercise we had carried out in May. Those bridges were indeed quite similar to the targets we were now about to tackle, but the Polish defenders of the Countess Weir bridges were basically 'friendly', while this time we could expect opposition that was decidedly unfriendly, and with much more to lose than just bridges.

My platoon, No. 25, was to fly in the first of the three gliders to go down on to the canal bridge. Each platoon was divided into sections, and the tasks of each seven-man section were considered. Finally, in cases where individuals had special tasks, these were also looked at in detail, since, working in darkness, it was essential that everyone knew what everyone else should be doing at any given time. If, for any reason, the detailed individual was not available to carry out the task, the others had to be aware of the requirements and able to carry it out.

31

The latest aerial photographs were very useful, as they showed the bridges and surrounding terrain in great detail. There was also a large-scale model and we were assured that every house, outbuilding, tree, bush, hedge, gateway, ditch and fortification had been meticulously recorded. Even if a pane of glass in one of the windows had been broken, we were assured, it would be shown!

Intelligence Reports and aerial photographs said that within the past few days, probably as a result of a visit by Field Marshal Rommel, local people had been recruited to erect huge poles in the proposed landing zones. Such a pole could easily smash a troop-carrying glider, as the landing speed of a fully laden glider is between eighty and one hundred miles per hour and at such a speed it would only need the wing to touch a pole to reduce the flimsy craft to matchwood. Even landing on an airfield in daylight posed risks in such a lightly constructed machine, so landing on rough ground in darkness might be expected to pose a few additional hazards and the poles were something that we could well have done without.

For this special mission we were fortunate in having been allocated the best pilots that the Glider Pilot Regiment could produce. They were cool and efficient characters who informed us that although we may lose a wing or two, they were confident that they would be able to put us down close to our targets, and fully expected to finish the trip the right way up!

At 1700 hours we had tea and strolled over to a large tent to see a film show. There was little else to do because, now that our mission had been disclosed, the camp was sealed; no one could get in or out. Afterwards we rushed to the NAAFI tent where we queued for a glass of beer, but became fed up with the long wait, gave up and returned to our tent where we played cards, turning in eventually at around 2200 hours.

It was hot inside the small tent and I suspect that, like me, few of the others slept soundly. On my mind was the thought that the task that had been allocated to us seemed so great for so small a force. To be the only Allied unit in France, even if for only a short time, facing whatever German forces might be thrown at us, seemed a daunting prospect.

What if the Germans counter-attacked before the Paras came in to reinforce us? What if the seaborne forces didn't break through the German defences in time to take over the positions we were holding? Although everything was planned down to the smallest detail, it was clear to us that there were so many possibilities for everything to go badly wrong.

I have never made a secret of the fact that I, like every one of my colleagues, thought that the whole scheme was little more than a suicide mission. A tiny force of around 180 men was to crash-land in gliders without heavy weapons or armoured vehicles, to capture a couple of bridges from the Nazis, with no guarantee of being relieved or supported for some hours at the very least. Even if we succeeded in taking the bridges – which was in itself quite possible as we had surprise on our side – the task of holding them until reinforcements got to us by air or fought their way through from the beaches seemed like a pipedream.

I smoked a great many cigarettes on the night after the first briefing, just about the longest night I can ever remember, and as such the most appropriate, if uncomfortable, start to D-Day, – later to be dubbed "The Longest Day".

Conditions on 5 June were far from ideal for an airborne operation, but apparently if there were further delays the seaborne forces would have run into difficulties because of the height of the tides, and there were many more of the seaborne troops than there were of us. We were told therefore that, weather permitting, we were to take off that evening, and we all knew that it was going to happen, whatever the weather.

We had an easy day, checking equipment and carrying out final briefings. Everyone was keyed up and the air felt charged with tension. Latest intelligence reports informed us that within the past few days the 12th SS Panzer Division and 21st Panzer Divisions (30,000 men with 300 tanks) had both moved into the area around Caen, some five miles from our targets. 12th SS Panzer Division 'Hitler Jugend' were the elite of the zealous Hitler Youth Movement and Nazi fanatics every one. Upon hearing this unwelcome news, the general feeling was expressed by one and all as "Just our bloody luck!"

After an early tea we saw another film, then rushed to the

NAAFI tent for a final pint of beer but all too soon came the strident and unsympathetic command, "Get Dressed".

Fully equipped, we looked like pack mules. Everything that we would need during the next few days we had to carry ourselves. The glider pilots had warned Major Howard about the dangers of over-loading, and he ordered that we should all be weighed in our fully loaded condition. The average weight was then calculated – for our glider it was 231 pounds – but most of us subsequently took on extra loads, such as pouches of Mills grenades and bandoliers of .303 ammunition, so the exercise of weighing everyone earlier was really something of a farce. Later, when the glider pilots were debriefed, every one of them said that they were hopelessly overloaded.

Nonetheless, we clambered on to trucks that took us on the short ride to the airfield where we sorted ourselves into Sections and Platoons, drank hot tea and sat around on the edge of the runway smoking heavily and cracking corny jokes. The gliders were already in position behind their Halifax bombers, which were to be our glider tugs.

Nervously we waited to clamber aboard. We kept busy, smearing our recently issued multi-coloured grease paint on our hands, necks and faces so that our white skin would not show up in the dark. Then, at 2200 hours, the order rang out "emplane" and we clambered aboard the gliders, wishing each other good luck, singing and joking. Once aboard the jokes continued, and on the surface there was an air of good humour but it did not cover the strong undercurrent of tension.

As I strapped myself into my seat I became aware that I was becoming increasingly scared. Both Major John Howard, commanding the *Coup de Main* force, and our Platoon Commander, Lieutenant Den Brotheridge, were travelling in our glider. As they came aboard, having said their farewells to the 'Top Brass' who were standing around on the edge of the runway, they wished us all "Good Luck" and we responded in our various ways. Then, to let the Top Brass know that they had made a good choice in selecting us for this special mission, we sang for all we were worth.

At 2256 hours the steady hum of the bomber engines suddenly

increased to a deafening roar. My muscles tightened, a cold shiver ran up my spine, I went hot and cold, and sang all the louder to stop my teeth from chattering. Suddenly there was a violent jerk and a loud "twang" as our tug plane took up the slack on the 125-foot towrope. The glider rolled slowly forward and my muscles tightened as the flying plywood box gathered speed, momentarily left the ground, then set down again with a heavy thump and, finally, a jerk as with a loud roaring of the bomber's engines we became airborne. The other five gliders were to follow at one-minute intervals.

I experienced an interesting psychological change in the few minutes before and immediately after take off.

As I had climbed aboard and strapped myself into my seat I felt tense, strange and extremely frightened, much as I imagined a condemned man must feel on his last morning when he is being led from the condemned cell to the gallows. It was as if I were in a fantasy dream world and I thought that at any moment I would wake up from this unreality and find that I was back in the barrack room at Bulford Camp.

Laughing and singing, each one of us attempted to show the others that we were not frightened, but personally I knew that I was scared half to death. The idea of carrying out a night-time airborne landing of such a small force into the midst of the German army seemed to me to be a sure way of getting killed, yet at the moment that the glider parted company with the ground I experienced an inexplicable change. The feeling of terror vanished and was replaced by exhilaration. I felt as if I were on top of the world. The hand of destiny had guided me to this point in my life and I remember thinking, "You've had it, chum. It's no good worrying any more . . . the die is cast; what will be will be, and there is nothing that you can do about it", and so I sat back to enjoy my first trip to continental Europe.

Part 2

A NORMANDY DIARY

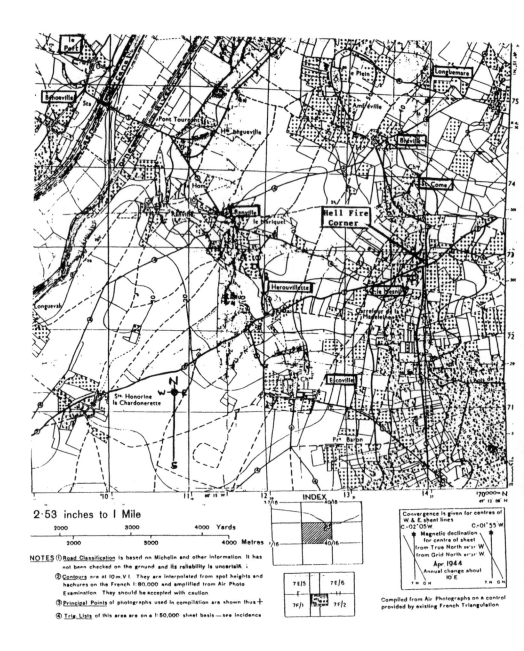

Chapter 4

THE LONGEST DAY

D-Day – Bénouville, Tuesday, 6 June

It was many years later that I understood for the first time that we did not head south as soon as we were airborne. To avoid clashing with the two American Airborne Divisions, who were to carry out missions parallel with ours, we first flew some seventy miles eastwards on leaving Tarrant Rushton. At an assembly area in West Sussex, between Worthing and Bognor Regis, we crossed the coast and headed for France.

To disguise our mission, our six gliders were towed over the coast in the midst of a large bomber force. It was hoped that, as, one by one, we were cast-off, those down below would assume that we were bombers that had been hit. The towing Halifax bomber and the Horsa glider are much the same size and in the darkness, and at such a height, it was unlikely that anyone would notice the difference.

It was about an hour after take-off when the Glider Pilots announced that we were approaching the French coast. Not that we needed telling since the reception committee was self-evident; to the front of us the sky was lit by a great carpet of flak. Numerous multi-coloured flashes of anti-aircraft shells, streams of coloured tracer and other missiles were exploding like an enormous fireworks display.

The time was just coming up to midnight and, although the full invasion would not start for several hours, for us 'D-Day' had already arrived.

39

As we drew level with the thickest of the flak and were beginning to make out the coastline, there came the familiar 'twang', and jerk of the tow-rope, followed by almost total silence which, from past experience, told us that we had parted company from the towing bomber.

While in tow there had been a continuous high-pitched scream of wind forcing its way through the cracks and crevices in the thin fabric covering of the wooden fuselage. The noise was increased by the fact that the door had been opened to facilitate rapid exit once we landed.

As we approached the coast the order was given to keep quiet. Hardly a sound could be heard as the bombers flew onwards on a diversionary inland bombing mission.

Once a fully laden Horsa glider is released by its tow plane it has just one way to go – downwards. Unlike the small sport gliders that can soar upwards on the slightest current of air, a fully-laden Horsa just keeps plummeting earthwards and I have the greatest respect and admiration for the Glider Pilots who have to make an immediate decision. If they misjudge their approach, unlike the pilots of the powered plane, they cannot go around again for another try. Theirs is a one-off decision as they swoop towards the ground at a speed approaching one hundred miles per hour.

Immediately after cast-off we had gone into a steep dive, a manoeuvre that had more than one purpose. Firstly of course the pilots knew exactly where we were and exactly the point we had to reach. Having no alternative to descent, they had to lose height at a rate which would allow us to arrive at the landing zone alongside the bridges with no further height to lose. To arrive at the landing zone while still too high, and then circling around to lose height is not a good idea when you are being shot at. Secondly, the German flak was ranged at the bomber formation, and rapid descent took us away from the immediate danger of flak damage. Thirdly, it was hoped that observers on the ground would assume that the rapidly descending glider was a crippled bomber on its way down.

From around 6000 feet we plummeted earthwards at what felt to us like breakneck speed until we were within 1000 feet of the ground, where we levelled out to glide more slowly down and take two sweeping right-hand turns to position ourselves for the run-in to the landing zone.

Now our pilot had seen his destination and turned and settled into his final approach. We seemed for an instant to be suspended in space, and then we were on the way down.

With our bodies tensed and weapons tightly gripped, the Senior Pilot, Staff Sergeant Jim Wallwork, yelled, "Link Arms", and we knew that at any moment we would touch down. The time was 0015 hours as we all held tight and braced ourselves for touchdown.

There was the usual slight bump, a small jerk and a much heavier thump, as the glider made contact with the ground, but only for a moment. It jerked again, shuddered, left the ground for a second or two, bumped over the rough surface and lurched forward like a bucking bronco.

We sped forward, bouncing up and down on our hard wooden seats as the vehicle lost contact with the ground, then came down again with another heavy thump, a tug and a jerk. For a few moments it appeared that we were in for a comparatively smooth landing, but just as that thought flashed through my mind the darkness suddenly filled with a stream of brilliant sparks as the glider lost its wheels and the skid hit some stony ground. There followed a sound like a giant canvas sheet being viciously ripped apart, then a mighty crash like a clap of thunder and my body seemed to be moving in several directions at once. Moments later the crippled glider skidded and bounced over the uneven ground to slide finally to a juddering halt, whereupon I found myself perched in a very strange position at an uneven angle.

I peered into a misty blue and greyish haze. From somewhere out in endless space there zoomed towards me a long tracer-like stream of multi-coloured lights, like a host of shooting stars that moved towards me at high speed. I realized after a moment that I was not being shot at. I was simply concussed and seeing stars!

The noise from the landing had ceased very suddenly and was replaced by an ominous silence. No one stirred, nothing moved. My immediate thought was "God help me – we must all be dead". The peace, after all the din and commotion, was unexpected and eerie. Then some of the others began to stir and the realization that

41

we were not all dead came quickly as bodies began unstrapping themselves and moving around in the darkness of the glider's shattered interior.

If the pilots had done a good job – which they had, although we did not yet know it – we were now in the remains of a very flimsy vehicle adjacent to a bridge held by armed Germans. I thought that this was probably not the healthiest place to be sitting around daydreaming, and the same idea obviously occurred to the others at just about the same instant. The whole interior of the glider erupted into a hive of furious activity as everyone sought their various weapons and equipment.

The exit door had been right beside my seat. Now there was only a mass of twisted wood and fabric across the doorway and we had to use the butts of our rifles to smash our way out.

When it was my turn, I clambered out and dropped to the ground. I glanced around from beneath the glider's tilted wing and saw the canal bridge's massive steel superstructure towering above me. The pilots had done a fantastic job in bringing the slithering, bouncing and crippled glider to a halt with its nose buried into the canal bank and within seventy-five yards of the bridge.

As I moved forward I glanced back towards the glider and saw that the entire front had been smashed inwards – almost back to the wing. There had been some twenty feet of structure forward of my seat, which was just below the front edge of the wing. Now there was a twisted mass of wreckage. I had been very lucky, but I thought that those who were forward of me must have been badly smashed up or killed. There was no time to think about this, however. The medics would take care of the injured. The job of my twenty-one-man Platoon, together with Major Howard, his Wireless Operator and the five Royal Engineers, was to fight our way across to the west side of the bridge as quickly as possible.

The tall superstructure appeared to shimmer in the moonlight. A few of the lads were already up ahead and, not wishing to be left behind in this exposed place, I made haste to join them. Major Howard was already on the approach to the bridge and shouted, "Come on, boys. This is it !"

Charging forward, we reached the wide steel bridge, letting fly with rifles and automatics, and threw grenades, shouting at the top of our voices to frighten the German defenders and to boost our own morale.

An enemy machine gun on the far side of the bridge chattered into life. We returned fire and kept going, with our Platoon Commander Lieutenant Brotheridge, leading the way. The machine gun was firing long bursts as we charged, and Brotheridge, who was at the very front of the charge, was hit and fell to the ground mortally wounded.[1]

Later, when we learned what had happened, every one of us was really distressed that Lieutenant Brotheridge should have been killed in that way and at the very start of our mission. He was a man for whom we all had the greatest respect. Like all our Airborne officers, he had never asked us to do anything that he would not do himself. It was typical of him to have been ahead of the rest of us in the flat-out charge across the bridge.

As we neared the far side of the bridge, still shouting, firing our weapons and lobbing hand grenades, the Germans jumped to their feet and ran for their lives, scattering in all directions. Relief, exhilaration, incredulity – I experienced all these feelings upon realizing that we had taken the bridge.

The first part of our mission had been accomplished and now we had to hold on to what we had gained until reinforcements arrived, the first of whom, the Paras, were expected to join us within the hour.

The three gliders allocated to the canal bridge landed within minutes of each other and with almost pin-point accuracy, although one broke in half by a small pond in which unfortunately one of the lads was drowned, having become trapped within the wreckage. Only minutes after landing the canal bridge was in our hands and we were keen to know what was happening at the river bridge. In due course, to our immense relief and pleasure, a runner came over and reported that, although only two of their three gliders had landed, they had also captured their bridge.

By thirty minutes past midnight we had taken both bridges and our Company Commander was able to transmit the coded wireless signal "Ham and Jam" to tell High Command that both of the bridges had been captured intact.

Now began our anxious wait for the arrival of reinforcements,

43

the wait that we all knew would be the most nerve-racking aspect of the operation. Pathfinder parachutists were scheduled to jump more or less as our gliders were landing, and their task was to set up marker lights nearby to guide in the reinforcements, 7th Parachute Battalion, who were due to jump about thirty minutes later.

We expected the Paras to reach us within an hour and, with the bridges now in our hands, we had to defend them against whatever counter-attack might be made. Still operating to the detailed plan rehearsed at the briefings before our departure, we took up our prearranged defensive positions. Our seven-man section moved a short distance down to the west side of the canal and took up positions astride a single-track railway that ran from Ouistreham to Caen along the top of the embankment.

We removed our heavy equipment and unstrapped our small lightweight entrenching tools. These had a short wooden shaft, with a metal head having a small pick and spade. The pickhead was about one and half inches wide and the spade about eight inches. This was our only digging implement – not the most effective tool, but just about the maximum that we could carry on top of everything else. They were not very useful on hard ground and even in soft soil they could lift little more than a handful of earth. They did, however, enable us to scrape shallow indentations in the ballast stones of the railway track to a depth sufficient to place our prone bodies below ground level. This offered us some protection against an enemy counter-attack, which we were sure would soon be launched.

Apart from the scraping and chinking noise of our entrenching tools against the ballast stones all was surprisingly quiet until the peace was suddenly interrupted by the sound of powerful engines from the west, somewhere around Bénouville. The accompanying clanking, rattling and squealing noises heralded the movement of tanks, and very obviously they were coming our way.

For tanks to arrive so quickly was terrifying and we stopped digging as they drew nearer. Our main concern was their size, as we had nothing to stop larger tanks. No doubt the guards who had fled from the bridge had been able to warn a nearby unit of our arrival and the tanks were sent to investigate. By now they were less than fifty yards to my rear and moving towards the bridge.

Suddenly I heard the familiar crack as one of the lads by the bridge fired a PIAT (Projector, Infantry, Anti-Tank) weapon. This was never a popular weapon with us, as we considered it rather ineffective. It stood on a short bipod and fired a fat missile which was not very accurate beyond fifty to seventy-five yards – and, at that range, if you fired and missed the target there was insufficient time to reload before the tank fired back at you. We had all been trained to use these weapons and, frankly, we were thoroughly sceptical about their effectiveness against real tanks. To our utter amazement, however, within a second or so of the PIAT being fired there was a mighty explosion quickly followed by shouts and screams, and it was obvious that an effective hit had been scored on the leading tank.

I learned later that this timely feat had been performed by Sergeant 'Wagger' Thornton, who had landed in glider number six, next to the Orne river bridge. Because of the light opposition over there he had come with a platoon of reinforcements to us at the canal bridge. The main enemy forces were known to be located at Bénouville and Le Port, and they would have to cross the canal bridge to get to the river bridge, and so it was clearly most important to hold the canal bridge.

The tank that was hit was a light machine, fortunately for us all, but still it burned very nicely, illuminating the bridge structure with a huge blaze of orange, red and yellow. There followed the sound of exploding ammunition as the tank 'brewed up'.

The following tanks were obviously not keen to chance their luck, so with much revving of engines and general commotion they withdrew in disorder. This was not really surprising, because an hour before they had been simply a unit in a largely unopposed army of occupation, and now, suddenly, they were having their tanks blown up and they could not have had any idea about what they were up against. As far as they could tell our force could have been anything from just a handful of paratroops to something much more formidable.

This uncertainty on the part of the enemy was to buy us valuable time. It is very probable that the Germans could have over-run our positions at the time of the attack by the tanks if they had realized how few in number we were. Our night arrival undoubtedly led to confusion in the German ranks – as intended – and bought us the valuable time we needed. 'Wagger' Thornton's successful attack on the enemy tank would certainly lead the enemy to assume that we had a significant anti-tank capability, which would have reinforced their caution about launching an all-out attack on a force whose strength they could not assess accurately until daybreak. If the Paras could get to us in time, although equipped much as we were, with not much other than small arms and a few additional PIATs, we stood a chance of holding out until the seaborne forces got through to us from the beaches.

After the tanks were driven off we settled down to await the arrival of the Paras. All was quiet again until the parachute transports came overhead, when the German anti-aircraft guns and ground forces began firing into the night sky.

The first few planes flew over with little opposition, but those that followed ran into heavy flak and at least one took a direct hit, was set on fire and came hurtling down like a comet from about 3000 feet. I couldn't see anything of them in the darkness but I hoped that the Paras and aircrew had been able to bail out before it crashed, since it hit the ground with such force that no one on board could possibly have survived the impact.[2]

As soon as the Paras had dropped, Major Howard began sending out pre-arranged 'Victory V' signals to guide them to the bridges, using a shrill whistle to send out the Morse code 'V' – dot dot dot dash.

The 'brewed-up' tank, still burning, was also a helpful marker for the Paras, although they must have been apprehensive upon seeing such signs of violent action so soon after the beginning of the operation.

The Paras should have been with us within an hour but it was obvious from the way that they were being carried by the wind that they were being scattered over a wide area and not within the compact dropping zone that had been planned. The result of all the confusion was that it was around 0230 hours before the first of them arrived, and then only in dribs and drabs. They were badly scattered, some of them hopelessly so, making it impossible for them to regroup at the designated dropping zone. Instead they were banding together in twos and threes, trying to make their way to our positions through unfamiliar wooded countryside in the darkness. Most were finding the river or the canal and following it until they came to the bridges.

Unfortunately the Germans were using the same method to get to us. It became very tricky as figures suddenly appeared in the darkness. It was impossible to tell whether they were friend or foe until they got to within whispering distance and we challenged them with a pre-arranged password. We whispered 'V', and the correct response was 'for Victory'.

A German patrol which came close to us was challenged, then cut down by the light machine-gun fire when they failed to respond with the password. Killed with them were three of our Paras whom they had taken prisoner, and who obviously had declined to supply the password at the appropriate time, and so paid with their lives, along with the German patrol that had captured them. It was tragic bad luck, but a hazard of war.

What other action occurred that night was sporadic, but nerve-racking. Incredibly, the German officer responsible for the defence of the bridges, dismayed that his bridges had been captured, arrived at the river bridge in his staff car, leapt out with pistol in hand and was promptly hit and wounded by our small arms fire. A despatch rider on a motorcycle, following the staff car, was killed at the same time.

The commander had been assigned from 21st Panzer Division to command the bridge defences, and, although his troops were from much less exalted units, and luckily for us not too effective, he himself was an obvious fanatic. When wounded, he called out for our men to shoot him, to finish him off. They declined to oblige him, but he later died from his wounds anyway and so no doubt he would have felt that honour had been satisfied!

Generally the night was quieter than we had expected but with the dawn came Germans in droves and from all directions. Under cover of darkness their snipers had climbed into tall trees and buildings and from daylight onwards began firing their high-powered rifles with deadly accuracy. My first indication was the distant 'crack' as they fired and, almost instantaneously, one of our lads would crash to the ground. They were fantastic marksmen and seldom let off a shot without hitting what they were aiming at. We quickly learned to respect these highly skilled Germans who were well concealed several hundred yards away, yet could pick off a man who only had the top of his head above ground level.

With no ammunition to spare we knew that there was no point in blazing away at every high tree and building in the surrounding area. In any event we were reluctant to disclose our defensive positions and firepower. We knew that the Germans could still have had little idea of our strength and hoped that they had over-estimated our strength, so we were not keen to help them revise their estimates.

All that we could do was to lie doggo and keep a sharp eye open for a definite target. When we had to move it was a case of crawling rapidly across open spaces and, when we thought that we were reasonably concealed from view, jumping to our feet and running for dear life!

Soon after daybreak a Spitfire came straight at us at tree-top height and we all ducked and held our breath, expecting that the pilot was unaware that the bridge was in Allied hands. To everyone's surprise, however, the aircraft appeared to be in no hurry and the pilot threw a package from his opened cockpit. It landed with remarkable accuracy close to the bridge. When it had been recovered it was found to contain the first editions of the daily newspapers!

German troops had begun moving towards us from daylight onwards, probing and attacking, but during the hours before dawn a good number of the scattered Paras had managed to reach us and with their added firepower we were able to repulse successive waves of attack.

We would have given a great deal to have possessed some heavy mortars and artillery, but knew that through the rest of the day we would have to rely upon our small arms – rifles, Sten guns, a few light machine guns, small two inch mortars and two PIATs.

The Germans, on the other hand, were bringing up heavier firepower. It was some consolation to us that, because we were surrounded and they were attacking us from all sides, it was not possible for them to use heavy artillery. By now they were becoming aware that we were only a small Airborne force and they were probably confident that they could wipe us out with overwhelming numbers of infantry.

Apart from the night-time visitors, the Germans sent no more tanks, for which fact we were all profoundly relieved. Although our trusty PIAT may have knocked out one light tank under cover of darkness, the two we possessed, plus those that the Paras might have, would certainly be useless in the face of an all-out attack by heavier machines.

One effective anti-tank weapon we did gain, however – a German gun set into a concrete pit on the south side of the canal bridge. During the morning an enemy gunboat came up the canal from the direction of Caen. Some of the lads fired the gun and the boat did a fast about turn and sped southwards.

(The story of that gunboat might have ended there, but I was to learn many years after the war that our gunnery was better than we had realized, because we all thought the shot must have missed by a mile. However, a member of 7th Para, now in Canada, told me how his section, defending the southern outskirts of Bénouville, was instructed to attack the vessel as it passed his position. He was delighted to observe a direct hit from the gun at the canal bridge, forcing the gunboat to turn and run!)

Later a second gunboat approached from the north. The liberated gun on the south side of the bridge could not be fired northwards, but a couple of the lads had nipped off with a PIAT and kept well down below the level of the canal bank until the boat drew level. Then they bobbed up and let fly with a PIAT bomb. The missile exploded against its side at just above water level. The boat quickly pulled over to the bank and after a brief exchange of fire the crew surrendered.

Our command structure, officers and NCOs, had taken an alarming number of casualties. We had been in action for only a few hours and it was likely to be several more before we could expect any help from the seaborne forces. We had absolutely no knowledge of how things were going at the beaches, and in any case the beaches were several miles away, with the ground between them and our own positions sure to be fiercely defended; and of course, we were surrounded.

Den Brotheridge, our Platoon Commander, had already been lost, having died from his wounds soon after we landed, and our Platoon Sergeant was injured during the glider's crash-landing. By midmorning our Section Corporal had been wounded. I didn't know how the rest of our glider-borne force was making out but I gathered that most of our officers and sergeants were out of action, and nothing had been heard of the missing glider.

One good piece of news I learned after daybreak was that, although the front of our glider had been badly smashed in, such that survival of the pilots seemed unlikely, both of them had indeed survived – injured but alive and receiving medical attention. Although with a badly cut head, Jim Wallwork, together with other reasonably fit pilots from other gliders, spent the first few hours after landing gathering ammunition from the shattered gliders and distributing it to the bridge defenders.

As soon as we came under the fire of the enemy snipers we had taken advantage of the much improved protection of the existing German trenches, but later in the morning our seven-man Section was ordered to leave the comparative protection of the bridge defences.

It was to the small village of Le Port that we were directed, on the higher ground just to the north-west of the canal bridge. During the night Le Port had been occupied by units of the 7th Parachute Battalion who were now under intensive attack by elements of the 21st Panzer Division. Moving with great caution, out of respect for the German snipers who appeared to have every inch of open ground well covered, we reached the outskirts of the village. There we came across a battle-weary young officer who told us that his Company had been virtually wiped out. They had been on the far side of the village and had been under constant attack by a large force since dawn. This seemed to sum up our problem – we were becoming fewer with each passing hour, while the enemy, now fully mobilized, was committing more and more forces to the battle.

While I was on my way up to Le Port, our bridges were visited by a lone enemy aircraft, a fighter bomber, evidently making a last-ditch attempt to deny the use of the bridge to the Allied forces, who by now were starting to make inroads off the beaches. A well-aimed bomb hit the canal bridge, but by some miracle it failed to explode, bouncing harmlessly off into the canal.[3]

Meanwhile, before becoming involved in the fight around the village of Le Port, we found a quiet spot beneath a tree to have a bite to eat. I had eaten nothing since leaving England and was glad to open my twenty-four-hour ration pack which consisted of a few dry biscuits, boiled sweets and a bar of unsweetened chocolate. I chewed a hard biscuit and sucked a sweet. It was not much, but for a short time it took my mind off the thought of food, until suddenly our 'meal' was interrupted by a long burst from an enemy heavy machine gun.

The stream of bullets ripped through the tree, inches above our heads, showering us with twigs and leaves. At that moment the 7th Para Battalion's Commanding Officer, Lieutenant Colonel Pine-Coffin, accompanied by a young officer, appeared next to our tree, crouching to keep below the line of the machine-gun fire, and busily looking all around, taking in the picture. The two of them paused momentarily, glanced up at the splintered tree and the Colonel said to his companion, "That is not too healthy old boy. He's firing just a shade too close for comfort. We had better deal with him, eh?"

With Stens tucked under their arms, they wandered off southwards in a leisurely manner and disappeared through a gap in a nearby hedge. A few moments later came the rat-a-tat-tat 'of two Stens, followed by complete silence.

Soon they reappeared with broad smiles upon their faces, looked towards us and the Colonel said, "Well lads, that's fixed him up". With a casual wave they continued strolling on their way, two grand officers who gave the impression of having not a care in the world, although they must have realized that the situation was fast becoming desperate.

In retrospect, it seems likely that these two officers were the direct cause of our presence in Le Port, in that they had just successfully requested some support from our small force holding the bridges, and they were now on their way back to their men in the beleaguered village. Years later I realized that the young Officer who had accompanied the Para Commander was Richard Todd, the film actor, who resumed his career after the war and appropriately played the role of Major John Howard in the film *The Longest Day*. No other actor could have had quite the same feel for the role as he had!

The village of Le Port was not large, but when we arrived only a small part was still under our control. The Germans had already gained the western and southern areas and the centre was a no-man's-land.

It was a typical old Normandy village of narrow winding streets with small cottages set close together, mainly in short terraces. Nearly all fronted directly onto the street and, at the rear, had medium-sized walled gardens. At the end of those on the eastern side were orchards and small fields enclosed by low walls or thick hedges.

On arrival at the outskirts of the village we made contact with the Paras who directed us to defend a short row of cottages just to the south of the church. It was inside one of these cottages that I found a partly used laundry book which I stuffed into my tunic pocket. This was the notebook in which I was to scribble my daily recollections during the coming weeks and months of my stay in Normandy.

Having gained access to one of the cottages from the rear, two of us went upstairs while the others stayed below. Peering through the front window, we realized that the Germans were occupying a cottage directly across the narrow street. We lobbed a couple of hand grenades through their window and scampered downstairs and waited until they retaliated with their stick grenades. As soon as these exploded in the bedroom above, we ran back up the stairs and repeated the process.

Because of the danger of being pinned down we soon found it necessary to vacate the first cottage by nipping out of the back door, over the side garden wall, and entering the next one. There were not enough of us to take up all-round defensive positions or to occupy every cottage along the terrace and eventually, as the Germans crossed the street and gained access to adjoining cottages, we were forced to withdraw to avoid being cut off.

With Germans occupying buildings on either side of ours we decided to carry out a fast withdrawal by running down the back garden and out through a gate in the end wall. As we did so the garden was raked by machine-gun fire, but we all got clear without being hit.

We moved into a small field on the eastern fringe of the village and immediately to the south of the church. In our new position it would be difficult for the enemy to carry out a surprise attack as we spread out and lay down in the longish grass. We were screened from the cottages by the tall back garden wall. If we covered the gateway and the churchyard, we felt fairly secure.

Soon a German peered cautiously through the gateway. We ducked down and kept still. Then another appeared and, obviously assuming that we had vacated the area, they both stepped out into the field. Despite our shortage of ammunition, all seven of us opened fire with everything we had – including even a Sten gun that was being carried by Lance Corporal Minns, who had taken over our Section when our NCO, Corporal Webb, had been wounded at the canal bridge. The two Germans could hardly have known what hit them and they crashed to the ground and made no further movement.

At the front, the church was separated from the road by a high wall. We could hear Germans on the other side barking orders to each other. Two of us slithered through the tall grass to climb over the low wall that separated the south side of the church from our field. Once within the churchyard, we darted from gravestone to gravestone, until close enough to the much higher front boundary wall to lob over a couple of grenades, before turning and running back to the field.

As we ran back into the field the grenades exploded and we had the satisfaction of hearing screams from someone in the roadway. Suddenly, in perfect English, a German shouted, "You English in the church. You are surrounded and cannot escape. Leave your weapons behind and come out through the church gate and no harm will come to you."

Two of the others jumped over the wall along the southern edge of the churchyard to hurl the last of our grenades over the wall, shouting, "Have these, then. That's all we're giving up."

It was fortunate that we chose not to take up the offer of surrender as we learned later that during the earlier fighting around the village the Germans had overrun the 7th Para

Regimental Aid Post and had murdered all of the wounded where they lay. At the same time they shot all the Medical Orderlies and the Regimental Padre, Captain Percy Parry. The Medical Orderlies were all dedicated Quakers who carried no weapons.

With no more grenades and very low on ammunition, we shared out our remaining rounds which were sufficient to part-stock our rifles and the Bren light machine gun, both of which used the same .303 bullet. We had no idea of what was happening elsewhere around the village and did not know if any more of our lads were still in action and if, like us, they had run low on ammo and were conserving stocks.

After all the earlier din of battle it suddenly became very quiet. Even the Germans had stopped shouting to each other, when suddenly, in the uncanny stillness of that spring day, I heard a sound that will live with me for the rest of my days. From somewhere to our north, well beyond the churchyard and probably beyond the village, I heard a sound that made the hairs stand up on the back of my neck – a sound like the wild wailing of banshees. Almost immediately I realized that it was high-pitched music carried towards me on the breeze that was coming from the direction of the coast.

One of the lads shouted "It's them – it's the Commando!" and we all let out a cheer as the noise grew louder and we recognized it as the high-pitched and uneven wailing of *bagpipes*! It may sound suspiciously like a scene from a Hollywood western movie, on a par with the bugle sounding 'Charge' as the cavalry arrives in the nick of time, but it really did happen like that.

No 4 Commando had come off the beach at 'Sword', smashing its way through the German defences to Ouistreham, and fighting all the way down the canal bank to Le Port. For us, excessively tired young soldiers, out of ammunition and in an impossible position, the sense of relief and exhilaration can only be guessed at. To know that the seaborne forces were ashore and moving inland was also a cause for enormous relief and satisfaction. We were English every one, and always ready to have a bit of fun at the expense of Scotsmen and their pipes, but those wild wailing bagpipes were like the sound of Heaven. The raucous noise came to me more sweetly than any music that I had ever heard. It was like hearing a reprieve of sentence, which in effect it really was.

Shouting and cheering, we all expressed our joy together and, abandoning all caution, were up on our feet and leapt over the wall into the churchyard again, yelling things like "Now you Jerry bastards, you've got a real fight on your hands".

Suddenly, as if in response to our lack of caution, and from just above our heads somewhere up in the church tower, a fast-firing enemy machine gun burst into life. We dived for the cover of the nearest gravestones, but then realized that he was not firing at us, but towards the Commando.

During the time that we had been in the adjoining field we had nipped in and out of the churchyard a couple of times and had felt fairly secure. It was odd that the German machine-gunner had not fired at us previously, and that he was now still not firing at us but at the approaching Commando. It was possible that he could not see us from his position of concealment up in the church, or that he had only recently got inside the building and taken up his position. However, we had been watching the churchyard and had not seen him, so perhaps he had got in from the other side of the building. It was also a possibility that he had been aware of us, but that, having seen the approaching Commando, he had decided that they presented a better target than our seven-man Section. We had been spread out in the grass in the adjoining field, and to fire at us would have given away his position.[4]

From the churchyard we could see nothing of the machine-gunner, so we ran back to the field and fired our last few rounds at the upper part of the church in the hope of keeping him quiet. He ignored us and continued to fire long bursts towards the Commando.

After a quick discussion we decided to rush the church, get inside and dislodge him from there. However, just as the decision was made, we heard the Commando in the street beyond the churchyard's front wall. They were accompanied by two Sherman tanks which halted, swung their guns over the wall and fired with a deafening crash, blasting away the top of the church tower.[5]

When the firing stopped we went back into the churchyard, out through the front gate, and greeted the Commando and assisted them in clearing out the few remaining Germans. Most had fled once the reinforcements had arrived and we were ordered to return to our Company.

No 4 Commando, led by Lord Lovat, marched through Le Port, down into Bénouville, then over the bridges and out into the countryside beyond. As they crossed the canal bridge they ran into the same problem that we had suffered throughout the day: the snipers who had harassed us began picking them off.

Now that our stock of ammunition had been replenished we fired in what we thought was the general direction of the snipers' location. The need to stop these deadly accurate marksmen became more acute when the Commando drove a 'liberated' horse and cart across the bridge. About halfway across a shot rang out and the horse was killed, blocking the bridge.

Someone spotted a well-concealed pillbox set into the west side of the canal bank several hundred yards to the south of the bridge. Our newly fledged 'gunners', now conversant with the workings of the captured German gun, fired two or three rounds that narrowly missed the target, and then scored a direct hit. We all cheered until, after a few minutes, as another Section marched across the bridge, the same snipers fired again and another man fell to the ground. Some Paras or Airborne Engineers made their way down the canal embankment and, with high explosives, finally put on end to the troublesome snipers who had taken a fair toll during the course of the day.

Almost incredibly, the Longest Day was, for us, long enough to include a few humorous moments.

At the time of the visit by the first enemy gunboat, Corporal "Bill" Bailey and some of his Section were in the concrete emplacement that housed the German gun. I had found a well-constructed German trench nearby and, conscious of enemy snipers, had crawled over to see how things were going with them. "Bill" was sitting in the bottom of the gun pit with his tin mess can filled with water, into which he had placed a 'Mixed Monkey" tea cube. This consisted of a small square cube made of powered tea, sugar and milk and, when added to hot water, made a quite diabolical brew which bore little resemblance to tea and could only really be described as a hot drink. The mess can had been placed upon a small heater appliance which consisted of a small metal crosspiece below which was a platform upon which was placed a solidified methylated spirit tablet, rather like a flat round moth-ball. If one could get them to ignite, which was never easy, they gave off just sufficient heat to warm up a small can of water. The tablets gave off a purple flame and a really foul smell!

On field training exercises we had already discovered that heating anything on these small gadgets was a slow process and, as we had been so busy, I doubt that anyone else had found the time to attempt a brew up under our present battle conditions. Our Bill, however, was a Londoner through and through, and to him a cuppa was more than just a beverage – it was almost a religion!

While he had been quietly squatting in the bottom of the pit watching over his brew, Wally Parr, Gus Gardner[6] and Bill Gray had been examining the captured gun. They were deep in discussion about how it might work and if it was safe to put such an old weapon to the test.

As they were working out how to aim it, by pure chance the enemy gunboat appeared. Their excitement and furious activity when the gunboat appeared did not deflect Bill from his brewing-up, and eventually Gus Gardner pulled or pushed whatever it was that fired the thing. There was a blinding flash and a great crash like a clap of thunder, accompanied by clouds of smoke. It was evidently a rather old gun and had probably not been fired for many years, and the gun pit was immediately showered with dirt and concrete dust.

As the dust and smoke began to clear the surprised silence was shattered by a loud howl of anguish from Bill Bailey. Just at the very moment that the gun had fired, his can of water was on the verge of coming to the boil (or as near as it was ever likely to get). He was furious, 'Yer bloody idiots – look what you've bleedin' done – it took me over 'arf an hour 'ter get this bloody tin of water 'ot, and just as I am about ready ter make a brew of tea yer 'ave ter find out 'ow that bloody gun works – look at me mess can."

What had been almost a passable imitation of a brew of tea was now more like a can of porridge, having been half filled with dirt and cement dust. He really looked a sorry sight, sitting in the base of the gun pit, his can of tea ruined, and his face, thinning hair and clothing coated in dirt and dust.

Wally tried to pacify him by pointing towards the gunboat, but Bill was inconsolable. "All that you 'ave done is ter bloody well ruin me cuppa," he moaned. We just couldn't help it. Everyone except Bill was splitting his sides with laughter.

Another event that caused great merriment occurred when a team of Italian forced labourers arrived to erect anti-airlanding poles. We had been advised by French Intelligence that these were to be erected and were grateful that we did not find them in position when we landed. The delay in erecting them was apparently the responsibility of these Italian workers, and they evidently feared the wrath of their German masters much more than the threat posed by us.

In a big second lift, code-named 'Mallard', the remainder of our Regiment and the Royal Ulster Rifles, along with some of the Devons, were due to take off from England in a fleet of gliders at 1900 hours. Due to lack of suitable landing areas only a limited number could be put down. Even so, at 2100 hours the whole sky to our north was filled with countless tug planes and their gliders, supported by circling fighter planes for protection against the Luftwaffe.

Two enemy fighter planes did chance their luck, however, swooping in from the direction of the setting sun hoping for soft targets. When they spotted the Spitfires they executed a sharp right-hand turn and sped away southwards hotly pursued by the 'Spits' which dived towards them from a higher altitude, rapidly overhauling the fleeing Germans which they despatched with a few bursts of fire, sending them crashing to the ground. There was a sudden spurt of fire and a mighty explosion as they both hit the high ground to our south. The cheer that went up at this event was long and sustained, as we all took heart from this demonstration of the air superiority that was making our job possible and that would protect us from aerial attack in the months to come.

Unfortunately, however, this did not mean that our comrades in the gliders escaped attention from the enemy. The ground forces and flak guns were busy, and once the landings took place the snipers turned their attention from us in our trenches to the new arrivals who made better targets.

The gliders need open ground in which to land, and in many

cases the newly arrived men had to sprint for considerable distances before they could find reasonable cover.

Once the glider landings had taken place we settled down to await the arrival of the main British force that was to follow the Commando in from the beach. It was almost dark when the Advance Guard of the Warwicks arrived to take over our positions around the bridges.

With the arrival of the British 3rd Army we now had a direct link with the beachhead. This enabled us to move our wounded back to receive more advanced treatment than had been available from our doctor and medics who, like us, had had to travel with just the bare minimum of equipment they needed.

Our wounded had been more fortunate than those of 7th Para. Alongside the canal was a café owned by M. Georges Gondrée, who made his premises available as a Medical Aid Post as soon as he realized that the British had landed, and he and his family helped to tend the wounded. It is said that M. Gondrée dug up many bottles of champagne – buried in the garden years before so that they would not be taken by the Germans – and he treated one and all to free drinks. I must say, however, that no one in our section was fortunate enough to be on the receiving end of this hospitality, as the Germans kept us far too busy for that.

Once darkness fell it became quiet around the bridges. I slid into a roadside ditch and immediately fell asleep.

Between 2200 and 2300 hours apparently over a thousand pairs of hobnailed boots and an assortment of vehicles passed along the road within a few feet of my head, but I heard nothing of them.

And so ended D-Day, one of the most momentous days in the Second World War, but those of us who survived this first day knew only too well that the battle to wrest Europe from the Nazis had only just begun.

What we didn't know at that time was that the Allied bridge-head would be effectively contained by the German forces for many long weeks thereafter, and that we would be staying here to defend our inland Airborne bridgehead area until the German forces could be pushed back.

Chapter 5

HÉROUVILLETTE AND ESCOVILLE

D + 1 – Hérouvillette and Escoville – Wednesday, 7 June

Apart from my profound sleep in the ditch, which had lasted all too short a time – only an hour or so – I had been virtually without sleep for forty-eight hours. None of the other lads was in any better shape because most of them, like me, had slept very little during the last night at Transit Camp, as we were full of apprehension at the thought of the daunting task that lay ahead. Since then we had been in continuous action of one sort or another, but, despite this, soon after midnight we were ordered to "fall in, ready to move off".

Loading most of our heavier gear on to the liberated cart that had been abandoned by the Commando, we were obliged to push it ourselves, since unfortunately we no longer had a horse. A group of us placed our shoulders against the rear of the cart and with someone steering by the front shafts we slowly trundled forward in the wake of the Company.

At around 0300 hours we arrived at what we assumed was Ranville. Here we were to rendezvous with the rest of our Battalion, together with other glider-borne units who had landed at zone 'W' to the west of Bénouville and Le Port and who were now making their way to the Battalion's assembly area at Ranville.

As we approached the village we came under fire. Although surprised at this reception, our officers concluded that a few Germans had infiltrated the area so we shot our way through the light opposition only to meet heavier fire-power in the village centre, which forced a hasty retreat and a hurried discussion among the officers. They concluded that in the dark we had somehow by-passed Ranville and entered Hérouvillette, which was to be the Regiment's battle objective at dawn.

At about the same time that we accomplished our rendezvous, the survivors from our missing glider also rejoined us. Their tug-plane had gone off course and released them several miles too far to the east. The glider pilots had seen a river, but it was the Dives, not the Orne, and they had landed close to one of its inland bridges near Varaville. Realizing that they had landed in the wrong place, they had headed west and after a daylong journey, much of it through the flooded Dives valley and up to their chests in water, they had managed to rejoin us. They had lost two killed and one wounded during skirmishes with enemy forces, and several others were missing, probably killed or captured, although it was hoped that they might make it back to us later.[1]

Tired to the point of total exhaustion, we were allowed to get a little more sleep near Ranville, but were roused before dawn to make the short journey into Hérouvillette, but now in full battalion strength.

As our Company had already been in action, it was placed in reserve, but we gathered that the lead units met little opposition and were then able to continue southwards to the next village, Escoville.

At around 0830 hours we arrived at Hérouvillette, by which time the leading units were probably already entering Escoville but we knew nothing of their progress.

Each of the Division's nine battalions had been given special tasks to ensure that a firm airborne bridgehead was secured, our battalion's objective being to capture and hold Escoville.

Escoville was another typical small Normandy village. On its northern outskirts was a château standing in large grounds that stretched to the main road that ran through the centre of the village from east to west. (I visited Escoville in 1995 and tried to find the château but it had not been rebuilt after the liberation of France, following its destruction by German bombardment during one of the fierce battles fought during mid-July, 1944. One account has

61

it that the Germans demolished it when they withdrew, to deny its shelter to the British.)

Along the road were scattered some cottages and farm buildings. At the back of the properties on the south side of the road was an apron of orchards and a well-wooded area which was on gently rising ground, while beyond there was open farmland.

After meeting small pockets of resistance the spearhead reached the northern outskirts at around 1000 hours. According to Intelligence reports – and so far they had proved to be extremely accurate – the village was heavily defended, yet we had met with little of the resistance we had expected, which was odd to say the least, and we all felt uncomfortable.

It was quiet and peaceful when most of us reached the centre of the village, and we were congratulating ourselves for having gained the Regimental objective without a real fight, but our self-satisfaction was premature.

It was about 1100 hours when all hell broke loose. The Germans were dug in on wooded and rising ground to the south of the village from where they had been watching us move into their trap. They opened fire with a massive bombardment.

Most of our Platoon was in a small coppice that formed part of the château's grounds and, as shells and mortar bombs exploded in the trees above, we were showered with bits of trees, whole branches and red-hot shrapnel.

There was no point in lying on the ground as that only exposed more of our bodies to the stuff that was coming down from above. Nor could we stand up and shelter against the tree trunks, as they were too slender to give any real protection and well-positioned machine guns and snipers were firing directly into our position from their higher vantage point.

All around me I saw men falling to the ground, killed or wounded; it was sheer murder, trapped as we were in what was effectively a killing-field. The Germans then opened fire with their deadly 88mm and 75mm guns which were either self-propelled or mounted on their heavier tanks which had been well dug into a reverse slope with just their turrets above ground level.

During my stay in Normandy I got to know the German 88mm weapon very well and learned very quickly to give it a lot of respect. This version of it, mounted in a tank chassis as a tank destroyer-cum-self-propelled artillery piece, was fearsomely effective and we came across it all too often. Not only was it a very versatile and deadly weapon, but German gunnery in general was usually highly accurate, and these examples were no exceptions.

The 88s were not very far away and were firing through open sights in much the same way as we used our rifles, and they were wreaking havoc. As the barrage continued, one of our six-pounder anti-tank guns was wheeled into the gateway of the château's drive with the intention of knocking out the SPs on which the 88s were mounted, which it was very capable of doing despite being a relatively light and small-calibre gun. It was quite able to destroy these enemy vehicles when used in anti-tank mode, being equipped with special tank-destroying ammunition, but unfortunately for us our gun didn't even get a shot off before it received a direct hit from one of the 88s.

The crew had loaded the gun and had swivelled it round to point at the nearest 88 SP when we saw a flash from the muzzle of the 88, heard the brief high-pitched scream of the shell, ending with a blinding flash of light and a mighty explosion. As the blue-grey smoke cleared around the gateway I saw that the little gun had suffered a direct hit. It had been blown backward about six feet, and all that was left were the shattered remains of gun and crew.

In our exposed position nearby we were completely pinned down. We could neither advance nor retire. Most of us had crawled forward to take advantage of the only real shelter available, which was the low wall that separated the château's grounds from the road.

When the German heavy weapons ceased firing, it usually meant that their infantry was advancing towards us, and this was exactly what was happening now. The noise of the shelling and mortaring stopped quite suddenly and was replaced by small arms fire – sporadic bursts from machine gun and sub-machine gun – and uncoordinated rifle fire. The German infantry were moving forward through the orchards and wooded area along the south side of the village, firing their weapons as they advanced.

We were justifiably wary of meeting the enemy in hand-to-hand combat. Intelligence had reported that the fanatical 'Hitler Jugend' 12th SS Panzer Division was in the area and that they were considered to be the elite among the Panzer Divisions. These were no run-of-the-mill German soldiers – if such a thing existed – but out-and-out Nazi fanatics, hand-picked from the ranks of the zealous Hitler Youth movement. They were little more than kids in many cases, but exceptionally highly trained and very mobile. They were carried from place to place at speed in armoured troop carriers, supported by light, medium and heavy tanks, as well as the deadly self-propelled 88s, and they were all very ready to die for Führer and Fatherland. It was very likely that we were up against them, or alternatively it had to be the equally tough and totally professional 21st Panzer Division, hardened and experienced veterans of several campaigns, including the North African theatre. With either we knew that we were in a very tight spot in a battle in which we did not have the initiative.

One of our Sections was sheltering in the road behind the low wall on the other side of the street and adjacent to the wood through which the main thrust of the attack was coming. Another section on our left had managed to get into some farm buildings. Our Section, with a few odds and ends from other units, was within the château grounds, behind its perimeter wall on the north side of the street.

As the enemy advanced bullets were chipping the tree trunks just above our heads and bits of stone and dust were coming off the top of our low wall. From the first salvo our position had been hopeless.

I crawled along the wall to the gateway where our six-pounder had been knocked out. Peering round the stone gatepost I was horrified to find myself looking at hordes of German infantry advancing down the track opposite the gateway! They saw me immediately and a hail of small-arms fire spattered around the entrance to the gateway, but with little accuracy as they were firing from the hip as they advanced.

I dived back behind the wall, severely shaken by what I had seen, and, shouting to the others, I took out a No. 36 hand grenade. In my panic and haste I fumbled with the safety pin and nearly blew myself up as I released the firing pin before I threw the grenade.

This meant that the very short fuse was already burning while the grenade was still in my hand. As it transpired, this was an advantage for there is only a few seconds' delay between the release of the firing pin and explosion of the grenade.

Although I could not see what happened, I judged from my experience with the Mills grenade during training that I would have thrown it about thirty yards and that it probably exploded just as it hit the ground. This gave no time for those at the front of the enemy attack to dive for cover.

Some of the others had also hurled grenades, which caused a succession of explosions, which were certainly effective as we heard screams of pain from injured Germans.

As this was happening I turned my head and glanced along the wall, where to my amazement I saw our Section Lance Corporal Minns standing up with a Bren light machine gun propped between his body and one of the larger trees. As cool as can be, he was carefully firing long bursts towards the now disorganized enemy infantry. Seeing him standing there without being hit encouraged me to leap to my feet and open fire with my rifle, giving Minns the opportunity to load another magazine and fire another long burst. The Germans were partly bottled up in the track down which they had been advancing, and now they were falling to the ground like ninepins.

For the moment we had halted their advance, but with their superiority of numbers it was obvious that they would soon be coming at us again.

"Crawl back while I try to keep them busy," shouted Minns.

To make the Germans keep their heads down for a few precious extra seconds we threw a few more grenades, then let fly with rifles and Sten guns before diving to the ground and crawling towards the château.

Once the decision had been made to vacate the limited protection of the front wall we had to move really quickly.[2] Once the Germans realized that we were pulling back they would cross the road into the château grounds, and if we were still there when they arrived our chances of getting anything other than a bullet in the back would be so close to zero as to make no difference.

I had already seen so much desperate action that day that if I

65

had time to stop to think about it, which naturally I did not, I would have realized that if it were to continue like this my chances of surviving must be very slim. The day was not nearly over, and for me it was destined to be a day full of desperate fighting, narrow escapes from death and all the unpleasantness which war brings.

The worst of such horrors were always those which were avoidable – things that happened stupidly and unnecessarily. One such incident occurred just at this moment, as we were falling back under the cover of Lance Corporal Minns's heroic covering fire.

With bullets chipping the tree trunks only a foot or two above our heads, we could only slither along the ground as fast as possible. One lad who was crawling alongside me became panic stricken and shouted, "I'm not stopping here to be killed I'm going to make a run for it".

As he began to get to his feet I reached out to grab him, cursing and shouting, "Keep down you bloody fool. You haven't got a chance."

They were the last words he heard. Before he could get his body into an upright position there was a long burst from an enemy automatic and he crashed back to the ground with a line of bullet holes across his back and shoulders, his blood spattering over me as I lay prostrate just behind him.

The 88s, as well as mortars and machine guns, opened up again soon after the infantry attack had stalled, and as we crawled away two of the others were hit, either by shrapnel or bullets, and our seven-man Section was now down to four.

We had covered a fair amount of ground and were within a short distance of some outbuildings and a high wall. Taking a chance, but still crouching low, we dashed for the cover of the wall that ran in an easterly direction, and, although we drew small-arms fire, we made it without taking any more casualties.

There seemed no chance of getting out of the village by heading northward since that area was now under heavy bombardment. We quickly decided to follow the wall eastwards, which took us away from the area taking the most punishment from the enemy artillery, and away from the main thrust of the attack.

Coming towards us from the direction in which we were now moving I heard the rumbling of tanks and the sound of one of our

Bren light machine guns firing long bursts. It may be thought that one machine gun sounds very much like another, and this may be true in some cases, but the sound of the Bren was quite distinctive and not to be mistaken for the fast-firing German machine guns. We knew that if we kept moving toward the sound of the chattering Bren we would at least meet up with some of our lads who were still in action.

We came to an alley that connected with the main road. This was just beyond the built-up area of the village. Some of the lads from No. 22 Platoon were sheltering in ditches on either side of the road. As soon as they spotted us they shouted a warning that an enemy machine gun was firing directly into the alley from an opposite track to the south.

On the outskirts of the village the main road was slightly sunken, with a large cornfield on its south side. Along the western edge of the field ran the track from which the enemy machine gun was firing. The lads of 22 Platoon were obviously pinned down but the prospect of getting into one of the roadside ditches seemed to be a better idea than staying in my present somewhat exposed spot, so we dashed across the alley and dived into the nearest ditch.

After a brief rest we crossed to the south side. On the far side of the large cornfield were more well-positioned enemy machine guns. From time to time someone would pop up and take a quick look southwards to ascertain whether the enemy might be on the move and coming our way, which provoked long bursts of machine-gun fire every time.

Suddenly I heard tanks moving to our east. At a fork in the road a few hundred yards in that direction I saw tanks approaching the main road from the left-hand fork, from the north. As they came up to the road I had a good view of them, and to my delight I recognized them as our Airborne Light Reconnaissance tanks.

Some of the lads from 22 Platoon beckoned them to come forward in the hope that we could use their cover to allow us to withdraw. They moved towards us cautiously but after a short distance they stopped, then went into reverse and were soon back to the fork junction where they swivelled round and sped away northwards.

Confused, I eased my body up the roadside bank and, looking eastwards again, I now saw more tanks. They were coming up from the south and were much larger than those that had just disappeared, but I could not identify them positively.

"More tanks coming up from the South", I shouted, "They're bigger I don't think they're ours". From a position nearer to the fork junction, and presumably with a better view, the Platoon Sergeant shouted back, "Don't you worry. They're ours all right".

The new arrivals reached the fork junction and stopped. From the tops of the two leading tanks people were peering at us through field glasses. Several of the lads nearer to them, where the road was deeply sunken so that they were out of sight of the enemy machine guns, were standing in the road and beckoning to the tanks, which nonetheless did not appear anxious to move towards us.

Behind the two leading tanks I could see two or three more. Then I noticed that around these tanks and moving from the south fork and into the north one were long lines of infantry.

I knew that the Paras were working in the area to our east, but these were coming up from the south, the direction from which the enemy attack had been launched. If these were our tanks and the troops were the Paras, I wondered why the enemy weapons on the far side of the cornfield were not firing at them. If they could see us they could almost certainly see the tanks and troops at the fork junction. Yet they did not open fire.

This was enough to convince me that we were in danger. The tanks suddenly revved their engines and began moving slowly toward us.

I shouted across to the others, "I don't know about you lot, but I still think they could be bloody Germans and I'm getting out of this road until I know who they are".

"Please your bloody self," responded the Platoon Sergeant impatiently, underlining his point with an emphatic "but my platoon stays here."

The other three in our little group of four agreed with me that, as this was not our Platoon, our safest option was to be found in making ourselves scarce until we had established the identity of the new and strangely reticent arrivals. We crawled up the roadside bank and slithered into the adjoining cornfield, which we disturbed as little as possible as we didn't want to alert the enemy machine-gunners or the tank crews.

In single file we moved forward and covered a distance of possibly thirty yards in a southerly direction then veered off to the west and back towards the built-up area of the village. Before we had made much progress we heard the chatter of machine guns from the sunken road that we had just left, followed by shouts and screams. I whispered to the others, "I said those bloody tanks were probably German didn't I?" But there was no pleasure to be had from being right in such circumstances. Without a further word we began crawling forward in a common desire to put as much space as possible between us and the tanks.

We came to the edge of the field and the track that ran along its western border. We knew that the Germans had a machine gun firing directly down this track, but across the other side was an orchard and a row of cottages. We had no way of knowing whether any of the cottages were occupied or by whom, but the prospect of putting solid walls between us and those tanks seemed like a good idea and the risk was worth taking.

Getting into line abreast at the edge of the field, on the word "Go", we made a dash across the track, all four together, and dived into the orchard. Predictably, as we did so the track was raked by a long burst from the machine gun. Luckily the machine-gunner's reflexes were not fast enough, and the four of us made it without being hit. We were now out of sight of the machine-gunner and we were also screened from the tanks by the trees in the orchard.

Being now reasonably well concealed, I got to my feet and looked back towards the sunken road. I saw that the lead tank had its offside track in the north side ditch and the one following had its track in the south side ditch and both were firing their machine guns.

The lads from 22 Platoon didn't have a chance. Those still in the ditches were being run over by the tanks. We were glad to see that some were standing in the road with their hands above their heads, so we hoped that they might at least get away with being

69

taken prisoner. I learned much later that some were in fact captured. Bob Ambrose, who was probably one of those I saw surrendering, was taken prisoner, and later wrote an account of his time in captivity.[3]

We moved off rapidly westwards across the orchard, in case the tanks came looking for us. Approaching the row of cottages, and taking great care not to be seen by whoever might be in occupation, we progressed cautiously from one end of the row towards the other, scanning the cottages from a respectable distance and from behind cover as we looked for signs of activity. About halfway along we spotted movement in an upper window and froze to the spot. After a while the figure reappeared and we recognized him as one of the lads from Company HQ. Now our problem was to make contact without being shot at by our own side. We were approaching the cottage from the south, the direction from which the enemy had attacked. Our lads would not expect any of us to be coming from that direction.

We crept forward until we were level with the back of the occupied cottage which was separated from the orchard by a high boundary wall with a tall and solid gate. Then I called quietly to the soldier by name. After a short pause a voice from the back garden called back.

"Is that you Eddie?"

"Yes", I replied. "There are four of us and it ain't healthy out here. For Christ's sake open this bloody gate."

"You're bloody lucky we didn't shoot the lot of you," came the reply from beyond the gate.

"If you don't open this bloody gate the Germans will do that for you," I replied tersely.

The gate swung open and we dashed inside and found some of our own Company HQ people and a few remnants from other Platoons, all under the command of Major Howard, whose head was swathed in blood-stained bandages, having been hit by a sniper earlier in the day.

With the arrival of the four of us, the cottage now contained about a dozen men of various ranks, and we all busied ourselves barricading the lower windows and doors with whatever furniture was to hand. As far as anyone knew we were the only British left in the village and presumably the attacking Germans had bypassed us.

The time passed slowly, but to our great relief towards the end of the afternoon a counter-attack was launched on the western side of the village. Our cottage had not come under attack previously, which implied that our presence was not known to the enemy, and with the distraction caused by the counter-attack we felt it was reasonably safe to make a move. We got out from the east side and without making any further contact with the enemy we made our way carefully back to Hérouvillette where we rejoined the Regiment.

It was estimated that we had suffered about sixty casualties, which was worrying. Our only consolation was that we were sure that the Germans had incurred even higher losses.

With everyone pulling out of Escoville in such a hurry, a fair amount of equipment, ammunition, weapons, medical supplies and rations had been abandoned. Since communication with the beachhead was still intermittent and irregular, we could not afford to leave such supplies behind. We were also unable to rely on supplies dropped from the air, as in this heavily wooded country-side they tended to land in inaccessible places.

Early in the evening a group of us were detailed to go back into the village to salvage whatever we could. We approached it with a great deal of caution, but were relieved to discover that the Germans, not wishing to make artillery targets of themselves, appeared to have pulled out. They had established their main defensive line somewhat to the south of the village itself, where they could settle their tanks into hull-down positions on the higher ground.

The first thing we found when we got there was our old cart, which we loaded with anything that we could conveniently grab, and there was a lot of it to be had.

With our heavy load of salvaged supplies, and with plenty of sweating and swearing, we manhandled the heavily laden cart back towards our new area.

In the gathering dusk, when we were about midway between

the two villages, an enemy fighter plane spotted us. It swooped over us to get a good look, coming very low, and then executed a steep 180-degree turn and zoomed back towards us. When we realized that it was coming back to have a go at us, we scattered in all directions, leaping into ditches or under the cart, as the aircraft attacked with all guns blazing. It was very fortunate that no one was hit, because if we had taken even a single casualty it is doubtful that the survivors would have had enough strength to get the heavily laden cart back to our lines.

While we were undergoing our adventures with the cart, others went in to remove our dead, who were later buried in the church-yard at Hérouvillette.

'D' Company began the day with its Company HQ at full strength, plus four Platoons each with about twenty-seven or twenty-eight men. In the evening those who had survived Escoville were divided into two under-strength Platoons. Platoons originally designated Nos. 22, 23, 24 and 25 no longer existed. The new ones were designated 'A' and 'B'. Lieutenant Sweeney was put in command of 'B' Platoon, while I now found myself in 'A' Platoon commanded by Captain Priday. He, together with the unfortunate No. 22 Platoon, had rejoined us only that morning after having fought their way through to rendezvous with us at Hérouvillette when No. 4 glider had gone astray.

At about 2100 hours we had our first cooked meal since arriving in France. With the loss of rations in Escoville, the meal was small, and by the time I got mine it was not very hot. The heated tinned stew and tinned potatoes, however, washed down with a mug of the foul-tasting 'Mixed Monkey' tea, tasted as good as any meal that I could ever remember. Perhaps the fact that against all the odds I had survived this terrible day had something to do with the pleasure of the lukewarm food.

Now, after the frantic activity and continuous action that had occurred all day, I was feeling an incredible relief at having somehow come through it all. I was also delighted beyond words to see that brave Lance-Corporal Minns had also survived and had rejoined us at Hérouvillette.

D + 2 – Hérouvillette – Thursday, 8 June

In our new positions we quickly settled into a routine. The first night was divided into spells of guard duty and digging out new defensive trenches.

The position allocated for my trench was on a bank overlooking a large field between the two villages. The bank was topped by a thick prickly hedge interspersed with mature trees whose roots seemed to be everywhere.

To be effective, a trench suitable for two men needs to be about six feet long, two feet wide and over five feet deep. It was no easy task to dig out such a trench with a small implement like the entrenching tool supplied to airborne troops. As mentioned earlier in this narrative, it could lift very little soil at a time, and its modest weight meant that it could not be swung down to penetrate the earth by its momentum. Using this implement needed continuous muscle power, and in ground that was full of tree roots this was a tedious and frustrating experience.

In addition, since it was certain that the enemy would have patrols out to discover our positions, we had to work as quietly as possible. Consequently, between trench digging and guard duty I managed to get only about two hours' sleep.

An hour before daylight everyone was alerted and watching the front in anticipation of a dawn attack. When this did not materialize at daybreak we were permitted to leave our trenches in ones and twos to make our way to Company HQ which was located in a nearby caravan.

For the first time since landing we were able to get a wash and shave, but with just one small problem. The entire Company had pooled whatever we had been able to salvage from Escoville, and for ablution purposes this amounted to five razors and washing kits which had to be shared between about sixty men.

Shaving in cold water with blunt razor blades was an uncomfortable experience, but after a quick wash, a shave and a bite to eat we returned to our trenches and continued with the overnight dig, taking turns to watch the front for enemy activity.

The day passed slowly as we watched and waited. During the afternoon a few of us went out into the adjoining fields, crawling most of the time to keep out of sight of snipers. We badly needed to recover some of the Parachute containers that had been dropped during the past two days. A container might hold rations, medical supplies, weapons, ammunition, or just about anything. Since we were now short of everything, any container that could be recovered would be of use to someone.

We didn't empty them when we found them, but we would drag the entire container back to our positions as they served a double purpose. Not only did they hold valuable supplies but, once emptied, could be filled with earth dug from the trenches and placed across the top of the trench on raised earth mounds at either end to form an excellent protective roof. With our experience of shrapnel coming down from above, we well understood the value of having a solid roof above our trenches.

Unfortunately many of the containers were in high trees. German snipers tended to find a position close to trees draped with containers and anyone attempting to recover them was very likely to be shot at.

In the evening I went out with a five-man patrol to explore the area to our east. We made our way slowly to a farmhouse about 500 yards from our positions. We could not risk entering as the Germans were known to be around and it was more than likely that they would be in occupation.

We moved eastwards until we came to a road and wooded slope, where we settled down for some time to watch and listen for any sign of enemy activity, but heard and saw nothing so returned quietly to our lines.

We had understood that the Paras and the Commando were located along the wooded slope, but we had not seen or heard anything of them. This was a cause for concern because if they were not in fact there it meant that there was a wide gap between them and us.

Our knowledge of what was going on around us was scant, so as soon as we reported back another patrol was sent out in a slightly different direction to add to our fund of information about our immediate surroundings. After returning we went to our respective trenches for spells of guard duty. I managed to get about two hours' sleep before the dawn 'stand to'.

D + 3 – Hérouvillette – Friday, 9 June

During the afternoon 'C' Company went into Escoville to establish whether the Germans were still around. As they approached the village, enemy artillery including 88s, mortars, machine guns and tanks opened fire with all the fury of the attack of two days earlier.

With thick hedgerows and trees between the village and us, it was impossible to see what was going on, but from the din we soon realized that 'C' Company had run into trouble. It was not long before they came streaming back to our lines. They had bumped into the spearhead of a massive attacking force. If nothing else, it gave us advance warning of what we could expect.

As 'C' Company fell back, the German gunners ranged their barrage to follow their retreat, so that they were followed yard by yard by vast quantities of shells, mortar bombs and bullets. The barrage soon reached our positions and we came under intensive fire.

Such was the weight and strength of the enemy attack that we might well have expected to be in real trouble had they overrun our lines. By now, however, we had the support of heavy artillery which had arrived from the beaches, putting down our own massive bombardment upon Escoville, and so the attack failed. The Germans, caught out in the open, suffered heavy casualties and were forced to withdraw, leaving behind five large Mark IV and V tanks, a light tank, an armoured car and a lot of dead infantry. The armoured car was found to be in good working order and was driven back to our lines for future use.

We also suffered many casualties and, very sadly, among several killed was Lance Corporal Minns, hit by a bullet which was deflected from his bayonet scabbard and penetrated his heart.[4]

Although our casualties were high enough, it was estimated that the Germans had lost around 400 killed, with many more wounded, some of whom they left behind, and we heard them shouting and screaming for help throughout the night. Some of these were unfortunate foot soldiers who had been sheltering behind their tanks when the bombardment was in progress. As the offensive ground to a halt the tanks went into reverse, presumably

75

on orders received by radio, and several of their infantry were killed or maimed by not being able to get out of the way quickly enough.

French civilians informed us that the Germans had more than forty large tanks around Escoville. When the first wave was knocked out they decided not to risk any more.

D + 4 – Hérouvillette – Saturday, 10 June

Although it had gone quiet along our front, at the top of the wooded slope running up to the village of Bréville to our east a big battle was in progress. Perhaps having concluded that Hérouvillette was too well defended, the Germans had probed the area to our east and found their way through the wide gap between us and the Paras on the higher ground which rose up along the entire eastern side of the Airborne bridgehead.

However, during the day an infantry battalion had been brought in to help fill the gap, so that, although the enemy had made some progress, they soon ran into the new arrivals who were equipped with heavy machine guns and back-up artillery, which brought the attack to a halt.

We spent the day tidying up and improving defences, but otherwise there was not much activity.

In the afternoon some enemy fighter planes found our positions and strafed us, but by now we were very well dug in, and we suffered no further casualties.

Later in the evening we were sent out on another patrol to the farmhouse, now occupied by the Paras. We made contact after a quiet exchange of passwords which, for security purposes, were changed every day so that if the enemy overheard them they could not be used on another day.

Throughout the night our big guns pounded the enemy positions. It was a comfort to know, as we listened to the regular crump, crump sound as they fired, that they were on our side. The sound of the big guns at work was impressive, commencing with the crump as a shell was fired, changing to a high-pitched whine as they gained height and, as they passed overhead, a flapping sound like the beating wings of some enormous bird.

The heavy artillery of both sides was always active during darkness when supplies and reinforcements were on the move, which was normally the case where the Germans were concerned. The RAF domination of the skies made it very difficult and risky for them to move anything during daylight.

From time to time a larger enemy shell would explode close to our positions, shaking the surrounding ground, but in general we were almost certainly not the intended target. Both sides occasionally fired shells that were under-powered, or a gun from either side could be wrongly ranged, which could be unlucky for us. When we knew that this was happening, we would count off the guns as they fired, keeping well down in our trenches when it came to the turn of the badly ranged weapon to fire.

D + 5 – Hérouvillette – Sunday, 11 June

At 'stand to' Jerry gave us his customary dawn hammering and our lines took a thorough working-over, an exercise which we called a 'stonk'.

Since the village of Escoville was our regimental objective our senior officers would not be happy until it was in our hands. Accordingly, another well-armed fighting patrol went out 'to stir things up', and stir things up they certainly did, a veritable hornets' nest in fact. As the patrol withdrew they attracted an enormous amount of German fire, the overspill of which shells, bombs and bullets, landed on us in Hérouvillette.

Although our airborne commanders seemed to place the capture of Escoville high on their priority list, the Germans for some reason displayed a similar tenacity and concern to retain the village. It remained under effective German control, together with the area immediately south of the village, until the middle of August, which meant that the vicinity of the village remained a dangerous no-man's-land for us throughout all this time.

When the enemy big guns opened up it became very uncomfortable and remained that way for most of the day. Movement above ground was severely restricted and trips to the Company cooking area were out of the question.

Cigarettes were running low, and while we were not allowed to smoke during the hours of darkness, for fear of giving our positions away during the day we tended to smoke heavily. A small supply of fags always came up with the ration packs irrespective of whether we smoked or not. Now that supplies were running low we smokers began checking with the known non-smokers only to find that most of them, like us, were now smoking like factory chimneys!

D + 6 – Hérouvillette – Monday, 12 June

Enemy patrols were extremely active during the night and we came in for several heavy bombardments throughout the day; obviously more trouble was brewing. That evening and throughout the night there was considerable activity along the wooded slope to the east. It was not clear exactly what was going on, but since D-Day the Paras and the Commando had been involved in several battles in the area.

The slope was simply the eastern side of the Orne River valley, and the crest ran from north to south along the length of our inland bridgehead. From the crest the entire Orne valley area was overlooked. Thus, whoever controlled the high ground enjoyed wide views westwards to the canal. It was clearly a danger, since this allowed them to overlook the bridges over which had to come all our supplies from the beaches.

The Germans held a large area of this valley slope and our senior officers decided that they must be driven off at all costs. Our largest field guns and the even larger guns of the offshore battleships were giving the hilltop a real pounding.[5]

When the guns stopped firing the Paras, with some of the Devons from our Airlanding Brigade, plus the Commando and units of the newly arrived 51st Highland Division, launched a massive attack.

The night sky was well lit as both sides fired illuminating flares. Heavy, medium and light machine guns opened fire, along with automatic weapons, rifles, and exploding grenades. Viewed from our trenches a mile from the battleground it was a fantastic sight. It was certainly one of the biggest attacks that we had yet launched. It made our efforts around Escoville seem a very modest affair. We did not, however, escape scot-free since a fair amount of stray stuff from the German big guns exploded around us.

Needless to say, with such a din no one got any sleep. In any case we were warned that if the Germans fared badly along the hillside some of their other units might well launch a powerful attack upon us in the hope of drawing some of the heavy fire-power away from the hillside. We were placed on full alert.

Chapter 6

THE CHÂTEAU ST COME AND BRÉVILLE

D + 7 – Hérouvillette/St. Come – Tuesday, 13 June

In the early hours we were roused and ordered to pack everything and be ready to move out at short notice.

Because the 51st Highland Division had just moved into our area, some of the lads got the bright idea that we were being pulled out and taken home. There was some justification for this assumption because before we left England we had been told that we were only to be used to capture the bridges and form a bridgehead around them. At such time as the seaborne forces were able to reach us we would be returned to England and prepared for further airborne operations in the immediate future. We had done all that had been asked of us and, by all accounts, the Generals were pleased with the way that we had carried out our tasks.

(As it turned out, perhaps they were a little too pleased. It is a well-attested matter of record that Montgomery was reluctant to trust some of his other divisions to protect his left flank if he pulled out the 6th Airborne.)

When we seized the bridges at the very start of D-Day we were all that existed of the Allied forces in Normandy, establishing a small Airborne bridgehead, which we ourselves had to defend throughout the next twelve weeks. This area was filled from the rear by further Airborne landings and the seaborne landings, to form just a part of the total Allied Normandy bridgehead. To our front, however, there were only Panzer divisions. This meant that we were left for three months on the very perimeter of the Allied bridgehead, battling for control of the cluster of villages on the east bank of the River Orne. We were never further than a few miles from the Orne river bridge, usually dug in, and virtually as close to the German front line as it was possible to get.

The Germans were now throwing everything into holding the line to contain the Allied forces, and if possible to throw them back into the sea, and some very heavy fighting had been taking place at critical points along our part of the front.

At around 0400 hours we were quietly ordered to fall in in sections, ready to move off. We advanced eastwards up the lane towards the higher ground of the Orne river valley. This was a very odd route to be taking if we were being pulled out!

The battle for the eastern bank of the Orne valley had not gone according to plan. The enemy's commanding position overlooking the entire airborne bridgehead was unacceptable to Montgomery and it was considered essential to clear the whole area of enemy forces.

The Germans on the other hand were obviously keen to retain their strategically important vantage point and were defending it with great resolve and ferocity. Although they had been driven back in most places, we had suffered heavy casualties and the enemy still held part of the higher ground on the slopes over-looking our bridges and the area for miles around them. We were being sent in to add extra weight to the battle that was still raging up there.

It began to pelt with rain as we moved slowly forward. The Regiment was spread across a wide area of the slopes and we had to reach our new locations by jumping over ditches, pushing through thick hedges and along muddy tracks in almost total dark-ness and through unfamiliar territory.

As we trudged up a track we passed some of the Paras who were being pulled out. They had been badly mauled. Most had blood-soaked field dressings covering various parts of their bodies and they looked badly shaken.

It took about three hours to cover the mile or so to the top of the east bank of the Orne, arriving around 0700 hours. For the first time we saw the carnage of the night-time battle as we met up with the shattered remnants from those units that had been involved. All around was evidence of brutal warfare such as I had never seen before; it was horrific, a scene that will stay with me for the rest of my life.

Before long we encountered the lads of the Highland Division, and here was shell shock on a massive scale. The poor devils stood around in groups, dazed, staring at us through vacant and bewildered eyes.

I had never seen the result of warfare so grimly demonstrated, with every ditch, gully, hedgerow, track and roadway strewn with dead and shattered bodies of both British and German soldiers of various units. Every square foot of ground seemed to be strewn with parts of human bodies, shattered, burnt, some still burning or smouldering. All around was to be seen equipment, weapons, clothing, ammunition, grenades, guns, vehicles and tanks. Half-used belts of machine-gun bullets lay beside twisted and broken weapons. Tins of food, mess tins, packets of biscuits were scattered everywhere, along with just about everything else that British and German troops might carry.

We moved up the drive that led to the Château St. Come, stepping around what the day before had been Sherman tanks and armoured troop carriers. Now they were simply twisted, smouldering and burnt-out wrecks. Beneath one burning tank were the shrivelled and blackened remains of two burnt bodies.

The sheer hell of the night-time battle became even more apparent as we moved around the château grounds seeking out any enemy who may still be about, while we looked for suitable positions in which to dig trenches in anticipation of a counter-attack.

Just along the road, the village of Bréville had been reduced to little more than a pile of rubble. The château had fared no better. The main building stood in a clearing amidst woodland and was surrounded by its own grounds and outbuildings.

By the driveway was a small copse in which we found some of the 51st Highland Division. Beyond the copse and cowering in a nearby ditch we found a young Scot, still in deep shock, white as a ghost and literally shaking from head to toe.

With teeth chattering uncontrollably he told us that while the battle was still raging his Section had been cut off and surrounded

82

by Germans. Cornered and outnumbered, they had to surrender. They were disarmed and marched away by men carrying sub-machine guns. In a courtyard by the château they were ordered to line up against a wall. Their captors stepped back a few paces and opened fire with their automatics. As his comrades began to fall he, at the end of the row, fell with them. There he lay for some considerable time, too terrified to move in case they should return and finish him. Once he was certain that they had gone he crawled into the ditch where we found him.

After asking other Highland lads to take care of him, we walked to where he had indicated and found, at the foot of a whitewashed and blood-spattered wall, a row of dead Scots. Nearby were several dead Germans. From one, for identification purposes, I extracted a wallet, which contained very little but gave an indication that the man was proud of his status. He still carried an identity card issued by the Hitler Jugend which stated that he was born at the end of September, 1925. This meant that he was even younger than I was and, in April, 1936, still five months short of his eleventh birthday, he had joined Hitler's Nazi party youth movement.

There were also two postcard-size photographs of the boy, one in the grey denim type working uniform in which he was now clad, the other in his dress uniform, on the collar of which was the double lightning bolt insignia of the SS. On the back was a hand-written date indicating that he joined the SS at some time before his seventeenth birthday.[1]

From beneath the body of this dead young Nazi I extracted an item that was a high priority on my survival shopping-list, a fast-firing Schmeisser sub-machine gun. In this close and heavily wooded countryside I reckoned that it would be far more useful defensively than my single-shot bolt-action service rifle.

I would have no problem in obtaining ammunition for the Schmeisser, as it used the same 9mm round used by our Sten gun, a decision taken by the British in anticipation of capturing large quantities of German supplies during the invasion. The British Sten gun, however, was the simplest of weapons, effective but utterly crude in its utility construction, while, in complete contrast, my newly acquired Schmeisser was a work of art and engineering,

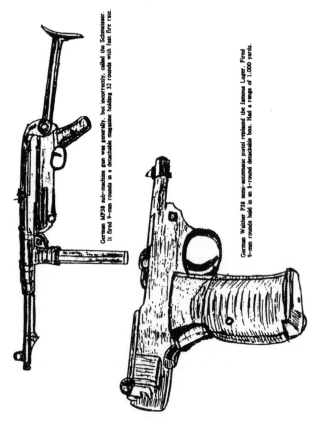

German MP38 sub-machine gun was generally, but incorrectly, called the Schmeisser. It fired 9-mm rounds in a detachable magazine holding 32 rounds with fast fire rate.

German Walther P38 semi-automatic pistol replaced the famous Luger. Fired 9-mm rounds held in an 8-round detachable box. Had a range of 1,000 yards.

84

built to the highest German standards, and I was delighted to have it. This was not all, and I was able to complete my 'wish list' from the booty that was lying around everywhere. From the mass of abandoned equipment I acquired a black-faced German Army issue Helios wristwatch, made by the same Swiss firm that supplied the British Army, and a long-barrelled P38 pistol. This was another beautifully crafted weapon that took the same 9mm bullets as the Schmeisser and the Sten. As a bonus, I found a pair of lightweight German field glasses, which were often to be very useful when I was sniping.

The Helios watch was a great luxury and immensely useful to me, as wristwatches were scarce. When we needed to know the exact time, as for example at night when we had to take our turn at 'stag' duty, it was the usual practice to pass the NCO's watch from trench to trench, a risky business when we were being mortared or shelled.

In addition to weaponry, we were all able to acquire an assortment of picks, spades and other implements that would make future trench-digging easier.[2]

Once we had settled into our new positions the Para and 'Jocks' were withdrawn. They must have been thankful beyond measure to get away from that place. From accounts given to me, and from the independent evidence of survivors, the battle had been nothing less than sheer hell, with attack followed by counter-attack, hand-to-hand fighting, and the most horrific bombardment by heavy artillery. Throughout the raging battle the big guns from one side or the other, and sometimes both together, were blasting the combatants to smithereens while tearing enormous craters in the ground. Such was the ferocity of the engagement that the fact that there had been communication problems between the artillery and the front line was scarcely to be wondered at.

Once our officers had decided upon suitable defensive locations we were quickly involved in the tasks of watching the front for signs of enemy attack and digging out new trenches. The area was crawling with enemy snipers, however, and in the open parkland we presented easy targets as we dug our holes.

In an adjoining copse, which I judged to be about fifty by seventy yards, the trees had been torn to shreds, with torn-off branches

85

strewn around. Some of the taller trees had had their tops blasted away and the trunks were still smouldering. Within this small area I reckoned that there were at least twenty bodies, both British and German. It was difficult to be exact as few were whole and there were many detached arms, legs and heads. British lay across Germans and Germans on top of British. There were also, however, several dead who were virtually unmarked, killed by shell blast according to the official explanation.

This was very odd, and in the midst of the carnage I saw some amazing sights. The strange poses of some of the dead have been explained as having been caused by concussion – enormous forces from detonation of heavy calibre artillery shells close by, which killed them instantly but without tearing them to pieces.

In a hastily dug shallow shell-scrape was a Scot lying on his back and in his hand he held a set of fanned-out playing cards. At what stage of such a battle a man could have found the time to play a hand of cards I simply could not imagine!

Nearby lay a comrade, a Corporal with an Africa Star amongst his medal ribbons; he was at the foot of a tree stump, flat on his stomach and with a Thompson sub-machine gun pulled tightly against his shoulder. His finger was still curled round the trigger and his left eye was tightly closed, while his right was wide open and peering intently along the sights of his weapon, obviously taking aim and ready to fire.

Within a few yards, and directly opposite, at the base of another tree, lay a German in an almost identical position, holding a dagger in his still clenched fist. One knee was drawn up beneath his prone body and the other leg was straight out behind him. His arms were in corresponding positions and it appeared as if he was about to crawl forward to attack the Scot. The two appeared to have been killed at exactly the same instant.

A German was in the process of opening a box of ammunition and still had a hand on top of the box. Beside him lay his mate behind an empty machine gun, looking over his shoulder towards his companion. It was easy to imagine him saying, at the moment that death struck them, "Hurry up, the gun is empty".

There were other unmarked British and Germans in a variety of positions, a German lying flat upon the ground and still clutching a long handled stick grenade, another with a water bottle pressed to his lips, yet another placing a bandage on the arm of his wounded comrade.

Some were sitting up, others lying down. Some were on their backs with their hands in the air as if to ward off danger, others on their stomachs with faces pressed into the ground, or still clutching a helmet to their heads as if for added protection. And all around were great holes where massive shells had exploded. It was really very strange to see how these men had died so suddenly, and how, as corpses, they had remained posed as they were at the very final instant of their lives![3]

The scene was horrifying but the smell was even worse. The air was heavy and sickly with the smell of burnt or burning flesh and clothing, wood, leaves, grass, petrol, oil and cordite. The night-time rain had stopped soon after dawn and been replaced by warm sunshine which was already having its effect upon human flesh.

This was in one small segment of the battlefield. It was repeated all around the grounds of the château and up the slope running northwards to the nearby shattered village of Bréville. There I saw many other horrific sights, one of which was a weird tableau in which one of the Canadian Paras had been run through the middle of his body by a German bayonet, pinning him to a tree. At the instant that this was happening he had reached over the bent German and plunged his dagger into the middle of his opponent's back. The two had died at some time during the night but in daylight they were as they had been when they died together, still propping each other up.

Near the château were the remains of a block of stables. In the fury of the battle the stables had been set alight and some of the thoroughbred racehorses burnt to death in their looseboxes. Others had perhaps been more fortunate through a quick death when a large shell scored a direct hit, demolishing a large part of the building. Others had got out but perished around the area. The smell of the burning stables and horses added to the overall and unforgettable putrid stench.

So numerous were the various horrors that I witnessed on that day that I could only note a few of them in my diary. It is difficult to witness such a charnel house of death and destruction without being moved. However, every one of us knew that the same fate might be awaiting us and that we couldn't afford to be sentimental, and so, as we were all desperately short of fags, we were not slow to restock our supplies from those who had no further need of them.

The stables were far too close to our trenches for my liking and, if we were going to be there for very long, I knew that somehow or other we were going to have to bury the animals whose bodies were already swelling to twice their normal size.

We didn't know where the Germans had re-drawn their front line, but they remained quiet, although late in the afternoon we were heavily shelled by their artillery. By this time, however, we were well dug in and not too worried by the shelling. With all the wreckage that lay around we had no difficulty in finding suitable material for trench roofing.

Later in the evening I was part of a small recce patrol sent forward to establish contact with the enemy, who, apart from their snipers, had been understandably quiet throughout the day. They had taken at least as much punishment as we had. We saw and heard nothing of them, however, and we concluded that they had taken such a beating that they had moved well back to lick their wounds and reorganize themselves.

D + 8 – Château St. Come – Wednesday, 14 June

The day began with the normal stand to, followed by heavy and accurate shelling and mortaring from the enemy. Soon after breakfast I went out with an officer who led a small recce around the hedgerows to the front. He wanted to see the area and plot possible routes from which an attack might come, in particular the route along which tanks and self-propelled 88s might approach our positions.

German snipers were still infesting the area and taking a fair toll of men that we could ill afford to lose. To discourage their activities we snipers were sent forward in small groups to find a secluded spot from where we could watch the taller trees in which we guessed the enemy snipers would be located.

When a sniper fired, a telltale wisp of smoke could be seen. His position would then be given a real pasting, but they seldom worked alone, so that when we hit one, another would fire at us, so it was a case of firing and quickly moving to another location. Sometimes it was a matter of hurling a smoke grenade or two to cover our move. Using smoke was often a problem, however, because it worried Jerry, who took it as a prelude to an attack, and he would usually retaliate by mortaring and shelling the whole area.

In scouting around the deep ditches we came across many dead Germans and cattle. It certainly looked as though we had suffered heavy casualties, but Jerry had fared even worse.

Upon our return to Company lines we were delighted to find that a fresh supply of rations had arrived and, with them, a good supply of cigarettes, each of us receiving a tin of fifty.

The new trenches having been completed to the officers' satisfaction, we hoped that we might get some time off to relax and get in some badly-needed sleep. We had been getting in little more than the odd hour or two at a time since we had landed in Normandy. This was not to be the case, for, with the rations, we also received a large quantity of Dannert barbed wire which was heavy and had to be manhandled some thirty or forty yards out in front of the forward trenches.

The wire was in large-diameter rolls which were pulled out concertina fashion to make a high spiral barricade. It was strung out across the entire front, with two rows of the coiled wire topped by a third, and the whole then wired together to form an impressive defensive screen. Although of little effect against tanks, it was difficult for ground troops to get through it, as we had painfully learned during training.

We didn't object too much to this extra chore since it meant that if Jerry put in an attack his stick grenades could not easily reach our trenches from the far side of the wire.

In the evening a deafening explosion occurred to our rear. It was the result of a very unfortunate accident. To prevent tanks from smashing through our outer wire defences, the Regimental Pioneer Platoon had been instructed to lay an outer minefield. The Pioneers had driven up in a large truck and began unloading the boxes of ready-primed mines and stacking them in a neat pile. Some of the lads were inside the truck doing the unloading while the others stood around waiting for the job to be completed. Apparently, assuming that all the boxes had been off-loaded, one of the men in the truck found two or three loose mines, which he placed on top of the pile of boxes. Unfortunately his mate had lifted the last box and, without looking, dropped it down on top of the pile. The loose mines exploded and detonated the whole pile. When the smoke cleared all that was left of the mine-laying team and their truck was a very large hole in the ground. This sudden enormous explosion panicked Jerry who immediately put down a heavy stonk, which ended what had otherwise been a comparatively quiet day.

D + 9 – Château St. Come – Thursday, 15 June

It was a fairly quiet day, even though it started with the normal dawn stonk of between twenty and thirty mortar bombs and shells.

Later, we took turns in going out to the front on patrols and sniper hunts. One team decided upon an ingenious innovation – they took a PIAT with them. When a sniper was spotted a PIAT bomb was fired at the top of his tree. We had no way of measuring the success of their effort other than from the fact that several of us thought that fewer snipers were bothering us after this incident!

We were delighted to receive some more fags – a present from Monty – a nice thought since we understood our British Commander neither drank alcohol nor smoked. I guess that he understood that we lesser mortals were in need of the nerve-soothing weed!

The area in which we were located consisted of small fields and orchards surrounded by thick hedges set above wide and deep ditches. These provided secluded channels along which we could move unseen. In many places the hedges were overgrown and the topmost growth on one side of the ditch had entwined with that from the other side, and this provided additional cover, particularly from aircraft.

Where the ditches intersected they formed a sort of crossroads, a potential danger as they could be covered by a machine gun lying in wait for our patrols.

During the first few days use of these ditches was quite dangerous due to the fact that, having been neglected and over-grown, they contained a deep layer of dried leaves and twigs which rustled and snapped underfoot.

Some of the ditches were eight to ten feet deep and both sides made use of them, but we were now discouraging enemy use by establishing permanent well-armed 'Listening Posts' normally manned by a section of six or seven men. Like a typical guard duty, each section would spend two hours out in front and four hours back at the trenches. This soon became a permanent feature of our warfare and an added burden, since, from earlier losses, we were now short of manpower. Nevertheless, such a strategy was highly beneficial as it gave those back at the lines advance warning should the enemy mount an attack. It also discouraged Jerry from getting too close to our defensive positions and made life more difficult for his snipers.

Our days and nights followed a routine of trips to the Listening Posts, 'Stag' duty – our term for guard duty – back at the lines, with a brief time off to wash, shave and feed, and to get in the odd hour or two of sleep.

To keep us busy the officers also had us going back behind the lines to collect boxes of ammunition and rations from the delivery trucks. This meant that we were lugging yet more reels of Dannert barbed wire, and then laying it in rows, together with anti-tank and anti-personnel mines which were scattered in between the rows of Dannert and to which we fixed trip-wires.

Another chore that no one enjoyed was being detailed to dig new latrines. For reasons of hygiene these had to be well away from the trenches and out in the open. They were crude affairs consisting of a deep trench with Y-sprigs cut from stout tree branches and placed one at either end of a tree branch, forming a crude seat or perch across the top of the trench.

Those who began the dig were at risk from mortar bombs and shells, since, being out in the open, in the early stages there was nowhere to dive when a stonk began, and we were always open to attack by enemy aircraft. Fortunately, thanks to the RAF boys, there were very few Jerry strafers around. When they did attack, they tended not to go for the forward positions as they were too close to their own trenches. Their favourite targets were the so-called 'Rest Areas', half a mile or more behind the front line.

We tended to dig the latrine holes deeper than our slit trenches so that they took longer to fill. However, since all our food was delivered in Composite Packs, known as 'Compo rations' and came from tins, and the 'Mixed Monkey' tea cubes were, for many, an unwanted laxative, many had now developed what we called a 'Compo Tummy'.

I felt very sorry for anyone caught with his pants down when a stonk began, which guaranteed a loss of dignity if not loss of life. I was lucky, however, and, having been unaffected by compo tummy, I was able to visit the toilet at a time of my choosing. This was normally during the hours of darkness when the enemy concentrated their shelling and bombing on supply areas and routes, and tended not to bother with our well-dug trenches.

Another serious hygiene problem was that of the disposal of dead humans and animals. Some had been out in the open for several days and the stench was appalling. Even though one could duck down into a trench when bombs, shells and bullets were coming in, there was no getting away from the putrid smell of rotting flesh and the flies that they attracted. Human corpses were no great problem, but the larger cattle had to be dragged away. The only fortunate thing was that, due to the earlier bombardment, there were many deep craters into which we were able to drag the animals and cover them with a layer of soil, which helped to keep the smell down and the flies away.

D + 10, – Château St Come – Friday, 16 June

After the daily dawn bombardment it was usual for the stonk to ease off, but today was different. It increased steadily through the morning and had all the hallmarks of a softening-up process as the prelude to an attack. The one thing that we had quickly learnt about Jerry was that he was highly predictable and, as anticipated, the bombardment suddenly stopped and he launched an attack. The action was further down the crest of the valley, to our south, around a crossroads with which I was to become much more familiar in the near future. The squeaking of tracks and the roaring of engines could be heard clearly enough as Jerry moved his tanks around. Even the guttural sound of Germans barking out orders to each other testified to the fact that they were quite close to our positions, but we were so heavily enclosed that I saw nothing of them.

The attack was quickly repulsed, but the joy of this news was soon dampened when it suddenly began to pour with rain. Although our trenches now had gullies surrounding them to take away the worst of the water, because there had to be an open space between the trench and roof, there was no way of keeping the water out, and very soon the bottom of my trench began to fill. All that I could do was to use my mess tins to bail out as much as possible.

Trenches were normally two-man affairs. For mutual support, especially at night-time, and during heavy stonks, most preferred sharing with a companion. The usual arrangement was that they would sit with their backs against the end walls, using the heavy pack as a pillow or headrest, with feet overlapping in the middle of the trench. However, where a Section comprised an odd number of people it meant that someone had to go solo. I was always happy to be the odd man as this gave more room to spread out in the bottom of the trench.

Because his attack had been unsuccessful, Jerry covered his withdrawal by putting down a massive bombardment along the entire front, forcing everyone to spend the rest of the day and night deep down in our cramped and waterlogged holes in the ground. To make matters even worse our own heavy artillery and mortars gave the German positions immediately to our front a real battering. Since their front-line trenches were no more than a few hundred yards away our eardrums took a heavy pounding and, as a result of the almost continuous bombardment from both sides, it was impossible to get a wash, shave or cooked food. We had to rely on the meagre supply of hard rations that we kept inside our trenches.

D + 11 – Château St. Come – Saturday, 17 June

The day began with a variation on the usual dawn chorus when Jerry brought his 88s into play. The shells screamed in around the château drive and our adjoining trenches with deadly accuracy, and we wondered why, until someone pointed out that the tops of the tall tree trunks along the château drive were still smouldering and being fanned by the dawn breeze. They were glowing like a line of beacons and obviously Jerry was using them to good effect. We agreed that as soon as this deadly stonk finished we would set to and cut down the blasted trees.

It began to rain quite heavily and some of us were detailed to go to the Listening Post, but we saw nothing special, although we heard enemy tanks moving around. On the way back we fell foul of a sniper and one lad was hit in the leg. We had to drag him clear and help him to get back while we ducked and swerved to avoid becoming the sniper's next target. We made some sort of attempt to locate the sniper, but he was obviously well concealed, while we were obviously visible to him, so the odds were heavily in his favour and he got away with it.

By evening it was still pelting with rain and there was nothing I could do to prevent all my gear from becoming soaked. It was all very miserable and, as even the heavy rain did not extinguish the burning trees along the driveway, we cut them down just as we had threatened to.

D + 12 – Château St. Come – Sunday, 18 June

Throughout the night a big artillery duel took place. The flashes of exploding shells constantly lit up the sky and it was naturally very noisy. Apparently our Intelligence had some reason to believe that the Germans were about to launch a major offensive along our front. The big guns had been used in the hope of hitting them while they were moving about during the night and so disrupting their preparations.

Expecting an attack at any moment, we watched and waited all day long, but nothing out of the ordinary occurred. This meant, however, that we were constantly tensed, concentrating on our tiring and frustrating vigil, waiting for something that might have happened, but didn't. It must have been one of the rare occasions when Intelligence got it wrong. Normally they were spot on and seemed to know exactly what Jerry was planning to do.

D + 13 – Château St. Come – Monday, 19 June

In the dawn stonk the Company Sergeant Major was killed when a shell exploded near his trench and detonated his Gammon Anti-tank bombs. These bloody awful things were standard issue for us all and we hated them. They consisted of a sort of grenade or bomb, which was sticky and had a handle, resembling a large toffee apple. It was protected by a thin metal cover that was discarded when the bomb was about to be used. The bombs were highly sensitive and exploded with little encouragement. Standing orders were that these should be kept in every trench. If tanks overran us, the required procedure was to reach up and stick a bomb on the thin underside of the tank as it passed overhead.

From fear of the sensitivity of these infernal things, born of past experience with them, most of us dug a shallow hole within arm's reach of the trench and placed the bombs there. If tanks came our way we could grab a bomb or two before they arrived. The only occasions that we took them into the trench were when the officers came round on a tour of inspection! Since the CSM was a stickler for discipline and orders, he probably kept his bombs with him inside his trench, and when an enemy shell exploded nearby it set them off.

The same explosion that detonated the bombs that killed the CSM also wounded the Company Commander. He was in an adjoining trench and was hit by shrapnel. He was taken to the Regimental Aid Post where the shrapnel was removed and he was patched up and, very courageously, insisted on returning to the Company, when most would have accepted such a wound as a sure ticket back to Blighty!

It rained heavily throughout the day and for some strange reason two platoons of 'B' Company were ordered to launch an attack upon nearby enemy positions. This was a very unusual event as we were normally holding a defensive line and none of us could fathom what was going on. Perhaps someone thought that if Jerry were as miserable as we were he would not be alert. He was, however, very wide-awake and 'B' Company stirred up a viper's nest and were reported to be in deep trouble. We were ordered from our trenches and told that we were to put in a counter-attack to extricate 'B' Company.

In pouring rain and soaked to the skin, we were none too happy when told that 'B' Company had pulled back and we were now not needed. While it was reported that about a dozen Germans had been killed, 'B' Company Commander and five others were wounded and six were missing, and the Commander of 'S' Company, which was really an HQ Unit, had to take over the command of 'B' Company.

Jerry obviously assumed that 'B' Company's foray was the prelude to an all-out attack and immediately began plastering the entire front with artillery, mortars and 'Moaning Minnies'. The latter was a kind of rocket mortar, fired from a 6-barrelled launcher called a *Nebelwerfer* by the Germans. It was mounted on a light gun carriage that was towed by a truck or a half-track. The projectile could be described as being somewhat like a six-foot length of drainpipe filled with high explosives and scrap metal and stopped up at the end.

Moaning Minnies were designed to plaster a large area with shrapnel as a result of a single firing, since they launched all six missiles simultaneously. Because of their shape, instead of swishing through the air like the streamlined shells and rounded mortar bombs, the missiles went up to a high altitude and then came screaming down to earth with a very characteristic noise, exploding on impact with a fearsome crash that shook the surrounding ground. They had no accuracy and the six projectiles tended to spread out over a wide area. Although their explosive power could be devastating, they did little harm to those in well-dug trenches, unless they scored a direct hit, but the most notable feature about them was the blood-curdling noise that they made, screaming down from on high with a noise like a pack of wolves.

When I first heard them they put the fear of God into me.

If it was the Battalion Commanding Officer who initiated 'B' Company's abortive attack it most certainly backfired on him. Although Battalion HQ was behind the front line, Jerry may have thought that there were troops massing in that area ready to be launched into battle, so when he retaliated much of what he sent over was aimed at, and landed on or around, Battalion HQ. Several of the Battalion's longest-serving men were killed or wounded, including the Quartermaster.

Also killed in the same bombardment was Sergeant Major Johnny Crew who had been out to the front to observe the attack and was returning to report to HQ. He was caught in the open on his way back when the first batch of Moaning Minnies came down. He was my first drill sergeant when I joined up in March, 1941, and a long-serving member of the Regiment.

Johnny had been sitting at the side of the road as we moved forward to put in our counter-attack. I said something about what a bloody awful day it was to be putting in attacks and he replied with something like, "you bloody lot from 'D' Company are always moaning and complaining about something or other". This remark was very characteristic. Other units in the Battalion were perhaps a little envious that 'D' Company had been selected for the bridge job and 'tongue-in-cheek' cynical remarks such as this were just part of the everyday banter.

D + 14 – Château St. Come – Tuesday, 20 June

The bombardment of the previous evening continued throughout the night and at dawn it increased to a crescendo. Among the several casualties was the newly appointed Commander of 'B' Company, transferred from 'S' Company only the day before. He was killed on his early morning round while making himself known to the lads in his new command, and our Company Second-in Command, and my platoon commander, Captain Priday, then took over 'B' Company.

It continued to rain heavily throughout the day, but we were now all so wet that we were past caring. Then came the good news that we were to move back into a Rest Area at Le Mesnil, a mile or so south-west from our present position, but by no means a mile away from the front line. The Devons, or 'The Swedes' as we called them, arrived to take over our positions.

Our new location was about 400 yards behind the front line between the two forward Battalions, the Devons and the Royal Ulster Rifles, known to us as the 'Paddies'.

To the extent that we no longer had to watch the front or go out to the Listening Posts, Le Mesnil could be called a Rest Area. On the other hand it was within the general area where supplies were delivered, and so it was a prime target for enemy bombardment, and quiet it most certainly was not.

As always, having moved to a new position, our first job was to dig new trenches.

D + 15 – Le Mesnil – Wednesday, 21 June

The day was fairly quiet and we spent most of it putting finishing touches to the trenches.

For a change the weather was fine and, for the first time since we had been out here, we were able to change our underclothes and wash those that we discarded. It was a case of exchanging one set of wet clothes for another, but at least they were cleaner!

During the afternoon a small wounded pig wandered into our area and was promptly dispatched by a pistol shot, providing us with our first taste of fresh meat since arriving in Normandy. Unfortunately, firing a shot in the Rest Area was an unusual occurrence, which attracted the attention of several surrounding units who all came 'on the scrounge'. Alas, the little pig did not go very far, but at least it made for a pleasant change of diet.

When there was no shelling or mortaring, and when not given a specific duty, we would always have plenty to do. In general we might spend the time improving trenches, cleaning equipment and weapons and generally watching and waiting, but if sunny we might spend a little time relaxing next to our trenches, enjoying the sunshine. The frequent rainstorms of that summer meant that when we had some sunshine we would use it to dry out our clothing.

I did not let it be known generally that I was keeping notes about the daily events, so I would bring my diary up to date while inside the trench, usually when the shelling was not too severe. I was also careful to conceal my notes in the roof of my trench when I went out on patrol or sniping, as there was always an appreciable risk of capture.

D + 16 – Le Mesnil – Thursday, 22 June

The day was relatively peaceful, and we received a large supply of fags from Monty. These were very welcome, as we were all practically chain-smoking during the daylight hours. Even though our rest area was well to the rear, we seldom smoked at night for fear that the glow of cigarettes might be seen by an enemy patrol and the location noted for a future bombardment.

A few shells landed in and around our orchard, but this seemed to be part of a general stonk centred on another rest area about 300 yards to our right, and not aimed specifically at our positions.

D + 17 – Le Mesnil – Friday, 23 June

After the comparative peace of the previous day, we were forced to spend much of our time in the trenches due to heavy shelling, but, for the first time in seventeen days, we were able to have a bath – of sorts.

The bathhouse was the remains of a battered stable block and the bath was a tin-lined manger. Water was heated in discarded ration cans on the Company stove and carried across to the stable, dodging enemy missiles *en route*. It was a tricky operation, as Jerry seemed to be sending something over pretty regularly to keep us on our toes. Much of the precious water was lost on the short journey but we were able to strip off our clothes, splash tepid water over our bodies, rub in soap and rinse off and dry as best we could. Then we go back to our trenches, relieved to have got through the process unscathed. One lad, however, 'Gus' Gardner, was wounded by shrapnel, not too severely, while returning from bathing, and we joked with him that he would be the cleanest patient seen at the Aid Station for quite some time.

D + 18 – Le Mesnil – Saturday, 24 June

The weather was fine, enabling us to dry our clothing. Without dry clothing life could be really miserable.

A lone fighter plane came in to strafe us, but there were no casualties. The Allied air superiority was so overwhelming that it was in some ways surprising that any enemy aircraft would have the temerity, or the courage, to go out looking for targets to strafe, but in fact it was a fairly frequent occurrence, even though they almost always worked alone.

From our position high up the eastern side of the Orne valley, we had a fine view down the valley to Caen and Colombelles. Around dawn some of our bigger guns began a softening-up barrage in preparation for the assault on Caen. It continued throughout the morning and by lunchtime Caen was screened from view by a massive pall of smoke.

Colombelles is an industrial area on the outskirts of Caen. It contained factories, many with tall chimneys, which Jerry was using as observation posts. Some of the gunners had been firing at the chimneys in order to deprive the Germans of the services of these artillery observers. I would not have fancied being a German artillery observer officer perched on the top of one of those tall chimneys, with nothing to look forward to except to fall 300 feet or so amid a pile of bricks and rubble. So many of them seemed to be dedicated fanatics, although you did not need a crystal ball to see that the end for the Nazis was now just a question of 'how long'.

At around 2330 hours the enemy launched yet another heavy attack directed at the southern end of the high ground of the Orne valley, but once again they were beaten off and took heavy casualties.

D + 19 – Le Mesnil – Sunday, 25 June

In retaliation for having repulsed their attack during the night, Jerry opened up on us along the entire front during the early hours, with very heavy shelling along the whole front and, although we were in a so-called 'Rest Area', a lot of it landed on us.

We suffered several casualties, including four killed, and the shelling continued throughout the day.

Our big guns continued to pound Caen and Colombelles and during the hours of darkness the sky was continually lit by red tongues of flame as the guns fired. Whatever the German propaganda machine might be telling their troops, it must have been shattering for their morale to know that only three weeks after the landing the Allies had established such massive fire-power.

D + 20 – Le Mesnil – Monday, 26 June

During the night some of our bigger guns were moved into our area and our relative peace of the past few days was shattered by the violent crashes as the big stuff began firing from only a short distance to our rear. While we were always glad to know that if we were attacked we could call upon these big guns to fire upon the Germans, we were not overjoyed to have them so close at hand. Apart from the deafening noise, big guns need large ammunition stocks and these attract Germans like bees to a honey pot!

In some ways we were not too displeased to learn that our rest period was over and that we were to move up to the front line again, this time to Bréville. Indeed, we thought that the front line might now be more peaceful than the Rest Area, but we were wrong.

D + 21 – Bréville – Tuesday, 27 June

Bréville is just slightly to the north of the Château St Come, half a mile or so, and we soon learned that it was not a place to go to for a quiet time. It had a reputation as one of the hottest spots on our front and was subjected to almost continuous bombardment. About two weeks earlier a hard battle had been fought for control of the village, with No 6 Commando and the 1st Battalion of the Free French slugging it out with the German 314th Division. Although most of the village had been virtually destroyed, for once we were lucky and were allocated a reasonably sound terraced cottage as Platoon HQ, not that we were going to spend much time there.

Our new defensive positions were on the reverse side of the slope which led up to the village, and where, once again, we had to set to and dig fresh trenches. It always struck me as odd that whenever we moved into an area that had previously been occupied by other troops who, for their own protection, had built superb trenches, our officers had other ideas about the way each new location should be defended. They always ordered us to dig new ones. Worse was that, having dug them, we then had to fill in the old ones so that they could not be used by an attacking enemy! One compensation was that, since the older trenches were near our new ones, we could re-use their excellent roofing materials.

D + 22 – Bréville – Wednesday, 28 June

During the night we were heavily shelled, but the pressure eased after sun-up. There was still some sporadic activity by the German gunners, however, with the occasional in-bound shell, but no continuous bombardment, but this led to an amusing incident. One of the new trenches incorporated a huge cider barrel as sleeping quarters and was completely destroyed by a direct hit.

Fortunately the usual occupant of this trench was down at the cottage at the time. He was so upset by the destruction of his unique trench that we all set to and dug a new one for him.[4]

D + 23 – Bréville – Thursday, 29 June

At dawn a small group of us went forward on a Recce to Longuemare crossroads. It was some distance to the north-east and we had learnt from the 'Paddies' that it was a no-man's-land. It was a wooded area and provided concealed lines of approach for either side so that no one could establish a permanent post out there as it was too vulnerable to attack or ambush.

At the road junction was a farmhouse and outbuildings, from the upper floor of which it was possible for either side to observe the others' positions. We approached with caution but were seen and fired upon and forced to withdraw.

As we moved away we had frequently to dive for cover as the

Germans put down a steady flow of mortar bombs all along the route. They were probably aware that a new lot had moved into Bréville and wanted to make it clear that Longuemare was 'off limits'.

To round off the day a lone fighter plane flew in from the direction of the setting sun and, at just above tree-top level, strafed our new trenches with canon and machine-gun fire, but there were no casualties.

D + 24 – Bréville – Friday, 30 June

In retaliation for the previous day's pasting from the Germans, our heavy mortar platoon moved into an orchard to our rear and opened fire, giving Longuemare a short but really heavy hammering. "Oh God!" we exclaimed, "what the Hell have we done to deserve this?" and promptly dived for the protection of our trenches, since we knew exactly what would happen next.

Whenever our heavy mortars moved up close behind our lines and opened up with a short bombardment, Jerry would immediately retaliate with everything to hand. Of course by the time the position from which our mortars had fired had been plotted the mortar platoon had already withdrawn, leaving us to face whatever was sent over in reply.

Once again everyone was running low on fags. We were all hoping that the NAAFI, or someone, would soon be sending up fresh supplies. There was still the odd dead body out in no-man's-land, but by now so well decomposed that we didn't fancy smoking anything that they may still have had in their pockets.

D + 25 – Bréville – Saturday, 1 July

The spell of several fine days that we had enjoyed ended abruptly, as the weather changed quite dramatically and it rained heavily all day.

A brave Jerry pilot took advantage of the low cloud and mist and gave us a thorough working over. We dived for cover and one of the lads grabbed a light machine gun and opened fire at him. He was so low that we could clearly see the pilot's face as he peered down at us. Obviously he was trying to get a good look at our well-camouflaged positions. After his visit we had only just settled down when, to our surprise, another came flying in.

Strafing aircraft were fairly common, despite the fact that they were at great risk of attack by allied aircraft, and despite the fact that, at that stage of the war, the Germans had very little fuel to waste on unproductive missions. It is very possible that, although armed and aggressive, their main purpose was to take photographs of our positions. Though they did very little damage they were annoying, like wasps, and if you were out in the open when they appeared you were a fool if you didn't dive into the nearest ditch. On a day like this one, if you jumped into a ditch you could expect to get very wet and muddy. However, we could not really grumble about the occasional enemy plane since the skies were usually well patrolled by our own Spitfires, Hurricanes and rocket-firing Typhoons.

The Luftwaffe obviously gave our aircraft a very wide berth, and so did I after the time that I made the mistake of waving to a low-flying RAF Typhoon that came hurtling in my direction. I gave the pilot a cheery wave, only to be greeted by a burst of cannon fire in return. As the cannon shells exploded in the ground all around me I dived headlong into the nearest ditch, which fortunately was quite close.

Never again did I make the mistake of waving to a 'friendly' aircraft. Many had similar experiences, and reputedly the American pilots were the worst offenders, being not at all fussy about who or what they shot up, although personally I was never unlucky enough to be targeted by one of their number.

Not to be outdone by their gallant airmen, the German ground forces gave our area a heavy shelling and several shells hit our row of cottages but no one was hurt and, for the large amount that he sent over, very little damage was done. Jerry probably assumed that since it had been raining so heavily we would be sheltering in the cottages and getting dried out. No such luck!

In the late evening the Commando to our North sent out a strong fighting patrol. We had been warned that they were having a 'party', so, from past experience, we made sure that we were in our trenches when the attack went in, knowing that, in the usual way, Jerry would immediately retaliate by bombarding the entire front. In a short sharp skirmish the Commando kicked up a hell of a racket, thus making Jerry panic, obviously giving him the impression that this was the prelude to a large-scale night attack. We were glad to be well down in the trenches when he hit back, as he did, and with a vengeance.

D + 26 – Bréville – Sunday, 2 July

Jerry continued his panic stonking throughout the night and the rest of the day, so life became extremely uncomfortable. Instead of casually strolling down to the cottages for food and washing, it was a case of running, swerving, diving, crawling, then standing up and running like hell as soon as the stonk appeared to ease off for a moment.

Enemy shelling and mortaring was far more accurate than in the recent past. This was no random stonk. Jerry really seemed to have our new positions pinpointed. We could only surmise that one of those low-flying aircraft had taken photographs. Although our trenches were well camouflaged from the ground and air, we were making tracks in the wet grass as we made our trips back and forth between the trenches and the cottages. There was an obvious need to vary our route in future.

To add to our discomfort, it began to rain even harder than before so that, whenever we were out of our trenches, having to find cover in a hurry during the heavy stonk meant that we got very wet and muddy.

D + 27 – Bréville – Monday, 3 July

Our Gunners did their best to make life unpleasant for Jerry, hammering away mercilessly at his lines. Despite the abysmal weather, we sent out patrols as well, to keep him on his toes. I was not detailed to go out on any of these patrols, for which I was very grateful. There was no great joy in being cooped up in a muddy and waterlogged trench, but crawling through wet grass, mud and waterlogged ditches was even less enjoyable and a good deal more dangerous as well.

That's the
CRY
of the
1st American Army
near St Lô.

Who knows, perhaps

you

may be in the same desperate situation to-morrow.

AW 41.

Calling

S.O.S.

GERMANS

SEND US

DOCTORS !

NORMANDY – 1944. Typical double-sided German propoganda leaflets highly sought-after for use as toilet paper!

Welcome to the Continent!

Hallo, Boys!

Here you are at last, old chaps! We have been waiting for you long enough. Even though you are unwanted and altogether uninvited guests, you are not unexpected. You have given us plenty of time to get ready for your arrival.

You're quite right, Boys, there's a really swell least awaiting you; come and help yourselves. Many more of you will be coming over; that's a sure thing! Let'em all come — why not? We've laid a place for all of you at this invasion dinner-party. Who knows—and perhaps that is actually what we mean to do—whether we shan't' wait to dish it up until the last one of you has got here, so that each and every mother's son of you can share without any doubt in the good, the swell things from our kitchen.

Now then, at last, sit down, take your places, we're ready to serve you. You'll get a bellyful; once and for all, provided that your knives and forks don't fly out of your hands before you start to eat.

Whom have you got to thank for this invasion-dinner?

Of one thing you must be clear: you must eat up the soup into phich a certain Mr. Joe has crumbled your crackers for you. To the very last spoonful. It ist this Mr. Joe from Moscow that you have to thank for your present posi...on. Behind you lies the sea and Hell lies all around you. You've come more than a thousand miles over the mighty ocean to sacrifice your good American skin for Moscow and the Bolshies.

Don't forget this, now that you are laced ·····ith the toughest of all fighting!

What exactly do you want in Europe?

To defend America? Do you, the aggressors, want to uphold the banner of democracy and Freedom?! For us you are the aggressors, and we shall fight you to the last breath.

The American Continent has never been threatened by Germany but this is now the second time you are about to mix yourselves up in European affairs at the instigation of Jewish hate instincts and lust for power, although it is none of your business. Don't be surprised it we defend ourselves against you. Just as we don't interfere in your American affairs we don't want you to poke your noses into our business. It is no question of your defending America; you are fighting for capitalist, Bolshevist and Jewish interests. In actual fact you are only the tools, the victims of Stalin.

Don't forget your mothers.

The Bolshies are the sworn enemies of all culture: they are the destroyers of religion and family life. That's a fact that every American knows. It's ridiculous to suppose that the Bolshies have changed since the gory days of the Russian revolution.

Are your mothers and yours wives content that you are shedding your blood now for these devils? Surely not. If your mothers knew how hard are the battles awaiting you here and how few you will ever return from this hell of fire and blood, they would sure:, compel your President to put an end to this damned war. But of course they don't know.

Think of them when you are facing Death.
Die for Stalin — and Israel?

Obviously intended for American troops but dropped on the British Airborne Divisional bridgehead

D + 28 – Bréville – Tuesday, 4 July

This was another dismal grey day with frequent showers. I guessed that most of the Americans were probably wishing they were at home and not in Europe helping us!

To make an already lousy day even worse our people decided to put out a propaganda broadcast. This was achieved by a Jeep fitted with a public address system, which drove up close to the front line. They would spend several minutes putting out propaganda, but as it was in German none of us knew what was said. We were, however, well aware of the consequences and dived into our trenches, because whatever they said always made the Germans furious. It took them a short while to plot the approximate location of the Jeep with its PA system, and to get details to the gunners, and then the whole area came in for a real plastering. Of course by that time the Broadcast Unit had driven off at high speed and we poor devils were left to face the music.

In addition to this type of propaganda, both sides made frequent use of leaflets dropped from the air or fired in shells that exploded as air-bursts spreading the leaflets over a wide area. Both sides offered surrendering soldiers good food, comfort and medical attention, etc. The Germans would try to spook us by suggesting that the Americans were surrendering in droves, or were being pushed into the sea. Some examples of German propaganda leaflets which I collected as souvenirs can be seen on pages 106–7.

Although I never heard of anyone taking up the generous offers made in them, the leaflets had a particularly useful secondary purpose as they made ideal toilet paper which was always in short supply! Happily, as the Allies, with their air superiority, tended to drop more than the Germans, and as we were close to enemy lines, we always got a good supply from both sides!

D + 29 – Bréville – Wednesday, 5 July

For a change the weather was fine, the sun shone brightly and we were able to begin drying out our trenches, equipment and clothing. I was very despondent and was hoping that the spell of rain we had endured would be the last for a long time. I was fed up with so much rain; being soaked to the skin in a wet trench brought on a sense of misery that sapped the morale. Someone came up with the idea that it was all the shelling and explosions that were the cause of so much wet weather in the middle of what was supposed to be the summer.

I was told that we were to go out on some offensive patrolling and sniping. This would be a pleasant change after being cooped up in the wet trenches over the previous few days.

When I went down to the cottage for food I was told that the show was off, there would be no sniping expedition that day. As this left us with time on our hands a few of us decided to carry out a recce around the village in the hope of finding some fresh vegetables.

We tried one place and found a few onions. Our next call was to a field where we hoped to obtain potatoes. Those around the edge of the field, near protective cover, had already gone. We moved out into the middle and from nowhere a lone aircraft swooped down with all guns blazing. With no cover available we could only hit the ground and face the oncoming plane, so presenting the narrowest possible target. We could see the bullets and cannon shells ploughing into the ground around us, but no one was hit and when the aircraft passed overhead we were up on our feet and running to the nearest ditch.

Our evening meal was much improved by a few young spuds and onions, which went down well with the tinned bully beef.

I was told that the next day we would definitely go out sniping, which was something to look forward to.

D + 30 – Bréville – Thursday, 6 July

The Germans were quiet and we enjoyed a peaceful day, which enabled us to dry our clothing.

Late in the day three of us took off for a scouting and sniping trip into no-man's-land. We had plenty of fun but saw nothing worth taking a shot at and, since Jerry was not bothering us, it made no sense to stir him up, particularly as the other lads back in the line were still busy drying out.

D + 31 – Bréville – Friday, 7 July

Before dawn the three of us who had been out yesterday were sent on another trip. This time we aimed to reach the farmhouse at Longuemare. We wanted to be there early to see if the Germans occupied it during the night. If there was no sign of life we hoped to enter the house or at least the outbuildings. On the way there we heard the sound of many people digging trenches on the far side of the crossroads. One at a time, and flitting from cover to cover, we reached the farm and, after many stops to listen and observe, managed to get inside the farmhouse. From the upper floor we overlooked the road junction and saw a mass of Germans digging new trenches. While the other two stayed to observe, my job was to get back to Company lines and report to Major Howard.

We had several rows of wire with zigzag or staggered openings in front of the trenches and as I arrived a large dog followed me through. We tried to catch or shoot the wretched animal but it got away. With the possibility that it could lead an enemy force through our maze it was necessary to make extensive alterations to the layout, as a result of which I was not very popular!

After getting the OK from Regimental HQ, Major Howard organized and led a large and well-armed fighting patrol out to the farmhouse. After withdrawing the other snipers, we lined up along the edge of an adjoining orchard and, on a signal, let fly with rifles, automatics, machine guns and mortars. A few minutes later, having caused pandemonium, on the Major's signal we stopped firing and quickly withdrew to our lines.

Late in the day we saw a large bomber force flying overhead on its way to give Caen another heavy pasting. I doubted if there would be much of Caen left when this lot was all over; it really took a hammering.

D + 32 – Bréville/St. Come – Saturday, 8 July

To our surprise, early in the day we were told to pack up and move out. It was a pity, because after our efforts of the previous day we were just beginning to enjoy ourselves at this location.

110

We were being moved back into our old stamping grounds around the Château St. Come. During our absence the place had undergone a major clean-up. The dead had gone and any serviceable equipment had been removed. We were sent further forward than before, into an area to the north-east of the main building so that we were nearer to Bréville and Longuemare.

We took over from the 'Swedes' (Devons) and, for a pleasant change, we were allowed to make use of some of their trenches, at least for the time being. Our Platoon was spread out along the side of a deep ditch that overlooked a field that was about one hundred yards wide. On the far side was another deep ditch and hedge and beyond that a similar field. According to the Swedes, the enemy forces were dug in on the far side of the second field so that they were only about 200 yards away from our own positions.

Sniper Corporal Wally Parr and I went out on a recce and soon discovered that, like our earlier location at St. Come, the fields were all surrounded by deep ditches topped by thick hedges. The Swedes told us that the Germans in this sector made little use of the surrounding ditches.

We were quickly able to verify the information given to us by the Swedes. When we had moved a little further to the north-east, we soon came to ditches that were extensively overgrown, and it was obvious that no one in that area had made use of them in the recent past. From our vantage point we were looking over an orchard about 150 yards wide. It sloped away toward the east where there was a hedge, on the far side of which were the German trenches. Beyond their hedge was a field of ripening corn, providing a light backdrop to their positions. As they passed gaps in the hedgerow they were nicely silhouetted against the lighter background.

This was going to be a splendid place for sniping. We could clearly see Germans strolling up and down their hedgerow, quite oblivious to the fact that they were under observation. Although they provided many tempting targets we could not fire as we were only there to spy out the lie of the land and to seek suitable locations for future sniping expeditions. Our officers would want to know a lot more about these enemy positions before allowing us to open fire.

Wally and I spent much of the day out in no-man's-land and had plenty to report when we returned to company lines.

The battle for Caen was now in full swing and, although it was several miles to our south and not in direct view, I could see the great pall of smoke as the artillery and bombers softened it up in preparation for the assault.

D + 33 – Château St. Come – Sunday, 9 July

Before daybreak Wally Parr, Paddy O'Donnell and I set out for our new hedgerow. Before we could get into position a runner arrived to say the shoot was cancelled. The reason soon became apparent when, a short time later, an Artillery Forward Observation Officer and his Wireless Operator appeared. The F.O.O. needed to see the Germans before we sent them all to ground.

He had a quick look, gave some rapid instructions to the wireless operator and almost immediately a shell screamed in, passed through the hedge just above our heads and hit the field a few yards from where we lay! We need not have worried as it only sent up a puff of smoke. The F.O.O. gave further instructions whereupon another round came whistling in, landing right in the enemy positions. Satisfied that he had the correct range, he gave a cheery wave and was soon on his way, followed by the lad with a massive wireless on his back.

Although we could not shoot we were happy to stay to observe the enemy reaction. After their initial fright they soon recovered and were again strolling around. It was a fine sunny day and we were in no hurry to return to company lines, which were taking a battering, perhaps as a result of the two ranging shells. The German artillery seemed to operate on the simple principle of 'When in doubt, open up'. On such a day no-man's-land had its compensations; we were too close to the enemy for them to risk firing shells or other heavy stuff at us.

By lunchtime the battering along our front had died down and we returned to our lines for a bite to eat.

Unlike many of the commanders who went before him, Monty was keen to keep the rank-and-file in the picture. When we went to Company HQ for food, or for any other reason, the Company Commander or other senior officer, standing in front of a large map, would point out the positions of our armies. There was also comprehensive coverage of the enemy positions. The information was gleaned from various Intelligence sources, such as aerial reconnaissance, civilian reports and scouting trips, and was updated on a daily basis. One of the first things that most of us looked for was details of any new divisions moving into our area, as this might indicate that we were being withdrawn. On this occasion, however, the only news about our part of the bridgehead area was that the battle for Caen was going well.

D + 34 – Château St. Come – Monday, 10 July

A sunny spell, which had lasted for several days, came to an end, and it pelted with rain. To make life even more uncomfortable the big guns from both sides were pounding away and we came in for some really heavy stuff.

Things were easier towards the end of the day and two snipers went out, but soon returned with nothing to report. Presumably with all the shelling, bombing and rain the Germans, like us, were keeping down in their trenches.

I was hoping that the weather would improve, because the next day I was due to go out on another sniping expedition.

D + 35 – Château St. Come – Tuesday, 11 July

My hopes were fulfilled; it was a glorious day. The same team, Wally, Paddy and I, left early to be in position at daybreak.

When I went out sniping I invariably took my captured German weaponry along with me, the Schmeisser and the P38 pistol, as well as the Helios wristwatch of course. Wally and Paddy joked that if I were to be captured, Jerry would execute me on the spot for carrying such an arsenal of German equipment with me, but I always reckoned it was worth the risk. In all the grime and mud that we had to contend with, crawling through ditches and so

113

forth, the chances of having a weapon jam when it was most needed were pretty high, and I was of the opinion that it did no harm to have back-up defences.

It was quite likely that when their Stand-To ended, Jerry would be out of his trenches drying out after the rain of the previous day. This proved to be the case and we had no difficulty in spotting targets.

All was peace and tranquillity until Wally let fly at an excellent target. By the time he hit the ground the rest had dived for cover. It was a long time before they began to reappear, probably assuming that the man had been hit by a stray shot. I took careful aim at a hole in the hedgerow. It was well lit by the lighter background. Soon it filled as someone peered across the orchard towards us. I held my fire, hoping that it would encourage others to surface. After a short time the hole reappeared as the man moved away. Then it filled again. This time I gently squeezed the trigger and the target crashed backwards.

Paddy should have been the next to fire, but as I was closing the bolt on a fresh cartridge which I had just loaded into my rifle I saw a well-built German out in the open and exposed to my view from his head to his knees. I waited for a few seconds for Paddy to fire, but assumed that he could not see this target who began to move. I fired and almost certainly winged him as he let out a loud yell and disappeared from sight. Paddy was furious, and all the more so when I whispered, "Blast – I think that I only winged him!"

It was several hours before they got over the shock of two kills and a wounding. We had to wait until getting towards lunchtime before, once again, they began moving around, probably on their way to the cookhouse, and at last Paddy was rewarded for his long vigil.

Happy to have made a hit apiece, we reckoned that three 'kills' would mean that no further targets would appear, so we decided to call it a day and we returned to the lines.

In the afternoon we were heavily shelled, but the weather had changed soon after lunch and once again it had begun to pelt with rain, so not many people were out in the open and we took no casualties.

The day ended on a good note when, around teatime, fresh

supplies arrived and included *real tea*, sugar and tinned milk, which made a wonderful change from the foul 'Mixed Monkey' tea cubes. This new stuff really tasted like tea.

There was a severe stonk a short while later, and whether the fresh tea went to his Cockney head I don't know, but Wally Parr was hit by two chunks of shrapnel. I was not around when it happened, but I was told that the wounds were not too severe, but enough to put him out of action for some time.

Wally was a collector of interesting items! Apparently as he was being placed upon a stretcher he said to the medical orderlies, "'Ang on a minute mates". Then he called out to one of the lads, "Hey mate, do me a favour. Nip over to me trench and get the little pack for me. It will make a nice pillow as they cart me back to Blighty."

As he went he called out, "Don't worry mates – I'll be back!" Wally was one of those brave characters who seemed to be in his element during warfare.[5]

D + 36 – Château St. Come – Wednesday, 12 July

It wasn't a particularly bright day but soon after an excellent breakfast, with real tea again, Paddy and I made for 'our hedgerow'. On the way we met the standing patrol who were fed up, moaning and complaining because they should have been relieved. As we approached them, at first they thought that we were the long overdue relief patrol, and they were most unhappy to discover that we were not. We told them about the smashing breakfast that we had just enjoyed, then we all sat around chatting. The relief patrol did arrive finally, and the original patrol departed, muttering threats about what would happen the next time if by chance their positions should be reversed.

We wandered off along the hedgerow and Paddy got into a hide about thirty yards away from the patrol. I sauntered further along, but there was simply nothing to be seen. The Germans across the way had obviously learnt fast and were taking no chances.

After some time I got bored and decided to move further along in the hope of seeing some targets from a different vantage point.

After two or three stops I neared the end of the hedge and field. Suddenly, from down in the corner of the field, where deep ditches formed a crossroads, I heard a quiet cough and froze to the spot. As far as I knew no other snipers were around this area. I slung my rifle across my back, dropped to the ground and took out a smoke grenade in case I should need it. I took my liberated P38 pistol from my belt and began crawling backwards along the hedgerow.

I moved very cautiously, making no sound, and it took ages to get to Paddy. When I explained what had happened we both withdrew to the well-armed standing patrol and advised them that there was someone down in the far corner of the field. Their usual boredom quickly evaporated as they swung the machine gun round to cover the direction I had indicated. Paddy and I hurried back to the lines and reported to the Company Commander who decided that we should return to the standing patrol and, with their support, attack whoever was in the corner. When we advised the patrol of the plan, no one, including Paddy and me, was over-keen to hurry into the attack.

While we were sitting around, having a smoke and discussing tactics, a runner arrived to say that the attack was cancelled. I didn't mind one bit for whoever was in the ditch was well concealed and we would have to attack across an open field. If it turned out to be a strong enemy group we could all be in a lot of trouble!

Upon returning to the Company we two snipers were told by the Company Commander that, in the usual way, he had advised Regimental HQ that we were about to have a 'party' out to our front, and HQ passed the message up through the line. The reason for that procedure was so that other nearby units would know what was going on and would not fire at us.

It was someone higher up in the command structure who put a stop to the attack. Apparently there were some freelance French snipers working the area next to us and no one was quite sure of their location. We could not risk an attack on what might well have been people from our own side. We were told that we could only attack if we were certain that the occupiers were German, but I wasn't very keen to find out!

116

Surprise! Surprise! After yesterday's supply of fresh tea, etc., the supply bods really excelled themselves today by sending up *real white bread*! It tasted wonderful, a superb change from the usual hard biscuits.

There was one thing about this war – it certainly made you appreciate any fresh food on the rare occasions that it came your way.

D + 37/38 – Château St. Come – Thursday/Friday, 13/14 July

The Thursday was a lousy day with nothing special for me to note. The overcast sky of yesterday turned into heavy rain, which was always depressing if you lived in a trench, and we received our usual quota of mortar bombs and shells, but suffered no casualties.

We were wet and miserable and no one was sent out sniping. It would have been pointless anyway, as in this sort of weather Jerry would be no more likely to be standing around in the open than we were.

The next day was another quiet one, much like the day before. The only good news we heard was that Caen had fallen at last. The Generals had hoped and planned, rather optimistically, to capture Caen on D-Day, but just the same it was good to hear that it had finally fallen.[6]

Our own immediate thoughts were that with Caen now liberated perhaps there would be a spare Division to take over our positions so that we could go home.

D + 39 – Châeau St. Come – Saturday, 15 July

Although there had been many occasions since D-Day when I had my doubts that I would ever see it, I finally made my twentieth birthday. As far as the Army was concerned it was my twenty-second, since I had put my age up two years when I volunteered in March, 1941, and no one since that day had ever done anything to question it.

117

By way of a birthday present from Jerry a shell in the first batch that came over exploded within a few yards of my trench. The roof lifted up and came down again. The side walls expanded and contracted and for a few moments I lay in the bottom semi-stunned, my ears ringing and lights dancing behind my closed eyelids. In the same batch our Platoon Commander, Lieutenant 'Chalky' White, who had replaced Den Brotheridge who was killed on D-Day, was hit on the side of his head by shrapnel. The wound was not fatal, but it certainly meant that we would see no more of him for a while.

That was a nasty experience, but by midday I was fully recovered from the shaking up and I was out sniping again. As soon as I had settled into a hide I realized why things had been so quiet yesterday: a new lot had moved in. They were wandering up and down the hedgerow without a care in the world. It was a reasonably bright day and they presented some excellent targets.

I contemplated going back and getting one or two more snipers out, since, on this occasion, I was on my own. As I wondered what action to take a very large German stopped right in the middle of a gap in their hedge. It was my birthday and the target was just too tempting, so I let fly. The man leapt into the air and then fell flat upon his face and made no further movement.

It was such a pleasant day that I spent most of it wandering up and down the hedgerow, but did not see another worthwhile target. These new Germans obviously learnt fast, but I was, however, always surprised that every new lot seemed to learn from scratch. While in many ways the Germans were so efficient, when one outfit took over from another, it appeared that the outgoing personnel never informed the incoming replacements about the danger of the British snipers. In contrast, whenever we took over a new area we always made a point of asking about the opposition and any other information that would help us to survive without suffering unnecessary casualties.

D + 40 – Château St. Come – Sunday, 16 July

By way of a Sunday treat, the Company Commander decided that it would be a very good idea if those of us who were not doing anything special were to get out of our trenches and take a walk down to the bridges at Bénouville. None of us had seen our bridges since D-Day, so the idea was well received by the men, but as we left the protection of our trenches Jerry took it into his head to bombard us, which was not the best way to start a Sunday stroll.

With Lieutenant White out of action, his replacement, our new platoon officer, had just arrived, and his first task was to march us down to the bridges. As a fresh young officer he had his own ideas about how soldiers should march. We, on the other hand, had been wearing our boots almost continuously for forty-one days, and our once hard feet were now like lumps of soft putty. Our ideas about how battle-weary veteran campaigners should march were not exactly in line with those of our new Platoon Commander, and to say that our first meeting with him was not an auspicious occasion would be quite an understatement!

Although no textbook marching was done, we did eventually reach the bridges and were horrified to see them plastered with 'HD' (Highland Division) signs. Some of our lads talked of finding a tin of paint and writing 'D+3' across them, to indicate that the 'Jocks' had not been around when the bridges were captured by us.

Upon arrival I immediately made my way to my glider to seek the piece of fabric upon which I had written my name back at the airfield; it now seemed so long ago. Unfortunately I had written it on the underside of the nose which, in the crash, had been smashed into the ground. However, I found two pieces of the perspex that had once formed the glider cockpit and decided that they would make a reasonable substitute.[7]

Our bridges were now well back behind the line and had been taken over by the boys from Army and Corps HQs, who had never been nearer to the battlefields than they were now. They were a cocky lot, strutting around in their clean and well-pressed uniforms and highly polished boots. They regarded us with total disdain and made us feel like a bunch of tramps. It was made abundantly clear that scruffs like us should not be allowed to make their area untidy. Their obvious wish to see the back of us was soon granted when we were ordered to fall in to be marched back to our lines.

D + 41 – Château St Come – Monday, 17 July

At dawn a mist spread across the front. It was the first time I had seen an early morning mist like that. We were all a bit worried to see it, as it could easily have screened an enemy attack, in the same way as smoke. As the sun came up, however, the mist quickly cleared and the panic was over.

I spent most of the rest of the day sniping. I was almost sure that I got one, but not one hundred percent certain, so I could not chalk it up as a definite kill.

The listening patrol had reported that the night before they thought that someone had come close to their positions. I was ordered to investigate and I made my way to the area about which they had expressed their concern. I crawled up a bank close to where they were located and into an adjoining orchard. Within about ten yards I found tracks which indicated that someone had recently flattened the tall grass. I checked with the patrol that none of them had been out there. Assured that no one had, I advised them that someone had crawled to within spitting distance of their positions; it gave them quite a jolt.

When I reported to the Company Commander he instructed Paddy and me to set up an ambush. Just before sunset we left the listening post and crawled out into an adjoining orchard. We moved out through the long grass in a wide semi-circle hoping to get into a hedge above a ditch that was about seventy-five yards forward of our listening post. The idea was to lie in wait and then jump on anyone who might come along the ditch after dark.

As we approached the hedge we heard a noise coming from the ditch below. Someone was already there! We used our hands to signal to each other that a strategic withdrawal was the only appropriate action to take. We had moved a hell of a long way from our listening post and could not rely upon them for help; they probably couldn't even see us. Keeping flat upon the ground we swivelled round and began crawling back towards our side of the orchard but, all too soon came the familiar 'plop' sound as a mortar fired and seconds later the first bomb exploded. Then others fired in quick succession and bombs exploded all round us.

We crawled as fast as we could but expected that at any moment both of us would be blown to bits.

If Paddy and I had guardian angels watching over us they were working overtime during the time it took us to cover the seventy-five yards across that orchard. We finally made it to the far side and dived headfirst through the hedge and into the ditch. How we both survived that barrage of mortar bombs without getting so much as a scratch I will never know. I can only conclude that, because of the recent heavy rain, the grassy orchard ground was particularly soft so that the bombs penetrated well into the earth before exploding. This would have had the effect of throwing the shrapnel upwards rather than outwards. In fact the only scratches that we did get were made as we dived through the thick hedge!

After linking up with the listening post we took a long rest before returning to the lines and reporting to the Company Commander. After receiving our report he said, "Never mind chaps – better luck next time" I thought I had been lucky enough this time, without having to worry about next time.

As we walked back to our trenches I muttered to Paddy, "I don't know about you chum, but as far as I'm concerned, I hope that there will never be another next time, at least not like that one." Paddy nodded in agreement and we crawled wearily into our adjoining trenches. I was just about exhausted and I quickly fell asleep.

It seemed as if I had only just dropped off when, at 2330 hours, our new platoon Commander roused me. Staggering to my feet I clambered from the trench, while he informed me that he and I were going out on a night-time recce of the enemy forward positions as the 'higher-ups' wanted to establish whether the Germans had laid mines or trip wires in front of their positions. Apart from being totally exhausted from the earlier exertions, it was going to be no picnic crawling about in no-man's-land in the dark accompanied by an inexperienced young officer.

"A bloody fine party this is going to be," I thought to myself, and wished that Wally Parr, the Sniper Corporal, was still with us, as this would then have been his job and not mine!

At Company HQ, attired in camouflaged smocks over battle-dress, with web belt, black plimsolls on our feet, and faces and

121

hands blackened by soot from the cooker we made our way out to the forward listening post. We then waited for a few minutes, scrambled up the ditch bank, through the top hedge and out into the same wretched orchard from which Paddy and I had escaped only a few hours earlier. We were both armed with a couple of hand grenades and we each had an automatic pistol, his being regulation Army issue, mine being my liberated German P38.

I thought that this must be tempting fate just once too often, but we slithered quietly forward through the long grass and, with frequent stops to listen for enemy movement, gradually made our way across the orchard.

It was an exceedingly slow trip and my limbs ached like hell, but, after what seemed like hours, we finally arrived at the far side of the orchard, where we reached out with our finger tips to feel for mines or trip-wires, but found none. We were so close to the enemy positions that we could actually hear them whispering to each other. The officer tapped me and indicated that we should withdraw.

Silently we crawled away until we were well out into the middle of the orchard when I had an overwhelming desire to cough! I clamped a hand across my mouth and pinched my nose but still the cough came out like a clap of thunder. We froze to the spot and cringed down in the long grass waiting for all hell to break loose.

The Gods must have been with us. For some reason all that happened was that Jerry fired a parachute flare that cast a light over much of the orchard. The brilliant illumination from the flare might easily have been our undoing, as most of the trees had been badly blasted during past bombardments, but the one that we happened to be under still contained a fair amount of foliage and this cast a shadow over our prone bodies.

When the flare went out we waited a while, then crawled quickly back to the listening post. After all too short a rest, we returned to the Company where the officer reported to the Company Commander and I stood around like a spare file waiting to be torn off a strip for endangering the life of an officer.

He didn't mention the coughing incident, and as we walked away he said, "Well done. Now get some sleep. I expect you need it." Perhaps he wasn't such a 'regimental type' after all, or he was learning about our kind of warfare very quickly, and that would be no bad thing, for him as well as for us.

Once again I slid into my trench and was soon fast asleep, with just an hour or so to go before stand to.

D + 42 – Château St. Come – Tuesday, 18 July

At stand to I was almost fast asleep on my feet. I propped my body drunkenly forward against the front of the trench and peered bleary eyed into the semi-darkness. "Christ Almighty," I muttered "even after the events of last night they still can't let me off one lousy stand to."

Suddenly I was wide-awake as, from the north, came the sound of powerful engines and, within a few minutes, the whole sky appeared to be filled with aircraft. I had been impressed on D-Day by the mass of planes and gliders, but this lot was possibly an even more formidable force. Thousands of heavy bombers, escorted by hundreds of fighter planes, flew in from the sea like a continuous conveyor belt passing high overhead, flew on down to the area around Caen, dropped their bombs, circled and were soon on their way back to England for breakfast – lucky devils![8]

We didn't go out sniping and I took advantage of the interest in the activity to the east of Caen to slide down into the bottom of my trench and catch up on some badly needed sleep.

D + 43 – Château St. Come – Wednesday, 19 July

Paddy and I went out to our sniper hides before dawn and spotted a German standing in a gap, yawning his head off. We let fly together and put him back to sleep. Then we peppered away along their entire hedgerow, hoping to make them think that we were launching a dawn attack. We may not have hit any more but I guess that we caused a fair amount of panic. We stayed around for some while and had just decided to make our way back to the Company lines for breakfast when I spotted a German who must have had a similar idea. He flitted across two small gaps in his hedgerow and I selected the widest gap in front of him.

As he moved into the gap that I was covering I fired. He let out a loud yell and crashed to the ground to disappear from sight.

Back at our lines the rest of the day was quiet, but for some reason during the night we were heavily shelled. This was odd. Jerry didn't usually bother to shell us after dark when most would be down in the trenches.

D + 44 – Château St. Come – Thursday, 20 July

The enemy big guns were quite all day. British and Canadian forces were mounting a major effort towards Falaise, so it was possible that the guns had been pulled out and taken down there.

Perhaps the unusual shelling of the previous night was a last effort before pulling out. It was all very odd and out of keeping because we had come to rely upon German predictability. When something changed from the normal pattern, we would be apprehensive, not knowing what to expect.

Not only was there not much action by Jerry's heavy artillery, but very little else was going on either and the weather was fine, so, because I was not required for sniping I took advantage of the quiet spell to catch up on lost sleep.

My slit trench was cool and the warm weather drove a few insects into my 'home'. I awoke with a start when a large spider ran across my face. I never did like the things very much, but I suppose that if you live in a mud hole in the ground you must expect such visitors.

By far the worst insect problem, however, was mosquitoes. Because the Germans had flooded the nearby Dives valley, they had created swamp-like conditions that were ideal breeding grounds for these pests. At night-time it was particularly bad, especially out at the forward listening posts where, being close to enemy positions, everyone had to keep quiet once in place. In the damp, deep and often soggy ditches the 'mozzies' were to be found in great clouds. It became so bad that we were issued with a foul-smelling cream that was liberally spread over exposed skin.

However warm we were, when in the vicinity of these swarms of mosquitoes we kept our shirts buttoned up to the collar and covered our faces with a piece of camouflaged fine-mesh netting which we wore round our necks like a cravat or scarf. These helped to keep the 'mozzies' at bay but it was not unusual to find that those who had been out during the hours of darkness were still covered with bites.

A secondary problem with mosquitoes was that since there were so many they made a terrific noise as they flew around in great swarms. They could easily drown the sound of an approaching enemy patrol.

D + 45 – Château St. Come – Friday, 21 July

I went out sniping at first light, but it was a waste of time, as I didn't see one worthwhile target.

Two other snipers went out later and while they were out there was a short but fierce stonk, which kept us all down in our trenches. Upon returning, the two snipers found that their shared trench had taken a direct hit and made a hell of a mess of their kit and blankets. It made all of us think a bit. It was incredibly lucky that they were out sniping at the time, and that it was their trench that was hit, and not one of the others, nearly all of which were occupied. We felt pretty secure in our well-dug trenches, which could withstand near misses and even very near misses, but they could never be one hundred percent safe.

D + 46 – Château St. Come – Saturday, 22 July

Once again I was sent out on an early morning sniping trip. It became apparent very quickly that yet again a new lot had moved in across the field. The previous day not a German was to be seen, while today they were strolling around in the open. I had one 'kill' and a couple of 'probables'. My mate also got at least one as we peppered away at them for some while, returning eventually to the Company well pleased with our early morning effort.

It was bright and sunny when, after lunch, I crawled into my

125

trench for a few hours' sleep. While I slept the weather changed dramatically and I awoke with a start to find that my trench was well and truly flooded. This really surprised me as I had scrounged a couple of empty cans and two long planks of wood so that I had a raised and fairly comfortable bed; yet the water was lapping around my back. The sudden downpour must have been torrential.

When I looked around I realized that I was not the only one to have abandoned my waterlogged trench, and all the other trenches had been vacated by their very wet and uncomfortable owners, which was highly irregular.

At platoon HQ I found everyone crowding around the cooking stove. They had a good fire going and were doing their best to dry out. We kept the fire stoked up until it was almost dark and then returned to our waterlogged trenches.

I had retrieved my sodden blanket and by the evening it was almost dry. I baled out as much of the water as possible and settled down to a really uncomfortable night.

D + 47 – Château St. Come and Le Mesnil – Sunday, 23 July

The rain continued to pelt down throughout the night and the following morning. Everyone was thoroughly miserable and cursing the fact that we were supposed to have been out here for only ten days or so, but here we were now in our forty-eighth day and there seemed to be no immediate prospect of our being withdrawn.[9]

At midday we were withdrawn to the Rest Area near Le Mesnil with the expectation of having to dig out yet another set of trenches in the pouring rain.

1. The author in 1942, aged 18.

2. The cliffs and hills at Ilfracombe, North Devon, that we were ordered to climb, without any ropes or safety equipment, to impress the holidaying armaments factory workers (see p. 21).

3(a). Troop-carrying glider. Emplaning.

(b). A maximum glider load was 30 men (including two glider pilots).

(c). The Live Load. This picture gives the reader an excellent inside view of a glider load re
for action.

4. My Company Commander, Major John Howard, DSO, who led the coup-de-main force that captured the bridges over the Caen Canal and Orne River just after midnight on 5/6 June, 1944.

5. My Platoon Commander, Lieutenant Den Brotheridge, who was mortally wounded when leading the charge across the Caen Canal bridge moments after we had landed. He was the first Allied soldier to be killed in action on D-Day (see p. 43).

6. A rare German photograph of what was probably coup-de-main Glider No. 4 which should have been the first to land near the Orne River bridge but was tugged off course and landed beside the bridge over the River Dives to the east of Varaville and several miles away from the intended Landing Zone.

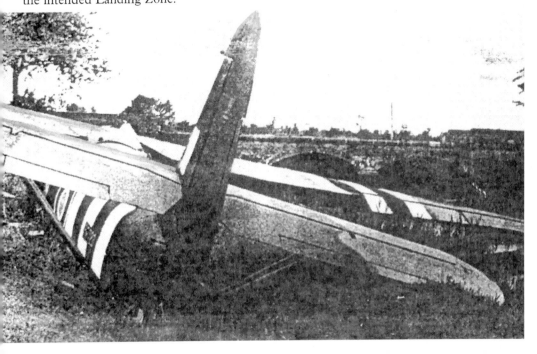

7. The church at Le Port from which, on D-Day, a German machine-gunner fired at the approaching Commando until put out of action by two Sherman tanks. (Note probable priest opening churchyard gate. The cart may well have contained bodies for burial (see p. 53.) (*Photo: Imperial War Museum.*)

8. "D" Company Snipers with Major Howard, St. Come, Normandy. Taken late July' 44 after Sniper Corporal Wally Parr had been wounded. (See p. 115.) From left to right: 'Wackers' Waite, 'Pete' Musty, 'Nobby' Clarke, Major Howard, 'Rocky' Bright, 'Paddy' O'Donnell, 'Eddie' Edwards. (*Photo: Major John Howard, DSO.*)

9. Copy of Hitler Youth membership card found on the body of a young German SS man lying close to the bodies of 51st Highland Division men executed by men carrying Schmeisser sub-machine guns. (I carried his Schmeisser as a secondary back-up weapon through most of the Normandy campaign.) *(See p. 83.)*

10. Captain J. M. A. Tillett, 1943. Adjutant 2nd Oxf & Bucks Light Infantry. Promoted to Major, he took over as "D" Company Commander in November, 1944, and successfully led the Company through the Ardennes and during the advance across Germany. He continued as "D" Company Commander until 1946. *(Photo: Col. J. M. A. Tillett.)*

11. January, 1945. The Ardennes. Troops in white snow suits during the 'Battle of the Bulge'. The snow was generally much deeper. *(See p.170 et seq.)* *(Photo : Imperial War Museum.)*

12. March, 1945. Germany. Horsa glider in which the author travelled for the assault over the Rhine. The starboard wingtip and aileron were shot away at 1,000ft and the tail section was hit by a shell as the glider slithered in to land adjacent to the objective, Hamminkeln railway station *(see p. 182).* *(Photo: Imperial War Museum.)*

16. Normandy, Spring 1984. This picture of the original Pegasus Bridge was taken from almost exactly where my 5-man Section took up a defensive position immediately after crossing the canal bridge to cover the southern approach. *(Photo: by courtesy of The News, Portsmouth.)*

17. Normandy, October, 1993. The original Pegasus Bridge being removed to make way for the new wider bridge, which is similar in appearance.

13. The author (in swimming trunks) on the Baltic coast, May, 1945.

14. The author in Palestine, 1946.

15. London, 1952. "D" Company Reunion: *Front row*: Evans; Ron Stock; 'Bill' Bailey; Major John Howard, DSO; Col. 'Tod' Sweeney, MC; 'Gus' Gardner. *Back row*; Arthur Roberts (?); 'Eddie' Edwards; Wally Parr; Glider Pilot Budds; Bob Hill; Harry Goodsir; 'Smokey' Howard.

Chapter 7

MOSTLY HELLFIRE CORNER

D + 48/50 – Le Mesnil – Monday/ Wednesday, 24/26 July.

For a pleasant change, and despite our fears, we were not required to carry out a fresh dig. This was perhaps fortunate because some of our big guns from way back were incorrectly ranged and several large shells exploded around our rest area, and we would have been caught in the open if we were all digging as usual. I would love to know what our people said when they got on the line to the gunners!

Although it was us and not they that were being hit, the Germans took offence, as usual, and promptly retaliated. We then had to endure a prolonged bombardment from them, which had the effect of encouraging us to improve the trenches that we had taken over.

It was another wet and uncomfortable day. The evening strafer put in his usual brief appearance and during the night an aircraft dropped a stick of anti-personnel bombs. This was something new and I didn't like it one bit. One of these bombs exploded near the latrines and another within fifty yards of my trench. They were not large – only about fifty to one hundred pounds – but went off with a hell of a bang and really shook the walls and roof of my trench.

The next day, 25 July, to my surprise and delight, I was issued with a brand new sniper rifle straight out from Ordnance. It was covered with a thick layer of grease and wrapped in greaseproof paper. I spent much of the day taking it apart and cleaning it. Until this time my rifle had been a completely standard issue Lee Enfield .303 MK. IV, with no telescopic sights, and this new weapon was much more suitable for sniping, especially for when we would leave our trenches and get moving again.

The gallant Luftwaffe varied their routine by carrying out an afternoon strafe, but there were no casualties.

I spent the most of the next day, Wednesday, sitting close to my trench cleaning the last of the grease from my rifle and generally admiring my new toy. It was a beautiful summer day with no bombardment aimed at us, so at the same time as I was preparing my new rifle, I had the time to clean my other weapons, the German P38 pistol and the Schmeisser sub-machine gun.

That evening we were strafed as usual by an enemy aircraft, but today in anticipation of the visit, some of the lads had set up a light machine gun to have a go at him. A Bren is not the best anti-aircraft weapon, but better than nothing, and who knows? The lads might have been lucky. As it happened they weren't, but at least it appeared to discourage the aircraft from hanging around or taking another run at us.

D + 51/52 – Le Mesnil – Thursday/Friday, 27/28 July

I was very keen to get to know my new rifle and accordingly I scrounged a couple of empty tins from the cookhouse. After warning the others that I would be shooting I went into a nearby field and propped the tins against a battered post. After walking back about 150 yards, I fixed the telescopic sight and fired. The tins kept jumping around so it was impossible to correct the sights. What I really needed was a few obliging Germans, but there were none to be had in this back area, so I returned.

By asking a few questions I discovered that no one from the forward units was out sniping, so I pestered the officers and eventually obtained permission to go out into no-man's-land. After finding a suitable spot in view of the German positions, and waiting for a little while, I saw a German in a small gap, took a quick aim and fired. Judging by the way he fell backwards I was satisfied that the weapon was correctly zeroed.

Like a kid with a new toy, I spent most of the afternoon and evening looking for more targets, but, to my great disappointment, none appeared. Eventually I returned to the Company lines where I found to my astonishment that the entire Battalion had packed up and gone.

I gathered my kit and went in search of them, and found that they had been moved even further back from the front line, still in the area of Le Mesnil but considerably further from the front line than we had been previously. Everyone was busy digging new trenches as I arrived, so there was nothing for me to do except to dump my kit and join in with everyone's favourite pastime – digging.

The following day was tough going for us – no shelling, no stonks, no sniping expeditions – but the entrenching went on relentlessly, and just as I expected I spent almost the entire day digging. Otherwise the new rest area was just the job – well back behind the lines, where we could have a real rest – but only after days of backbreaking digging.

D + 53/54 – Le Mesnil – Saturday/Sunday, 29/30 July

Our officers came round early to inspect our trenches, and they found fault with most of them – including mine – so much of the day was spent on improvements, but I didn't mind too much because the weather was fine and we were not being bothered by the Germans. Anyway, I hoped that with a bit of luck we would have a few days to rest after all this work.

Such was not to be the case. As we were putting the finishing touches to the trenches the order came to "Get yer kits on". I was stunned to be told that we were going up to the front line again. To me it seemed totally pointless. On our meagre rations, and through lack of regular exercise, we were far from fit. Our marathon dig had been for nothing. We would have been better off staying in the front line, but our officers considered it better to send us for a "rest", which meant continuous trench digging. There were times when the actions of our senior officers left me flabbergasted and very frustrated.

The Commando to the north of Bréville were on the move and we were to take over their positions. Once again we got down to the tiring business of digging a completely fresh set of trenches as our officers deemed the excellent Commando trenches unsuitable for us! However, on this occasion, there was some justification for their fussiness as we now had to cover a much wider area and we were being spread thinly across the ground. There were dangerously wide gaps between each trench, and this could be fatal if we were attacked.

The day passed, and we spent the following Sunday digging. Jerry added to our difficulties by pounding away at us, causing us to dig fast, frequently having to dive into what cover we could get from partly completed holes in the ground.

D + 55 – Bréville – Monday, 31 July

At stand-to the officers came round, found fault with most of the trenches, and we had to carry out extensive alterations; some even had to be re-sited! There was a mutinous spirit among the lads, as it was an exceptionally hot day to be endlessly digging. We all got on with the job, sweating and swearing and with much muttering and grumbling, but every man was thinking about what a bloody awful life we were living. I suppose that our officers felt that hard labour kept us usefully occupied and out of trouble!

Prolonged trench warfare was not what we were expecting when we came here. We did not want to be full-time trench diggers and we all longed to get out of the Normandy bridgehead and to get moving again, but it seemed that for some time longer we should be obliged to endure this hardship.[1]

D + 56/57 – Bréville – Tuesday/Wednesday, 31 July/1 August

On the Tuesday our trenches were finally approved and the weather was grand once again. Jerry left us in peace and it was hard to realize that we were still involved in the war.

This promised to be a better rest area than others of late. The only sound of war was the distant rumbling of guns. I saw a very large bomber force flying high above and heading south, but this time nobody seemed to know where they were going.

Later in the day I was notified that I was to go out scouting and possibly sniping the following day. This cheered me up tremendously as it would give me another chance to try the new rifle.

The Wednesday was peaceful and quiet, and I made a note in my diary that the war appeared to have passed us by and life had become a bit humdrum.[2]

As promised, I went out into the new area for most of the day but saw nothing of the Germans so I spent some time foraging for spuds, carrots and onions for the stew pot.

D + 58/59 – Bréville –
Thursday/Friday, 3/4 August

August 3rd was a beautiful day and the morning passed peacefully, but after lunch Jerry decided to remind us that he was still around by giving us a real pounding with shells, mortar bombs and Moaning Minnies. I had been thinking that the peace and quiet was too good to last, and regrettably I was right.

The next day I noted in my diary that Jerry must have moved some new people onto our front, who were letting us know that they had arrived. We were given a really thorough plastering.

After lunch, ducking and dodging incoming missiles, two of us went out to welcome the new folks across the way. No contact was made, which was entirely due to our respect for this new enemy unit. When up against quality opposition we had to use our knowledge, skill and patience to the fullest extent, knowing that a watchful enemy would punish unmercifully any mistake we might make while patrolling and spying out the land. The signs all pointed to the fact that a tough and professional unit was now facing us.

131

D + 60 – Bréville – Saturday, 5 August

We came under some severe pressure, being heavily shelled and mortared in three separate stonks. The weather remained fine and sunny but we saw little of it. With all the stuff they were sending over, the bottom of a well-dug trench seemed to be a good place to spend the day.

While I might have preferred to spend the day safely down in my trench, it was not to be as some of us were sent out sniping, but it was not a successful trip. We must have been spotted long before we saw anything of them, because we came under heavy and very accurate mortar fire. We soon realized that with yesterday's accurate bombardment and today's well concentrated mortaring, we were facing some very high quality enemy troops and this caused us once again to take the war very seriously indeed.

When you came up against good German troops, you knew it – they were exceptionally good.

D + 61 – Bréville – Sunday, 6 August

It was a miserable day, with accurate and concentrated bombardment from Jerry all through the day. I began to wonder if it would ever stop.

Just when I was wondering if things could possibly get worse, I heard that we were being moved down to Hell Fire Corner the next day.

Hellfire Corner was our name for the crossroads about a mile to the south of Château St. Come, a spot generally considered to be the hottest along the entire front. I had just about decided that the situation was as bad as it could get, but I was wrong.

D + 62 – Hellfire Corner – Monday, 7 August

Early in the day we gathered our paraphernalia, left the safety of our trenches and began the slow move on the three-quarter-mile journey to our new location, accompanied all along the route by a steady barrage of shells, mortars and Moaning Minnie rocket bombs. Life was not simply dangerous, it was extremely unpleasant.

The business of one entire battalion taking over from another is always a slow and dangerous process since those in position cannot move out until the incoming troops arrive. This means that in a deadly area such as Hellfire Corner far too many people are above ground as some clear out of trenches and others slide in.

While all this was going on Jerry was pounding the area mercilessly. I just wished that we could have done this move a few days ago when the entire front had been quiet. This was without doubt the most hairy move that we had yet made.

On a happier note, the trenches donated to us by the Devons in this new location were excellent. They had to be, since this road junction was the target of almost continuous enemy attention.

As we took over, the Swedes said they hoped that we would find their trenches comfortable as we would be spending most of our time in them!

I had only just settled in when I received a message to report to the Company Commander. Having finally made it to my allotted trench I was not very pleased at having to get out again. At Company HQ lads from other Platoons were gathering and, of all the weird things, we were informed that we were going on an outing to the invasion beaches! My first thought was that someone was pulling my leg.

However, it was not a joke and our trip had to begin by running, weaving, ducking and crawling down the hillside and away from the front line before we could reach our transport. Even though out of range of most of what Jerry was sending over, as soon as we had clambered on board the driver set off at high speed. Such was the reputation of Hellfire Corner that the driver acted as if Jerry was after him personally.

We crossed the River Orne and Caen Canal by way of our bridges, and we soon arrived at the beaches.

Without any preliminaries we were fallen in and marched on to the beach and told to sit down. Then, from an improvised stage, we were entertained by Forsythe, Seaman and Farrell. They were good and I thoroughly enjoyed their light entertainment, but all too soon we were loaded on to the truck and on our way back to the Battalion. As on the outward journey, the driver demonstrated his respect for the reputation of Hellfire Corner by stopping well short of the front line.

Up ahead, during our short absence, nothing had changed. The whole area was being pounded by the terrifying Moaning Minnies as well as heavy-calibre shells and large mortars.

We left the truck and were soon running and diving for cover, to avoid the incoming missiles. With each explosion as a shell or a mortar detonated, stones and clods of earth were continually falling upon our bodies as we lay on the ground. We reached Battalion HQ and quickly dispersed. From then on it was every man for himself.

At one stage, as I dived for the cover of a roadside ditch, I did a quick count and reckoned that as many as twenty enemy mortars and probably the same number of guns were in action. After several near misses I eventually found my Company and, with a sigh of relief, my trench. On reflection, I was by no means sure that the trip justified the risks involved in the journey.

D + 63 – Hellfire Corner – Tuesday, 8 August

The day was just as bad as the one before as far as stonking went. Something seemed to be exploding around the area every few seconds throughout the day. Whether Jerry had got wind of a general change along our front I do not know, but this was by far the worst bombardment, in terms of duration and severity, that I had yet experienced. Our only small consolation was that with the continuous bombardment everyone was kept down below ground – even the officers – so that they were not able to come round and tell us to undertake alterations to our trenches.

No one went out sniping from Hellfire Corner; to try it would be foolhardy and almost certainly fatal. Because of its strategic position, however, a good deal of the time was spent on 'Stag' duty, which meant getting up from the bottom of the trench and peering through the small front opening. When we were not on this duty we simply spent our time below ground.

D + 64/65 – Hellfire Corner – Wednesday/Thursday, 9/10 August

The heavy stonking calmed down a little. At dawn we were heavily shelled, but, by the standards of the past two days, I suppose I could say that we had a fairly quiet time. Staying below ground we waited for a break in the continuous stonk, but the next day was back to full-time stonking from Jerry.

Our new defensive positions were in the remains of what had once been a large orchard. Now virtually every tree had gone and the ground was a mass of shell holes. The call of nature, desire for food and a wash and shave, had forced me to leave the security of my trench during a brief lull. On the way back I was out in the open when a really large batch of missiles came screaming in. Shells, mortar bombs and Moaning Minnies were falling thick and fast. I literally dived headfirst into my trench as missiles began exploding all around the orchard. The stonk was so severe that the walls of my trench seemed to be vibrating all day long. I offered up my thanks to whoever had provided the massive roof that shook and shuddered continuously, yet remained intact.

D + 66 – Hellfire Corner – Friday, 11 August

The preceding days had been bloody awful, but today had something even more special in store for us.

Four of us were detailed to dig a new sanitary trench as the one that the Swedes had dug was nearly full. Although the location was some distance from the crossroads, which was Jerry's main target, it was still far too close to the danger area for my liking.

In the hot sun we began our dig. We were working in pairs, with two digging in the open field while the other pair took shelter in a nearby ditch. There were no trenches nearby since the contents of the latrine trench drained into the soil, so it could not be too close to our defensive positions.

When a new trench was being dug, the first few feet were always the most dangerous because there was nowhere to dive for cover when the missiles came screaming in. Lifting out the turf and topsoil was always the hardest part of any dig, but in this dangerous situation we dug fast and needed frequent rests. Sometimes all four of us were sheltering in the ditch during heavier stonks.

At one stage, with the trench only half-dug, all four of us were out in the open when a heavy stonk began. We were just about to change over and, with hindsight, it would have been wiser if the two diggers had returned to the ditch before the others left it, but we were anxious to get the job done and return to the comparative safety of our trenches. When the stonk began I moved quickest and hit the bottom of the trench, and the other three then piled in on top of me. I was battered, bruised and completely winded.

We decided to dig the trench deeper than usual and hoped that it would last throughout our stay, since no one wanted to see another dodgy dig like that, either for themselves or for any of the other lads.

The day ended pleasantly with a completely unexpected treat, when George and Beryl Formby suddenly arrived at the farm just behind our front line. Leaving only a minimum number of bods in the trenches, we ran down the hillside to the farm that, surprisingly, still possessed two large and fairly sound barns.

While George and Beryl stood in the doorway of one barn, the rest of us crowded into the opening of the one across the yard. We thought that it was really terrific – two stars of stage, screen and radio risking life and limb by coming to within a few hundred yards of one of the most dangerous areas along the entire front. To say simply that we admired their courage would not do justice to our feelings about these two wonderful people.

Fortunately, for once the area was fairly quiet but a few shells did come whining in and we realized, from long experience of the sound of shells in flight, that they were coming our way. Everyone dived for cover inside the two barns, and the shells exploded noisily enough, but far enough away to ensure that no one was hurt.

Eventually we went back to our trenches with a very warm feeling about how George and Beryl had taken such risks to show solidarity with us in the front line.

D + 67 – Hellfire Corner – Saturday, 12 August

On Saturday we heard the welcome news that Jerry was likely to be pulling out. Lieutenant Fox and a couple of lads were sent forward on a scouting trip. Unfortunately one of them set off a tripwire or stepped on a mine and was instantly killed and Freddie Fox and the other lad were badly wounded. It was damned bad luck for something like that to happen just at the moment that Jerry seemed at last to be on the run.

D + 68 – Le Mesnil – Sunday, 13 August

We were called from our trenches on the Sunday morning and told to assemble in the rear farmyard. We were being moved further back into a rest area around Le Mesnil again. Was this a prelude to an advance?

We were immediately issued with some extra junk to carry. This was a certain sign that we were about to be on the move; whenever we needed to be lightly clad and mobile someone always came up with the bright idea of giving us some extras to carry.

We were all raring to go and very keen to be on the move, although nothing more was heard of the matter that day.

D + 69 – Le Mesnil – Monday, 14 August

Jerry had gone very quiet. Had he moved out during the night?

Two of us were sent up to Hellfire corner to have a look around the area. As we came to the road junction we saw that in spite of the unusual quiet, no one was taking any chances. A Jeep appeared at high speed with driver and passengers ducking low. They had to make a right-hand turn at the junction, and did so without slowing down and I would swear that two wheels were completely off the ground!

Although we had a good look around the area beyond the road junction, we saw and heard nothing of the Germans. We dared to hope that they had already gone.

We went back and reported that all was very quiet.

D + 70 – Hellfire Corner –
Tuesday, 15 August

We had been in Normandy for seventy days or so and during that time we had never moved more than a few miles away from our bridges. Today, so we thought, it would be different, as we were ordered to "Kit up Ready to move off". And we did move – straight up the road and back into the trenches at Hellfire Corner!

What the hell was going on? I had only just clambered into a vacant trench at the end of a very quiet day when, from out of the blue, down came a heavy stonk. They gave us a real battering, almost as bad as anything they had dished out in the past.

Well, Jerry was definitely still around, so perhaps the sudden lull was because they were doing a change around, or perhaps they had been short of artillery ammunition. They certainly used ammunition at a prodigious rate, and we sometimes wondered why they hadn't used up their stockpiles, or why our total air superiority hadn't cut him off from fresh supplies or blown up the stocks he had to hand. We certainly received many unwelcome tons of German munitions almost every day, and we were only a small part of the front.

If this bombardment was an indication of the way this new lot intended to carry on, we could expect to be in for a long and uncomfortable stay. Whatever our intelligence reports may have discovered, the way Jerry was now hammering us gave no hint that he was anywhere near ready to pull out.

I felt sure that one of the missiles had exploded very close to my trench and when things eased up I popped up to have a quick look around, then realized that in my haste to dive for cover I had dropped my large pack by the trench entrance. It had been blown to bits. My only consolation was that if the bomb had been a foot or so nearer it would have exploded inside my trench entrance and it was better to have the pack blown to bits than me. It served to remind me that things could usually get worse.

D + 71 – Hellfire Corner – Wednesday, 16 August

I heard through the grapevine that, despite all the false alarms, the rumours and the disappointments, we were indeed likely to be on the move within the next day or so.

As Jerry was still sending over a lot of stuff, I spent much of the day in my trench, preparing for moving out, cleaning my various weapons and what was left of my equipment after losing my pack to the direct hit of the previous day.

Since the last week of July events elsewhere on the front had been developing rapidly and it was being said that over on the eastern side of the bridgehead the Yanks were now breaking out.

Rumours abounded, but in any case we now knew pretty much for sure that the German containment of the bridgehead was failing and that as soon as our armour could get moving Jerry would be encircled unless he pulled back. It was therefore certain that we would move forward just as soon as he moved back, but we could not be sure about exactly when that time would come.[3]

Our blankets, heavy gear, cooking utensils and food had been sent down the hill to Regimental HQ so it was really almost certain that we were on the move at last. After so many rumours and false alarms there was a general feeling amongst the lads that this time it was the real thing.

Chapter 8

THE ADVANCE TO THE SEINE

D + 72 – On the Move – Thursday, 17 August

Early in the morning, and not before time we all thought, the long-awaited advance began. After being cooped up in trenches for so long, it was a wonderful feeling to be on the move again. Jerry said farewell with a really heavy barrage along the entire front. Eventually all went quiet. He was on the run, off towards the east. We hoped he wouldn't stop running until he reached Germany, but, alas, it wasn't going to be quite as easy as that.

The advance began at 0930 hours but was hardly dramatic, more of an anti-climax after our high hopes for an easy advance. It was a tiring, stop-go process, a case of jump to your feet – advance a few hundred yards – stop – sit down at the roadside – up on your feet again for a few more yards – and so on, as the day wore on.

The cause of the problem was that Jerry was using tough and determined rearguards to cover his withdrawal. It took an entire morning for us to advance no more than a few hundred yards. However, we were not leading the advance. Other units were ahead of us and in contact with the retreating Germans. We had no idea what was happening up ahead and it was a pleasant sunny day, so we were able to take things easy. Jerry wasn't bothering us and we were no longer cooped up in holes in the ground, so we could enjoy the sunshine for a change.

At around 1700 hours we arrived at Gonneville-en-Auge where we spent the night.

D + 73 – On the Move – Friday, 18 August

The entire day was spent pushing slowly forwards, passing through the long-held German defensive positions where we saw something of the mess that our artillery had made of the roads and countryside. It was comforting to know that Jerry had been getting at least as much punishment as he had been dishing out.

Because we were some way behind the vanguard of the advance, we were not too sure about where we were going. The leaders were obviously responding to enemy tactics as appropriate, probing this way and that, and we just followed.

As we ourselves were nothing less than experts at trench digging, we took a great interest in the trenches produced by the Germans, which were truly excellent structures – massively built, sometimes with deep interconnecting passages between them, and with well constructed shelters.

The news filtered through that Allied forces were now established in the South of France after successful landings there on 15 August and this raised our spirits considerably.

D + 74 – On the Move – Saturday, 19 August

It was now 'D' Company's turn to take the lead in the advance towards Varaville. This meant that we would now be the first to come into contact with the German rearguard snipers.

As we neared the village the leading section came under fire from a German MG34 machine gun. Lance Corporal 'Smacker' Drew was killed and Corporal 'Smoky' Howard and Private Dancy were both badly wounded. It was very easy to slip into complacency and this incident was a grim reminder that the war was far from finished.

Two snipers, one of them being myself, were sent ahead to locate the machine gun and silence it. We thought the gun was located in or near some farm buildings a short way off, but the terrain thereabouts offered no chance of concealment for a direct approach, and we were forced to make a wide detour around, crawling and making painfully slow progress. We clambered through a hedge and worked our way around to the side of the buildings, with an officer and a section of men following in our wake, not far behind.

Ready to shoot up anything that we saw, we made a dash into the farmyard. As we did so, we heard a motor cycle engine roar into life. A motorbike with a crew of two men, complete with MG34 mounted on a sidecar, sped out of the farmyard and down the road. We fired wildly at the speeding machine, having no time to take a decent aim, but in an instant it was gone. We were a little bitter at having to let this successful enemy unit get away.

A quantity of British army equipment was strewn around the place, abandoned at some stage by the British, taken over by Jerry, and then in turn abandoned by him.

We moved on to Varaville, which had been captured the previous day by the Commando, and we took over from them. Once again, we saw some really excellent German fortifications and dugouts, where we spent the night.

I noticed that the German dugouts always had a strange smell. A different body odour, presumably because of a different diet, seemed to become locked into a place after long occupation, and persisted for quite some time afterwards.

D + 75 – On the Move – Sunday, 20 August

A Belgian reconnaissance unit had arrived the previous evening and they took over from us at Varaville so that we could continue our advance.

We were now at the River Dives, and with the problem of how to get across. We had been unable to break through along the coastal route and the decision was made that we would continue our easterly progress by crossing the river Dives at Troarn some five or six miles to the south.

We clambered aboard trucks, which drove us down to Troarn where Engineers had erected a pontoon bridge across the river. This was the only crossing place available, as the five bridges across the Dives – one at Troarn and the others further down the river – had been blown up by the Para on D-Day, to hold up the advance of German forces coming in from the east.

The centre part of the bridge at Troarn was completely demolished, so totally destroyed that the Germans had not even attempted to repair it. Apparently the Para had been badly scattered during their drop and had lost much of their equipment. Their commander decided to improvise by commandeering a Jeep and trailer, on which was loaded all the explosive they could find. He and some of his men then drove through the German defences and on to the bridge where they detonated their cargo – and with excellent effect, as could clearly be seen.

Reluctantly, we left our trucks on the west bank of the Dives and crossed the river on foot via the pontoon bridge.

D + 76 – On the Move – Monday, 21 August

Now, with the Dives safely crossed, we started to move eastwards, towards St. Richer.

At 0300 hours a long night march began in pouring rain. It was an incredibly tiring and difficult march, all of us virtually asleep as we marched, but, despite our state of extreme fatigue, we could hear the sound of a furious battle up ahead of us. The Commando that we had met earlier at Varaville had overtaken us again at some point, and had gone ahead to Brucourt, where they had set up a splendid ambush against a large German force that was moving down a hillside track.

Almost completely exhausted, at 0800 we arrived at Brucourt, where we witnessed the Commando's handiwork. Attacking from both sides of the track, they had trapped and then wiped out the enemy force, causing massive casualties. The hillside was strewn with German dead, upturned carts and abandoned weapons and equipment.

We took over from the battle-weary Commando and were told to dig in, but before we had time to do any digging the rest of the Battalion caught up with us and we were ordered to move on.

We pressed on until we arrived at a road junction just to the north of Heuland. One of our Companies pushed ahead to try to make contact with the retreating Germans, while we settled in for the night, fraternizing with the locals, handing around our cigarettes and chocolate, and even having a sing-song with them, until finally I got some much-needed sleep.

D + 77 – On the Move – Tuesday, 22 August

At dawn we began another march, ever eastwards along the main road. On the road between Heuland and Forges-de-Bionville we passed a well-organized French Red Cross Centre and the wreck of one of our bombers, or perhaps a transport aircraft, at the roadside. We trudged silently past.

Approaching Forges-de-Bionville, the village was heavily shelled by the Germans, forcing us to wait for the bombardment to stop. After a decent interval we began approaching the village centre, but there was a suspicious silence about the place. No locals appeared, which may have been because of the bombardment, but we would have expected to see a few of them by now, with the shelling over.

It did not take us long to realize that we had walked into an ambush from an enemy force consisting of two self-propelled 88mm guns protected by teams of well-trained and effective snipers. We took what cover we could find in the roadside ditches, while red-hot shrapnel from the exploding 88 shells flew through the air just inches above our heads.

A unit from the Devons had entered the village at about the same time as us and they had hastily abandoned their metal handcarts when the shelling and sniping started. From my ditch I could just see one of their abandoned handcarts, which was now so riddled with shrapnel impact that it resembled a sieve. This was clearly a very unhealthy place to loiter and I was wishing like hell that I was somewhere else.

A shell exploded quite close to me and I felt a thud in my back, while at the same time I was covered in a shower of dirt and small stones. I thought my last moment had come and tried moving my legs, but I couldn't feel them. Moving my hand to my back, I was relieved that there was no blood and, as my body moved, a large chunk of rock rolled from my back and fell into the ditch beside

144

me. Gradually the feeling returned to my legs and only then did I understand what had happened. I felt lucky to be alive and only a little bruised and winded.

I decided to move closer to the 88s to see if there was anything I could do. I started to slither forward in the ditch. A few others had the same idea, but unfortunately the snipers were acting as spotters and our every move was followed by the gunners. As our cover had now become inadequate to protect us from the exploding shells, we were obliged to make a dash for a nearby mound of earth which offered some protection from the shells as well as the snipers' bullets. From this point we fired towards the snipers, but we couldn't see them and it was more of a gesture than anything else.

Luckily, some of our lads had been able to work their way around the village to outflank the 88s, who were, however, alerted to the move by their sniper observers. Possibly fearing that the reason for the approach could be that our lads had some close-range anti-tank weapons, which in fact they did not, the SPs started their engines and sped off.

We soon realized, however, that the movements of the first two SPs were being covered by a second pair, much further off, and these began shelling the village immediately after the withdrawal of the first pair, and again we were pinned down until sunset.

We and the Devons had been pinned down for almost the whole day and we had nothing with which we could reply to the enemy 88s. I was never so happy to see the sun set as I was that day.

We knew that the German 88s and snipers were there to hold up our advance and so we knew that we had not seen the last of them. We had also now had an opportunity to observe their tactics, which were really very smart, using their resources economically and effectively. The lesson had cost us time and we had taken several casualties.

Starting out at first light, I was sent forward to try to spot the enemy 88s, but they were not around and we arrived at the village of Vauville where the locals informed us that the Germans had only just pulled out.

Pushing on to Tourgeville, we found a large German cemetery. From the dates on the wooden crosses, it was clear that our aerial

145

bomber forces and long-range artillery had inflicted heavy casualties during the preceding two months.

Nearby, we found the graves of five of our 6th Airborne Paras, as well as that of a Royal Canadian Airforce officer. The locals told us that nearly all these had died on D-Day. They were so many miles away from their dropping zones that they must have been badly scattered by the wind, or, more probably, their transport aircraft must have been off course and lost.

The same French villagers were keen to tell us about two Paras who landed in the vicinity and who were surrounded by a dozen Germans soon after landing. Called upon to surrender they opened fire with Stens, killing several Germans, and then they escaped from the midst of the confusion. No one knew what happened to them afterwards.

In the evening we enjoyed our first decent cooked meal for many a long day, and later I peeled off an extremely dirty pair of socks and put on another pair that were not quite as dirty. Such luxury!

The Belgian reconnaissance unit came in just before we settled down for some sleep, which was yet another taste of luxury as we slept in a hayloft, just about the most comfortable bed I had known since coming to Normandy.

D + 78 – On the Move – Wednesday, 23 August

At first light we were on our way eastwards from the village. At 1000 hours we came to what I will always remember as 'Hellfire Hill'. The hill was to the north, on our left, as we advanced towards St Arnoult, and we had to go up and across it before moving on to Touques, which was our Battalion's next objective.

We had been taking casualties continuously, and we had left some of our number buried in Vauville churchyard and some at Tourgeville Military Cemetery, but this was by far the worst experience of the advance to date.

Across the open hillside we had to negotiate a steep uphill track, which led up and around to the north-western outskirts of St Arnoult. This meant that we were completely exposed to the enemy mobile artillery, and we were continuously shelled by 88s firing from another nearby wooded hilltop, to the north-west and quite close to Touques.

As we ran, crawled and scrambled up the hill we were not much more than target practice for the German gunners. One lad, in his haste to scramble to safety at the top of the hill, dropped his airborne folding bike on the track up the hillside and the recently arrived Company Sergeant Major ordered him back to retrieve it. The lad was by no means keen to accept this order, and said so in forthright terms, responding with a rather panic-stricken invitation to the CSM: "If you want the bloody thing go and get it yourself". A second or two later an 88 shell blew the bike into a thousand bits as we watched in awe. I never learned whether or not the lad was subsequently on a charge for abandoning military equipment, refusing to obey an order or even for insubordination to the CSM, but he had the sympathy of every one of us.

Near the top of the hill, on the outskirts of St Arnoult, we were still taking punishment from the German 88s. An old French woman came out of her cottage to offer us shelter, but tragically she too was killed by a shell-burst from an 88 as she stood in her garden calling out to us.

When we reached the outskirts of St Arnoult we dug trenches on the far side of the hill, out of sight of the German guns, and we could hear Jerry not far away, also digging trenches by the sound of it. We were, however, in no position to investigate or to put in an attack. In our sheltered position we were out of sight of his artillery, and the location of the German trench-digging was back around the other side of the hill, from which we had recently extricated ourselves so gratefully.

After dark we went out on a fighting patrol, but heard and saw nothing of the Germans we had heard digging earlier.

We did, however, hear a terrible racket from a seemingly large force of men, who were very obviously not part of our own force, so we set up an ambush as they moved around the hillside below us. It turned out to be a group of French irregulars – resistance forces – who had been out all day harassing Jerry, and who were now making their way to who knows where, and in a very un-disciplined and incautious manner.

147

Had we been German forces, I fear that few of those noisy Frenchmen would have survived the night.

Not wishing to become involved with this noisy group, we kept very quiet and allowed them to pass without making contact as we felt that they would be more of a hindrance than a help.

D + 79 – On the Move – Thursday, 24 August

At dawn we were moving off the hillside and immediately met quite vigorous enemy resistance, with the dreaded self-propelled 88s in evidence yet again. They could be relied on to be where we would least like to see them, and lightly equipped infantry forces, such as ours, had no antidote for this effective German weapon and the skilful tactics with which it was employed.

Feeling fairly relaxed, being out of sight of the German gunners, we were looking forward to a good breakfast, which was being cooked by the HQ staff in a sheltered spot at the bottom of the hill. Hard biscuit had been our sole nourishment for some time, and when the CSM, who had just had his breakfast, announced that we were advancing again, breakfast or no breakfast, there were mutinous rumblings and a great deal of loud complaint. To appease us, someone in the HQ staff began handing out small tins of bully beef, one tin to be shared between four men.

Under fire at any time that the highly mobile Jerry 88s chose to hit us, we eventually made it to Touques, where we found that the Germans had earlier blown the bridge across the River Touques. The helpful locals, however, tied ropes to the front and stern of a large boat and used it as a ferry to pull us across the river.

We were now very badly in need of rest, having had very little sleep after the recent marching, shelling, trench-digging and night operations. However, the news on the east side of the river was that German forces had pulled out only minutes before our crossing, and the order was given that we were to pursue them up the steep hill and at the double.

At the top of the hill I was ready to drop from exhaustion, but our officers gave the order to spread out across the open country below, in the hope of making contact with the enemy. Two other snipers and I were ordered to patrol all the local farms and barns in the hope of spotting German rearguard units waiting in ambush.

Had we found a German ambush we were of course unlikely to have survived the experience, but happily we found no German rearguard units and they didn't find us. However, local farmers told us that they had been around, but had pulled out very recently.

The rest of the afternoon was spent scouting and patrolling over a wide area, until the advance recommenced in the early evening, ever eastwards, towards the River Seine.

The village of St Philebert was entered and passed with no further ambushes or heavy fighting and we met up with the Belgian reconnaissance group at Honfleur crossroads. We had left them behind us, but they had taken a different route and had overtaken us, but unhappily they had been ambushed and were badly shot up by 88s.

D + 80 – Manneville la Raoult – Friday, 25 August

A well-organized and determined group of really young German fanatics caused us plenty of trouble early on the Friday morning. We had been pressing on relentlessly when we came to wooded country from where they opened fire on us. There were not many of them, but they held us up very successfully, and before we could advance we had to kill all but two of them. These last two finally surrendered, and it was pitiful. They looked as if they should have been at school rather than on a battlefield dying for a lost cause.

Not much further ahead was our next objective, the village of Manneville-la-Raoult, which was on higher ground and separated from us by a densely wooded valley.

The Company Commander came to our lead position with the news that the village was occupied by a handful of demoralized troops who wouldn't put up much of a fight. The idea was to soften up the defenders by means of a barrage from our 25-pounder guns, after which we were supposed to stroll in and accept their surrender. It sounded too good to be true – and of course, it was.

Being on high ground ourselves, and the 25-pounder guns being a long way to the rear, the shells that were to soften up the enemy came screaming past us just a few feet above our heads. They came so close that I was at first convinced that they were wrongly ranged and that they were aimed at our own positions.

As soon as the bombardment ceased, we advanced, weapons at the ready, towards the village, and I was sent ahead to scout the approach, closely followed by the rest of our section.

We descended into the wooded valley, losing sight of the village ahead of us. As we reached the bottom of the valley a heavy machine gun opened up and we dived for cover. The village was now out of sight and I would have been very surprised if the defenders could see us, but the machine gun continued firing at someone or something.

I found a track, set well down with high banks, trees and hedges on either side, giving good cover for our advance, since the general direction of the track appeared to be towards the village. There were sporadic rifle shots, and occasional bursts of machine-gun fire, but once again we did not seem to be the intended targets.

I went ahead to scout the route, with the rest of the platoon following some way behind. Moving quickly but warily, always looking as far up the track as possible, and always noting any possible cover in case I should come under fire, I moved up towards the village. As I neared the top, sure enough I found that the track connected with the main street that ran through the village. On the left-hand corner where it joined the village street was the end of a terrace of two-storey cottages. I paused just short of the cottages, remaining concealed from the view of anyone in the main street.

Two other lads had now joined me and I was suddenly surprised to see a Jerry nip out of one of the cottages and disappear behind a building on the other side, but he was gone before I could get a shot at him.

We loosed off a couple of rounds at the building, hoping to get an estimate of the enemy position and strength by getting some return fire, but nothing happened.

We paused while the rest of our platoon began to catch up to where we were assembling. When Bill Gray, our light machine gunner, arrived, he set up his Bren on the wall in front of the cottages and fired a burst up the road, but immediately the wretched gun jammed. The magazine was quickly changed, just as two Germans appeared across the road. They were obviously not eager to stay around, however, and by the time we had loosed off a frantic hail of shots at them they had already disappeared behind cover.

Suddenly, and to our rear, came a sound. I looked around, startled, with the hairs on the back of my neck telling me that I was in immediate danger. I was alarmed to see a Jerry soldier standing there, high above our heads, with just the upper part of his body showing above the hedge along the top of the bank that rose from the side of the lane we were in. Behind the hedge was an orchard, or a garden of some sort, which we had not yet investigated, and it was a shock to discover that enemy were so close to us in such circumstances. However, to my relief, the man had his hands in the air, apparently as if to surrender, but he still held his Mauser rifle, horizontally above his head.

He started to shout, "Me good, me Russ, me good, Russ, Russ."

I wondered why a White Russian was fighting here in Normandy as I shouted to him, "Drop the weapon," and then in pidgin German, "Drappen ze Waffen".

I couldn't get to the man, as he was behind the thick hedge, and so I had no way of removing his weapon, nor did I seem able to communicate to him that he must throw down the wretched rifle. The scene was now commanding all our attention, with the result that we were no longer watching the street, from which direction there came the clattering sound of rapidly moving feet.

One lad swung around and shouted, "Look out – Germans," and at the same time from somewhere across the road an enemy machine gun opened fire with a long burst. The German up on the bank, still swaying in a drunken fashion, swung his rifle downwards with its business end pointing at me. A corporal standing next to me fired his Sten and simultaneously I fired my rifle from the hip. The German above the hedge fell backwards and at the same moment those further along the road dived for cover and began firing in our direction. We returned fire as we dived for cover below the low front-garden wall.

151

At this point if an enemy grenade had come our way it would have accounted for quite a few of us and we desperately needed to take up more dispersed positions. We rushed out into the main road firing from the hip and fanning out to right and to left so as to present the fewest targets to the enemy.

I went to the right hand with three others, leapt over a long wall to land in the orchard where the supposedly White Russian soldier had been. He was lying on the ground, apparently dead.

As we hit the ground German artillery and mortars opened fire and bombarded the village, presumably on the assumption that the village was now in our hands. When, after a few minutes of heavy bombardment, the enemy guns ceased firing we immediately set about clearing the row of cottages along our side of the road.

We had to work fast if we were to clear the village by nightfall as no one fancied sharing the place with an unknown number of Germans once it got dark.

To the front the houses were under direct fire from the enemy machine guns and snipers across the other side of the main road. Working our way along the backs of the properties, we hurled hand grenades and fired as we entered each house, some of which had been set ablaze during the bombardment.

We had cleared about six of the cottages when reinforcements arrived at the head of the same track we had used to get to the village. We shouted a warning as they reached the road, but in the din of battle presumably they did not hear us for they rushed straight across the main road directly towards the enemy machine guns. From our cottages we pumped bullets across the street and into the area where we thought that the Germans were located in the hope of keeping their heads down as the attack went in. Unfortunately we did not fully succeed and the officer leading the charge, Lieutenant Pat Bulford, and another chap were killed and several others wounded. The rest dived for what little cover was available and were promptly pinned down by the enemy fire.

While we fired across the road we were restricted by the fact that we were not too sure where our own lads were now located. I was watching a gap in the hedge at the side of a small orchard where I suspected a Jerry machine gun might be located. Eventually I saw the machine gunner and managed to hit him and so silence the gun, but no sooner had that one stopped firing when another opened up nearby and a stream of bullets came through the upper window through which I had fired. The wall behind me was pitted with a neat line of holes, so I moved quickly into another room and from the darkness of the back of that bedroom I peered out cautiously across the street hoping to spot the second machine gunner but he was too well concealed. Far from being demoralized, it seemed that this lot were prepared to defend the village to the bitter end.

Some of the lads worked their way along the backs of the cottages towards the north of the village where they hoped to cross the street and get round behind the well-concealed Germans across the way.

We soon discovered that the Germans had prepared the village as a strong defensive position and all the cottages that we now occupied had boxes of soil, and mattresses, furniture and timber under the windows. The ground-floor windows had been neatly boarded up, leaving loopholes through which they could fire. In many rooms there were tables and chairs positioned to allow the defenders at the loopholes to have supplies of ammunition and grenades easily to hand, providing yet more evidence of their determination to defend this place.

In some we found bottles of drink and glasses. We must have arrived sooner than they had expected as they did not have time to occupy these well-prepared fortified cottages. The few men who had been in them had fled across the street when we arrived, which was just as well for it made out task easier in clearing our side of the street.

In the normal course of events we would not consider drinking or eating anything that the Germans had left behind for fear of it having been poisoned, as had happened elsewhere. In the circumstances, however having caught them on the hop, we guessed that they would have had no time for such a sly tactic and, being tired, hungry and thirsty, we were glad to eat and drink whatever came to hand.

From an upstairs window I saw two of our lads bravely enter the orchard across the road within direct sight of the German machine gunners and snipers. Some of the men were pinned down around the orchard area and one had been wounded. One of the two lads was a medical orderly and the other a rifleman. They went to the middle of the orchard carrying a stretcher, placed it upon the ground and lifted the wounded man on to it. The Germans held their fire. Then the rifleman did a very stupid thing. When they had entered the orchard his rifle had been slung across his back. To prevent it getting in the way, as slung rifles always do, he had removed his weapon and placed it against a tree. Having put the wounded man on the stretcher, however, he then had to pick up his rifle, and he stood there holding it in both hands and gazing casually around.

Perhaps he did not realize that they were in full view of the enemy, who were holding their fire. He soon found out, however, when a single shot rang out from a German rifle. The rifleman fell to the ground wounded. After some while some of our medics were able to re-enter the orchard and removed both wounded men without a further shot being fired.

Such is the stupidity of warfare, where men hold their fire to help the enemy wounded, and then start trying to kill each other again.

Our well-fortified cottages were good protection for us, but we could do nothing about dislodging the German defenders while we stayed inside them, so we had no choice other than to move out. Avoiding any ground we knew to be covered by enemy fire, we made our way carefully towards the northern end of the village.

On the outskirts of the village we found a château standing in large and well-tended grounds. As the Germans made a point of using the large houses and châteaux as their local HQ, we crawled very cautiously across the grounds dodging between trees and bushes, making our way to the back of the building. There we discovered three fully laden carts, two of which had horses harnessed to them. The Germans had obviously been on the point of pulling out of the village when we arrived, but since the carts and their possessions were still there it was highly probable that they were still inside the building. We forced a ground-floor window and slid inside as silently as possible, with weapons and grenades at the ready.

The room was empty, but suddenly the door swung open and in staggered one of our lads, a most unusual character whom we

154

had nicknamed 'The Colonel' and whom we addressed as 'Col'. It was he who had incorporated a cider barrel in his trench some weeks before, and whose trench, including the famous barrel, was destroyed by a direct hit, fortunately while he was not in occupation.

Col stood swaying in the open doorway, as 'tight as a tick' and full of the joys of spring. He was a private soldier from a good family background, with a very noticeable public school accent. His 'posh' speech was in marked contrast to that of most of the London cockneys who made up the bulk of our outfit, hence our ironic choice of nickname for him.

He had not entered the village by the same route as our platoon, but had found a track leading on to the main road at the northern end of the village. At some point he had become separated from those he had been with and had then come across the château. Alone and unopposed, he had entered the château at some time considerably earlier in the day.

In slurred speech Col invited us to accompany him to the cellar where we were amazed to find a little old Frenchman and his wife, with a dozen or so Germans all around the large room. The Germans had stacked their weapons neatly in a corner and were cheerfully imbibing with Col and the French couple. I learned that the elderly gentleman was a long-retired high-ranking French army officer and presumably the local squire and owner of the château.

It was soon clear to me that when we first arrived in the village and the shooting had begun, the Germans, hearing that their escape route had been cut off, had surrendered to the Frenchman. He had been more than happy to hand his prisoners over to the first British soldier to arrive, who just happened to be none other than 'Col.'

Col's explanation of his actions that day were very vague; he may well have found some drink prior to entering the château, as a sober man would have been very brave indeed to have dared to enter the château alone. When he had received custody of a dozen prisoners of war, not knowing quite what to do with them, Col had invited them all to join him for a drink in the cellar.

Night was falling fast and most of the din of battle around the village had died down, so, with our band of captured Germans, their carts and supplies, and assisting our highly inebriated colleague, we made our way back into the village.

After handing over the prisoners, the order was given for us to return to our original row of fortified cottages, so I took our drunken colleague under my wing to keep him out of sight of our officers and the CSM.

It seemed best to let Col sleep off the booze, so as soon as we reentered our cottages he staggered off upstairs where I assumed he would find a bed.

The Germans across the way were still holding out and, after checking that none of them had slipped across the road and re-entered our cottages, I made my way upstairs to see if anything was to be seen of them, using a higher vantage point. As I looked out of the front window an enemy machine gun fired and a stream of tracer bullets hit the wall just over my head. As I had not fired, and was pretty sure that I could not possibly have been spotted in the half-light, I assumed that the Germans were simply firing at random, until a few moments later a shot rang out from some-where above my head. Since I was on the upper floor, I simply could not imagine where the shot had come from and had to duck very quickly as the Germans responded by firing another long burst into my room.

Keeping low, I slithered out onto the landing. Above my head was an open skylight and through this I could see my drunken comrade straddled across the ridge of the cottage roof, leaning against a chimney stack swaying back and forth and shouting, "I'll get 'em. Where the hell are those rats? I'll bloody well get 'em", at which he fired off another round from his rifle in the general direction of heaven.

I shouted, "Come down, you bloody fool. Do you want your drunken head blown off?"

Through bleary eyes he peered down at me, a drunken grin on his face as he said in slurred tones, "Eddie old man, don't you worry, I'll get 'em", and again he loosed off a wildly aimed shot which immediately brought yet another stream of bullets into the room below.

"You bloody fool Col," I shouted. "Come down before you get yourself killed."

In fact he was probably quite safe for the Germans would never expect anyone to be so stupid as to sit astride a rooftop when they had the cover of a well-fortified building down below, thus each time he fired they fired back into the rooms beneath. Exasperated, I explained, "OK. If you want you head blown off you can please yourself, but I'm going down to the ground floor because you're making it bloody unsafe up here."

Some say that God looks after idiots and drunkards and eventually, still quite unscathed, Col became bored with squatting on the rooftop and retired to rejoin me downstairs. We went off for a meal – a tin of slightly warmed stew, shared between four of us. It wasn't much, but at the end of that long day it made a very acceptable supper.

In the darkness the Germans, obviously not wishing to be overrun, left their positions and walked out into the main road with their hands in the air. By night-time, therefore, most of the village was in our hands.

Although the village was well stocked with drink, there was little food. Drinking on a near-empty stomach is never a good idea, and Col was not the only one to get a little tipsy that evening. Indeed, several of the boys got very drunk and I heard that the Sergeant Major put the Signal Corporal on a charge for being incapable of sending a message to battalion HQ to inform them that we had finally gained our objective.

Later that night I bumped into Col, still swigging away at a bottle of local hooch. This time he was celebrating the liberation of the village, in the company of a Frenchman. What the local man had to celebrate I cannot imagine, as our softening-up and the subsequent bombardment from the Germans had severely damaged many of the buildings and several had been set on fire.

As I had already assumed, the château had been a local German HQ and their main force had moved out an hour or so before we arrived, leaving behind two companies of cycle troops as a rearguard to delay our advance and allow the main force to get clear.

They had certainly done a good job since they held us up for a day and most of the following night. The intelligence report had said that we would only find a handful of demoralized, poor-quality troops ready to surrender. It had been very wide of the mark, but I shall always wonder whether we would have been able to take the village without a fight if we had managed to take the White Russian prisoner and the rest had seen that he had come to no harm.

As it happened, an unfortunate set of circumstances had arisen at the critical moment. This may have decided some of them to make a fight of it, even though not all of them would have realized that the Russian had been shot. It still concerns me, however, that I may have contributed to what might have been an unnecessary day-long battle which resulted in the loss of the lives of some brave comrades.

Others, with whom I have discussed this incident, have all been of the opinion that what happened was unavoidable. What seems to be the most likely explanation is that the White Russian – if indeed that is what he was – being aware that the Nazi cause was now hopeless, genuinely preferred capture by the British rather than to fight on and be killed. To fight on might well have led him eventually to fall into the hands of Soviet troops, with the certainty of facing summary execution. Second thoughts about surrendering, however, must have followed very quickly when he saw his mates launching their attack on us. Whether through duplicity or sheer indecision, he was foolish enough to point his rifle at us, and it cost him his life, and possibly caused the death of several others on both sides. Whatever the true explanation might be, it has always been an unpleasant memory for me, and has left me with a bad taste in my mouth.

Lieutenant Bulford and Private Bannatyle were both killed at Manneville-la-Raoult and are buried at Beuzeville. Several others, including 'Slick' Harris, were wounded during the day-long battle.

We stayed in the village overnight and collected a large number of prisoners.

D + 81 – On the Move – Saturday 26 August

At first light we started our preparations for moving out. Germans had been surrendering in small groups throughout the night and some of our Company were detailed to march the prisoners back behind our lines. The rest of us sat around along the roadside waiting for the order to move off.

While we were waiting, an officer who was cleaning his pistol accidentally loosed off a shot, which missed my face by inches and struck the roadside bank, which gave me a very nasty shock. I could not help thinking about how ironic it would have been if I has been killed by accident in such a fashion, after all the luck I had had when in action against the enemy.

Leaving the village we advanced through beautiful unspoilt open countryside to Foulbec, a distance of about seven miles, where we arrived at midday and started digging in, high up on the valley slopes of the west bank of the River Seine.

Here we were at last in sight of the River Seine. I felt like asking "May we go home now please?". We spent the night in a hayloft, which was a very welcome change.

D + 82/86 – Foulbec – Sunday/ Thursday, 27/31 August

For a change we had an easy time at Foulbec. We had no real need for trenches as we were not under fire, the Germans being far too busy trying to get away across the Seine. From our hillside vantage point we watched a massive aerial and artillery bombardment of German forces crossing the river far below our positions. It was a fantastic sight. I had been under severe bombardment myself many times, and I have seen others get the same or worse than I got, but I had never seen anyone take such a pounding as those Germans were getting. Unlike us when we were under such fire, they were not dug in of course, but completely exposed as they attempted to flee.

We had captured Foulbec, which was our objective, but some of our Airborne force had moved on further south along the river and had captured another small town, which had been in fact the objective of the 49th Infantry Division. We heard that these infantrymen were not too pleased that Airborne had moved in ahead of them and had stolen their thunder.

The next night we slept in a real house. It was marvellous, and we were beginning to feel that the end was in sight. Our officers,

159

however, as always, seemed to be in fear that we might become complacent, so they made sure we kept in top trench-digging form and we had to make constant amendments and improvements to our trenches. We all considered this to be a waste of time, as we supposed that by now the entire German army was across the Seine. Occasionally, however, there was a reminder that the enemy was still around, as when some Vickers heavy machine guns behind us, and higher up, opened fire at a convoy of German lorries moving through wooded country below, trying to make their way down towards the river. From time to time a lorry would take a direct hit and catch fire or explode, depending on what it was carrying.

We were not under any sort of bombardment and we were having a very relaxing time watching the German retreat like an epic piece of theatre being played in the vast panorama below us and away to the horizon.

The Vickers machine gunners, however, were not very relaxed at all. Some diehard German snipers were giving them a very hard time. I had been thinking that it was too good to last and, sure enough, towards the end of our stay in the Foulbec area I and some others were ordered to root out and dispose of the snipers, and so bring relief to the heavy machine-gun crews.

The snipers had the benefit of good concealment in the wooded country, while we had to move up to engage them, so we would certainly be spotted long before we saw them. Dodging from tree to tree, we moved too quickly and erratically for the German snipers to get a shot at any of us, and we managed neither to locate and destroy the snipers, nor to take any casualties ourselves. We did, however, keep them busy watching out for us and they did not dare continue their activities when they knew that a shot would reveal their positions, so at least the machine-gun crews got some relief.

On the last day of August all was peaceful for us, but the drama down below was continuing, with continuous RAF bombing and strafing attacks on anything moving on the eastern bank of the river.

German morale had clearly not collapsed at this stage, but at least it was weakening, and many were choosing to give up rather than to face what the RAF was dishing out. Some of them were even surrendering to French partisans, who brought in several prisoners who had been rounded up on our side of the river. Our morale, on the other hand was high. We were getting rest, better food, comfortable sleeping quarters and life was grand. As if on holiday, we were sitting around playing cards and watching the spectacular scene of German forces in full retreat and getting a good pasting.

D + 87 – Back to the Beaches – Friday, 1 September

Our life of leisure came to a sudden, but not unwelcome, end. We were to go home. It was true. The day we thought we would never see had finally arrived; it was not just another rumour!

We were roused very early and ordered to get ready to move out. No one was complaining this time. Loaded down as usual with all our gear, assembled and nervous with anticipation, we boarded the trucks that were to take us all the way back to the D-Day beaches.

It was an uncomfortable ride, bouncing around on the hard seats of the truck, but it was also a very strange sensation to pass through that quiet Normandy countryside which only a few days earlier had been the scene of bloody battles and horrifying events. At times it was impossible to imagine that it was the same country; the whole scene had an eerie sense of unreality about it.

Stiff and aching from the rough ride, and mighty relieved to climb down from the trucks, we found ourselves at the beach embarkation camp. Here we were to spend our last night on Normandy soil before sailing for home.

The sense of eeriness persisted. Were we really on our way home? The memories of the last time I was on British soil, sitting nervously in the Horsa glider, waiting to be thrown into real action for the first time, all that seemed like a lifetime away or something from a half-remembered dream. To me reality seemed to be only the danger and the discomfort of the trenches with the constant shelling, of seeing good men killed or maimed and hoping to avoid such a fate myself. When out of the trenches, there was always a

161

possibility of death from a sniper's bullet, or from a sudden stonk, and such conditions had marked us all and were ingrained into us too vividly to be instantly forgotten as soon as we were clear of immediate danger.

And yet, at other moments, the dream and the reality would change places, and it would appear to me as though it was the past three months that were unreal, and I felt as if this departure from Normandy was like awaking from the dream. It would take us all a long time to adjust.

D + 88/89 – Embarking – Saturday/Sunday, 2/3 September

Early in the morning we prepared to embark. It was windy and the sea was rough. Once aboard out landing craft we left the quay and smashed our way through the swell, making for our troopship at anchor a mile or so off the coast.

We were heavily laden, every man dressed in full kit and carrying a full complement of equipment. Even though encumbered in this way, we had only one way of boarding the troopship – by scaling nets hanging down from the ship. As the landing craft rose on the heavy swell, we had to jump for the nets and hang on for dear life, as the landing craft would then drop away in the waves until it was twenty feet or so below us. Having gained a foothold on the nets it was essential to climb quickly to avoid being crushed by the landing craft as it rode up, often on an even higher wave, and struck the side of the troopship. Many of the lads were simply unable to board in these conditions, and the boarding process had to be extended into the next day.

Finally, with a full complement at last, we weighed anchor at 1600 hours. Our Normandy adventure was at an end.

D + 90 – Southampton/Bulford – Monday, 4 September

We lay off in Southampton Sound overnight, docking at Southampton at 1600 hours, arriving to find the Regimental Band there at the dockside to greet us. I felt rather self-consciousness, and everything was still strange and unreal as we climbed into the trucks that were to take us back to Bulford Camp on Salisbury Plain.

On the way there were heavy rainstorms and for some reason the trucks got lost, so that it was 2100 hours before we finally found the camp, arriving to a hot meal which was more than welcome.

I returned to Spider Block and the Barrack Room. There, to underline the strange sense of unreality that was to stay with me for many months afterwards, and the memories that will stay with me for ever, were the many empty beds, previously occupied by those whom we had left in Normandy. Some of those beds belonged to men whom we saw die and whom we buried, or left behind for others to bury, others belonged to men too badly wounded ever to be able to rejoin us. These were to be constant grim reminders of the tragedy of warfare.

I felt extraordinarily lucky to have returned unscathed.

Part 3

BELGIUM AND GERMANY

Chapter 9

THE ARDENNES

Of the original one hundred and eighty men of the 'D' group of the 2nd Battalion Oxfordshire and Buckinghamshire Light Infantry who went to Normandy on D-Day only forty of us were left when we returned to Bulford Camp on Salisbury Plain England on 3 September, 1944.

There was a strange melancholy about the camp, a depressing feeling, like being in a house on the day after the funeral of the owner. The reality of what had happened was crystallizing in our minds, an awareness was developing that most of our missing comrades were gone for ever and that the lives of those of us who had returned had been permanently changed. Fortunately, the opportunity to brood or reflect too long on this state of affairs was avoided because we were sent on home leave.

Too soon our leave was over and we were back at Bulford. The depressed feeling of the place was gone. It was bustling with activity. The empty beds were now taken by new recruits, most of them without battle experience, and our knowledge and experience had to be passed on to them as quickly as possible. So it was that I took a hand in the instructing and training, which was an uplifting experience, being an 'old hand' with experience and tales to tell, even though my pupils were mostly no younger than I, often a year or two older. Our task was to teach them our ways of doing battle and how to maximize their chances of staying alive.

The training of our re-formed Company kept us busy until late December, at which time we were scheduled to go home on Christmas leave.

For 'D' Company, commanded by Major Howard, the training was, as ever, even more rigorous than for other units, as we just had to be the best. It was a profound shock therefore, to learn in mid-November that Major Howard had suffered a serious road accident. He had been travelling to Oxford by jeep, on his way home for a brief visit, when he had insisted on driving the jeep himself. In a narrow country road an American convoy of trucks was coming the other way, when somehow the jeep struck one of the trucks head-on. Everyone in the jeep survived, and, in fact, Major Howard survives to this day, but his active service career was over from that moment. He was in a serious condition for some time, but he tried to regain fitness too early after his discharge from hospital, succeeding only in injuring himself further and ensuring that he would never again see active duty. It was a great loss to 'D' Company, the Regiment and the Sixth Airborne Division.[1]

Captain Tillett had been our Battalion Adjutant during the Normandy campaign and it was he who was chosen to fill the void left by Major Howard. He was promoted to Major and went on to become a Colonel before he retired from the Army.

Our training continued throughout December and, with everyone looking forward to spending Christmas with their families, to say that we were disappointed to be told that all leave was cancelled is probably a completely unnecessary statement of the obvious.

Very soon after our return from Normandy the Airborne assault on Arnhem had taken place, an engagement that I was therefore fortunate enough to avoid. Had we been pulled out of Normandy a couple of weeks earlier, no doubt we might have been involved in the disaster at Arnhem. Everyone at the time was hoping that the Nazis were more or less finished, but it was clear that they still had the capacity to bring about serious reverses and it was not possible to be sure how much more damage they could still inflict. We may have missed Arnhem, but it was a lesson to us all that the Germans were resourceful, clever and ruthless opponents and there was still a lot of hard work to do before the war was over for us.

With the Allies closing in on Germany from east and west, the

Germans' greatest fear was of being overrun by the Soviets. Their fear was well-founded, since they fully expected to receive the same merciless treatment that they themselves had handed out in Eastern Europe when they had been winning comfortably in 1941 and 1942. Now, at the end of 1944, the Germans had much depleted their stocks of fuel and munitions, and logic suggested that the Eastern Front should have first call on what reserves were available. Hitler reasoned, however, that if the western Allies could be stopped and thrown back to the Belgian coast, they would never be able to recover, and the German forces arrayed against them could then be substantially redeployed against the Soviets.

So much for Hitler's theorizing. The reality for us was a nasty surprise, as the decision was taken immediately to shift us to the Ardennes to play a part in what has been called the "Battle of the Bulge".[2] An immediate shoring up of the shocked and wavering line of Allied forces in the Ardennes was essential, and 6th Airlanding Brigade was ordered in.

This was to be no Airborne landing for us, however. The Germans had struck at a time of foul weather, effectively denying the Allies their advantage of overwhelming air superiority. Large-scale airborne landings were almost impossible in such conditions. On the other hand, perhaps if it had not been for the heavy losses of gliders and pilots in the Arnhem campaign, even in that appalling weather some of us might have been dropped behind the German lines to hamper their advance or cut off their eventual retreat. In any event, the entire 6th Airborne Division was despatched to the Ardennes exclusively by surface transport. With virtually no time for any special preparation, we were transported by rail to Dover where we crossed the channel on the first ship to enter Calais harbour since its liberation.

It was Christmas morning when we disembarked and it was very cold. The canvas-covered trucks into which we were loaded were not the most comfortable way of travelling in those freezing conditions.

Our Christmas Day dinner was one of those unforgettable meals – it consisted of small tins of cold 'bully beef' – one tin to be shared by three men and eaten en route! While we were none too happy to be receiving such a Christmas meal, a former colleague from another Company later complained to me that 'D' Company, as usual, received favoured treatment. The lot of 'D' Company was always to be accused of receiving preferential treatment; it was part of the general banter in the Battalion. On this occasion my colleague's complaint was that his Company's even less memorable Christmas fare consisted of one small cheese sandwich per man.

After an overnight stop near Brussels an uncomfortable truck ride took us into the Ardennes. We arrived at last at a small town on the banks of a river, a tributary of the Meuse, where we met members of some other unit that was holding the place.

In general terms, 6th Airlanding Brigade were the first to arrive at the Meuse on 25 December, 1944, taking over from 71st Brigade (Welsh Division). Our battalion was at Givet and the Royal Ulster Rifles were with the Devons at Dinant.

Almost as soon as arriving, I was with a small detachment sent to support an American outfit guarding a narrow hump-backed bridge across the river. Our lorry stopped and we disembarked on the west bank of the river. The unit that we were to support or replace I remembered as being American, but the official record, which must be right, has it as a British outfit, but it didn't matter as we were not going to know them for very long. We had only just clambered from our lorry and greeted them when an elderly civilian crossed the bridge on his cycle, pointed to some high ground on the far side of the river, and said just one word, "Tigers!"

On hearing this, the members of the other outfit leapt into an assortment of vehicles and disappeared at high speed. They certainly showed no desire to hang around one moment longer than necessary when they knew what was coming.

Sure enough, very soon afterwards the German Tiger tanks crossed the bridge and our force of lightly equipped Airborne troops had nothing that could stop them. We had taken cover in the various buildings along the main street of the village, through which the Tigers now progressed, blasting away at the houses at point-blank range as they went. No doubt they would have spared the houses had it not been for the fact that we were using them as

170

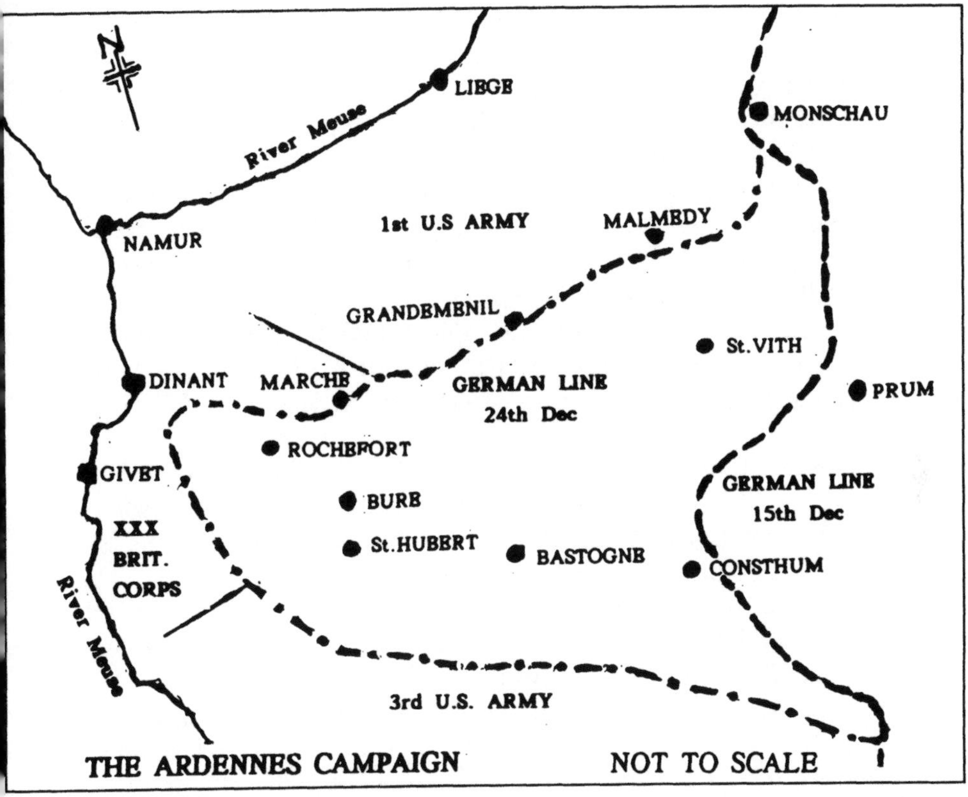
N
LIEGE
River Meuse
MONSCHAU
NAMUR
1st U.S ARMY
MALMEDY
GRANDEMENIL
St.VITH
DINANT
MARCHE
GERMAN LINE
24th Dec
PRUM
ROCHEFORT
GIVET
GERMAN LINE
15th Dec
BURE
XXX
BRIT.
CORPS
St.HUBERT
BASTOGNE
CONSTHUM
River Meuse
3rd U.S. ARMY
THE ARDENNES CAMPAIGN
NOT TO SCALE

cover from which to lob grenades at the tanks as they passed. It was a futile gesture, as we had nothing that would even scratch the Tigers, and we succeeded only in making them angry enough to cause massive damage to the houses.

As a tank passed us we would drop a couple of hand grenades on it from an upper window. By the time the tank had paused to investigate the irritation we were gone, having hurried downstairs and left via the back of the house, thereafter to enter other houses further along the street. The giant tanks would push the muzzles of their cannons right up to the lower storey windows and blow away the entire upper floors of the houses from which they had been attacked. This activity achieved absolutely nothing except the destruction of the houses, although possibly it made Jerry expend valuable rounds of tank ammunition that he couldn't easily replace and could ill afford to waste. We may possibly have delayed him a little as well.

After this first engagement with the enemy, we barely had time to familiarize ourselves with the new surroundings before we were off again, moving out before the end of December. Unlike Normandy, there was to be no digging in. This was to be a campaign of frequent advances, clearing villages and occupying them, then moving on to the next one.

Our first such move required a long march to Dréhance on the east bank of the Meuse near Dinant, but by 2 January it was decided to move again, this time to the east of Dinant, to the small village of Custinne.

Further south was the town of Resteigne, in which area the 5th Parachute Brigade had taken heavy casualties, so almost as soon as we arrived at Custinne it was move on again to Resteigne to support the Paras, arriving on 4 January.

Quite close to Resteigne was the village of Bure which was in enemy hands and where the Paras had been badly mauled by the Germans. 'D' Company saw little of the action here, but 'C' Company, under Major Granville, had been attached to 13th Para and they were in the thick of it, helping the Paras to clear and capture the village, mercifully without taking serious casualties themselves.

On 9 January it was time to move again, this time to Rochefort, crossing the River L'Homme the next day in pursuit of a German force that was retreating from the area. By this time the German offensive had petered out everywhere along the Ardennes front and, with shortages of munitions and other supplies, particularly fuel, they were pulling out of the area as quickly as possible, but in good order.

As the Germans retreated, we occupied a number of the villages that they had been holding, notably the villages of Wavreille and Forrers, and then Nassogne, still in the Meuse valley. We then headed away from the Meuse, heading generally northward through Belgium and into Holland, rejoining the river – called the Maas in Holland – at Grubbenvorst, almost 160 miles north of the Ardennes.

At each point of our progress en route our role was to occupy deserted farmhouses alongside the river bank. For this purpose we were split into small detachments, usually seven-man sections, and we would make our own way through the snow to our allocated positions,[3] remaining watchful and self-sufficient for a few days at each location.

While near the river we were under direct observation from German artillery for much of the time, and so we were unable to light fires during the hours of daylight and cooking was kept to a minimum. We had no experienced cook in our detachment anyway, so our diet was pancakes and eggs gathered from the chickens around the farms we were occupying. The eggs were fresh, of course, and, although it was a little monotonous, the diet was a lot better than the hard biscuit rations we had been given in Normandy.

We had to be very inconspicuous during the day, but at night we patrolled actively. We were equipped with white 'snow suits' to provide camouflage in the wintry landscape, and during the hours of darkness we spent much of the night patrolling our side of the river.

Word came to us from other units that the Germans were sending patrols across the river under cover of darkness to lie in wait for one of our own patrols to pass them, and they were then 'jumping' the last man, capturing or killing him. To counter this enemy tactic it was decided that on future patrols of, say, five or six men, an extra man would be added. His job was to hang well back so that when the supposedly last man was 'jumped', the lad hanging even further back – rather like a wicket-keeper's long stop in the game of cricket – would sound the alarm and enable our own patrol to attack the enemy.

As one of the more experienced snipers, on several occasions I was given the task of acting as the long stop or Tail-End Charlie. I did not enjoy this role, since quite obviously I was now the last man, and if the enemy patrols worked out what was happening, I would be the one to be jumped on. To this day, if anyone walks up behind me and prods me in the back I practically jump out of my skin! Fortunately, during many patrols we were never ambushed, so the idea was not put to the test.

During our night patrolling it was sometimes necessary to use small punt-like boats to cross the river in darkness to seek out enemy positions on the other side. These boats had a flat wooden floor, with canvas sides topped by a wooden rail; wooden upright struts jammed under the top rail propped up the sides. To say the least they were flimsy, and if they had folded up on us when we were in midstream, swimming while fully clad in those freezing conditions might well have proved fatal.

Knowing that the Germans were patrolling as actively as we were meant that we had to be very careful to avoid falling victims to our own kind of warfare. At the crack of dawn our patrol would leave the farmhouse and scout around the immediate area to seek out any Germans who might have crossed to our side of the river during the night. No direct contact with the enemy was ever made in this way, but once we saw deep tracks in the snow where a visiting German patrol had passed close to our buildings.

One morning at first light an artillery battery suddenly appeared on the top of the ridge above and behind our farmhouse. They had large field guns towed behind canvas covered trucks. I believe they could have been American units. Having moved into position, they promptly fired off a few rounds. In their highly exposed position they were immediately spotted by the Germans who retaliated by sending over a stream of shells, causing the gunners to withdraw very smartly.

Not unnaturally the Germans assumed that the farmhouse down below was probably being used as an Artillery Observation Post and they started bombarding our previously peaceful and quiet location. We cursed the gunners for their stupidity, but fortunately none of us was hurt by the shelling.

It was fairly boring to have to remain undercover during daylight hours, so much of our time was spent gambling with playing cards. I must have been a very bad gambler because in my Pay Book of that time I made the following entries:

22/12/44   30/- (i.e. thirty shillings – my last payment before leaving England. 30 shillings is approximately £1.50 in present money.) This was the usual amount I would draw.

4/1/45	300fr (Belgian) – (I can't remember how much this was in sterling).
31/1/45	16 Guilders (I noted at the time that this amounted to £10)!
11/2/45	5 Guilders.

(While in action in the Ardennes we had no opportunity to spend money in the usual way, so I can only assume that the large amounts drawn were to pay gambling debts.

1/3/45	30/- for 8 days' leave pay! (Through paying off my debts I must have been overdrawn so my pay was the minimum amount.)

We stayed on the River Meuse until the third week in February, but with very little to do in the final few days, as the Nazi forces were retreating into the German homeland. I found it satisfying to think that this place at least had seen the last of the Nazis.

We returned to England the same way we had come, in trucks to Calais and home by ship.

We lost very few men during the Ardennes campaign, and when we returned to Bulford it was very much "business as usual", training, drilling and wondering how much longer the war would continue and where we would next be used.

Chapter 10

ACROSS THE RHINE

Towards the end of February, 1945, we were back in camp at Bulford, having done our bit in the Ardennes. We had helped to shore up the line against which the Germans had succeeded only in exhausting themselves on their western front, and we had then done our share of chasing them back towards their own frontiers, and mercifully our casualties had been light. The point has to be made, however, that the Germans were not put to flight; as usual their retreat was skilfully handled and they withdrew in good order. It was clear that much remained to be done before Jerry was finished off once and for all, and that airborne landings were increasingly likely to be called for – and that meant us.

While Nazi Germany was not yet a spent force, the failure of their Ardennes offensive meant that they had used much of their remaining Western stocks of fuel and other resources without any gain. From now on they would use their much-diminished reserves with greater care, since there was nothing to be spared from the Eastern Front, where the Russian advance was relentless.

We were to discover very soon what the poor devils at Arnhem had already learned to their cost. Jerry knew that glider-borne infantry, as well as paratroopers, were sitting ducks when boxed up thirty or so at a time in a glider or paratroop transport, so that was the ideal time to attack them.

As for us, we could see that our next taste of action would be inside the German homeland, where the Germans could be relied upon to fight with more determination than ever, and, sure enough, barely a month was to pass before we were back in action.

LETTER

BY THE

COMMANDER-IN-CHIEF

ON

NON-FRATERNISATION

TO ALL OFFICERS AND MEN OF 21 ARMY GROUP

1. Twenty-seven years ago the Allies occupied Germany: but Germany has been at war ever since. Our Army took no revenge in 1918; it was more than considerate, and before a few weeks had passed many soldiers were adopted into German households. The enemy worked hard at being amiable. They believed that the occupation was due to treachery, and that their army had never been beaten. They remained unrepentant and attached to their worship of brute force.

2. The fight was continued by the German General Staff, who concealed war criminals and equipments, built up armaments, and trained a new striking force. To evade the Armistice terms they had to find sympathisers, and "organising sympathy" became a German industry. So accommodating were the occupying forces that the Germans came to believe we would never fight them again in any cause. From that moment to this their continued aggression has brought misery or death to millions, always under the familiar smoke screen of appeals for fair play and friendship, followed by the barrage of stark, brutal threats.

This time the Nazis have added to the experience of the last occupation; they have learned from the resistance movements of France, Belgium, Holland, and Norway. These are the type of instructions they are likely to give to their underground workers:

"Give the impression of submitting. Say you never liked the Nazis; they were the people responsible for the war. Argue that Germany has never had a fair chance. Get the soldiers arguing; they are not trained for it, and you are.

"Use old folks, girls, and children, and 'play up' every case of devastation or poverty. Ask the troops to your homes; sabotage or steal equipment, petrol or rations. Get troops to sell these things, if you can. Spread stories about Americans and Russians in the British zone, and about the British to other Allies."

3. Because of these facts, I want every soldier to be clear about "non-fraternisation". Peace does not exist merely because of a surrender. The Nazi influence penetrates everywhere, even into children's schools and churches. Our occupation of Germany is an act of war of which the first object is to destroy the Nazi system. There are Allied organisations whose work it is to single out, separate and destroy the dangerous elements in German life. It is too soon for you to distinguish between "good" and "bad" Germans: you have a positive part to play in winning the peace by a definite code of behaviour. In streets, houses, cafes, cinemas, etc., you must keep clear of Germans, man, woman and child, unless you meet them in the course of duty. You must not walk out with them, or shake hands, or visit their homes, or make them gifts, or take gifts from them. You must not play games with them or share any social event with them. In short, you must not fraternise with Germans at all.

4. To refrain from fraternisation is not easy. It requires self-discipline. But in Germany you will have to remember that laughing and eating and dancing with Germans would be bitterly resented by your own families, by millions of people who have suffered under the Gestapo and under the Luftwaffe's bombs, and by every Ally that Britain possesses. You will have to remember that these are the same Germans who, a short while ago, were drunk with victory, who were boasting what they as the Master Race would do to you as their slaves, who were applauding the utter disregard by their leaders of any form of decency or of honourable dealings: the same Germans whose brothers, sons and fathers were carrying out a system of mass murder and torture of defenceless civilians. You will have to remember that these same Germans are planning to make fools of you again and to escape the loathing which their actions deserve.

5. Our consciences are clear; "non-fraternisation" to us implies no revenge; we have no theory of master races. But a guilty nation must not only be convicted: it must realise its guilt. Only then can the first steps be taken to re-educate it, and bring it back into the society of decent humanity.

6. German discipline, though not our sort, is thorough. The people will judge you with no amateur eyes: and any slackness will be the cue for the resistance movements to intensify their efforts.

7. Be just; be firm; be correct; give orders, and don't argue. Last time we won the war and let the peace slip out of our hands. This time we must not ease off—we must win both the war and the peace.

B. L. Montgomery

Field-Marshal,
C-in-C 21 Army Group.

March, 1945.

PSS 1810 3.45

GERMANY - MARCH 1945   4-page booklet issued to all troops prior to Rhine crossing.

The operation planned for us was code-named 'Varsity', but before it took place some large-scale preparations were undertaken, including a massive practice airlift of the entire 17th American and 6th British Airborne Divisions as a trial run over eastern England.

A temporary camp in Essex was the location from which the operation would begin, and from where we took part in the trial run, which was very nearly a disaster. In full combat condition my platoon was loaded into a Horsa, and we became airborne along with a great many aircraft. In flight over Cambridge the tug plane developed an engine fault and suddenly we were in real trouble.

The only possible action was to cast off from the tug plane immediately. Luckily, our glider pilot was cool and businesslike, and shouted back to us to link arms in preparation for an unscheduled landing.

The Horsa had half a dozen small portholes along either side and I was peering through one of these to see what was happening. Already we were just a couple of hundred feet above the ground and losing height rapidly. As I watched buildings, grass, trees, hedges and fences flashing by at increasing speed, I was horrified to see a passenger train passing from right to left and directly in front of our flight path. I saw the passengers looking up at us as we swept over their heads just a few feet higher than the roofs of the carriages. A few seconds later we were skidding in to a perfect landing in a field on the outskirts of March in Cambridgeshire.

The local folk treated us as heroes, made us really welcome, took us into their homes and shared their meagre rations with us. When the pubs opened people were lining up to buy us drinks. We were having such a good time that when our Platoon Officer informed us that transport would shortly be arriving to return us to our camp in Essex a conspiracy was hatched immediately to enable our delightful but unscheduled holiday to continue. Some of the lads went to the outskirts of the town and misdirected the truck drivers as they came in search of us. When they finally tracked us down they were none too pleased that they had been sent on a wild goose chase, but no charges were brought against anyone as far as I remember.

Operation 'Varsity' began on 24 March, 1945. The target for

our battalion was the railway station at Hamminkeln, together with the Ringenberg road bridge over the River Issel, the railway bridge slightly to the north of the road bridge, and the road running westwards from Hamminkeln and Ringenberg.

The strategic aim was to capture these bridges and other objectives that would deny the enemy the opportunity to counter the assault across the Rhine by Montgomery's Second Army. The airborne bridgehead was then to be held until the Second Army broke through to relieve it.

The airfield of departure for our battalion was at Birch, in Essex, from where the take-off began at 0630 hours. About sixty aircraft, gliders and tugs, were queued for take-off.

A strange event occurred at this time. One of the corporals who had been with us in the Normandy campaign had by this time been promoted to sergeant of his Platoon. While waiting to enplane he had a premonition that the aircraft was fated and doomed. He ran off, only to be later detained, tried, stripped of his rank and sentenced to military detention. He might well have received a more severe sentence than a few months' detention had it not been for the fact that his premonition was justified. The glider in which he would have travelled took a direct hit and was destroyed with no survivors.

I have been told, although I have no personal recollection of the matter, that our Horsa was in fifth place in the queue for the runway. I do remember, however, that we were the last to get airborne, as our tow-rope snapped while we were on our take-off run, this being a not uncommon occurrence, since the tension in the rope was at its greatest as the glider accelerated while being dragged along the runway. A tractor was quickly sent down the runway to drag us back to the start line and eventually we were ready to go again, but now at the back of the queue. We were thus the last combination to leave, travelling toward Europe in grand isolation.

Our tug pilot, however – Wing Commander, later Group Captain, Alex Blythe – did not follow in the wake of the airborne armada. After a chat on the intercom with Stan Jarvis, our glider pilot, he had a new course plotted by his navigator in order to reduce the journey by a few miles and thus to arrive earlier. He

179

GERMANY. 6th Airlanding Brigade Glider Landing Zones on the morning of 24th March 1945.

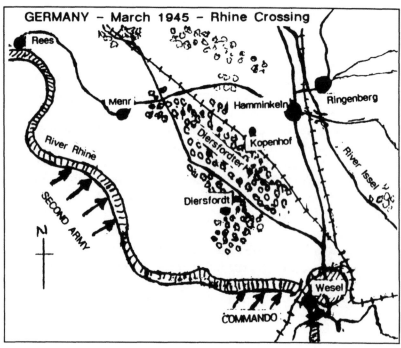

GERMANY – March 1945 – Rhine Crossing

intercepted the other aircraft exactly where he expected, close to the destination, and reinstated us close to our correct position in the formation. He was later full of admiration and praise for the precision navigation demonstrated by his colleagues.

Regrettably, the Germans knew only too well that we were on our way and they were ready and waiting. Following the British glider-borne landings in Normandy and Arnhem in 1944 the Germans had certainly realized that the most effective way to deal with the British troop-carrying Horsa, and the equally large and flimsy Hamilcar gliders was to hit them with incendiary bullets. Perhaps even tracer bullets were sufficient to set these large and slow gliders aflame long before they reached the ground.

Bullets zipped through one side of the flimsy plywood fuselage and out of the other as we approached our landing zone, and as we came in to land part of one wing, an aileron, and the tail section were shot to pieces by shellfire. Listening to the bullets ripping through woodwork around us was none too pleasant, but amazingly none of us was hit by them. Even more miraculously, unlike most of our comrades in other gliders and those paratroops who jumped, we suffered no casualties at all during the actual landing.

Stan Jarvis, our young RAF glider pilot, had been trained as an RAF pilot, but was hurriedly transferred to flying gliders for the Airborne forces because of the heavy loss of Army pilots at Arnhem. He put our Horsa down as close to the railway station as we could have wished. Many years later Stan recounted how, after we had all fled the wrecked glider, taking cover wherever we could amid a hail of incoming missiles and bullets, one of the lads said to him, "I know that before you left the airfield we asked you to get us as close as possible to the railway station, but if you had landed any closer we would have been in the ruddy booking office."

From the River Rhine to the landing zone the surface was already clouded by smoke from the guns and bombs and smoke-laying equipment used by the ground forces in preparation for crossing the Rhine. Stan Jarvis recalls how he cast off from Alex Blythe's Dakota tug aircraft while in dense smoke, with no sight of the ground whatsoever.

181

While he and his co-pilot, Peter Geddes, were looking desperately for clues as to our exact whereabouts, pieces of our glider were literally being shot away. As they identified a stretch of autobahn to the east of Hamminkeln, they steered towards where they would expect the railway station to be, while four feet of the starboard wing, together with most of the aileron, were blown off by a flak burst. He put us into a fairly steep dive as the tracer and machine-gun fire intensified and became more accurate. Then he saw the railway lines and the station, levelled off at about fifty feet and went in for his landing, skimming the fields and the posts and snag-wires that had been erected to discourage glider landings. The tail section was shot away just as we landed, but the cargo of men was intact, with no injuries whatsoever.

The official record shows that between 24 and 25 March, 1945, the regiment suffered one hundred and three killed. A normal company consisted of six officers and one hundred other ranks. At the end of 25 March our position was: 'A' Company, four officers and fifty-six other ranks; 'B' Company, two officers and forty-five other ranks; 'C' Company, four officers and fifty-two other ranks, and 'D' Company, three officers and fifty-eight other ranks. This was a truly awful rate of loss.

In total the British 6th Airborne Division had 1100 casualties and the American 17th Airborne Division suffered similar heavy losses. Many of the gliders were literally shot out of the sky and 100 members of the Glider Pilot Regiment and RAF men who flew the gliders also lost their lives. This was the price that had to be paid to overwhelm the German defenders and ensure the success of the land-based Rhine crossing.

Although we lost several men later, the losses were never again on such a scale and most of us who survived that horrendous landing made the 280-mile dash across northern Germany to meet up with the Russians near Wismar on the Baltic coast in early May. It was an eventful five weeks, most of which was spent marching and fighting, while always hoping that Jerry would throw in the towel and spare us any more misery.

The battle at Hamminkeln for the station and the Issel bridges was very bloody but short, and most of the opposition was out of action in one way or another within thirty-six hours. Stan Jarvis recalls that the surviving glider pilots had been given the task of managing the streams of German prisoners as they arrived. They had to be searched and relieved of anything other than personal effects as they stood facing a wall with their hands up. At one stage he noticed that a large amount of Dutch cash was accumulating from the pockets of one batch of prisoners and, upon questioning, they confessed to having raided a bank on the Dutch side of the Rhine just before being captured.

It is an interesting coincidence that some of the major milestones in my life should have occurred at the time of the Celtic New Year on 25 March. I knew about the Celtic New Year because both my parents were Celts, Irish in my mother's case, while my father was Welsh. Neither of them had a lot of time for the Christian culture that had supplanted the old ways of their ancestors, and when opportunity arose, being proud of their ancestry, they would revel in a kind of Celtic nostalgia. They frequently spoke to me about such matters, pointing out to me the wisdom and logic of starting the year at the time of the spring equinox.

It was on 25 March in 1941 that I volunteered to join the army while still some four months short of my seventeenth birthday. After Dunkirk, the army being woefully short of cannon fodder, I guess that the recruiting sergeant, who never asked to see my National Identity Card or any other form of identification, was happy not to question me concerning my statement that I was nearly nineteen. He probably even received a recruiting bonus when I signed up for seven years, which I had done on the assumption that it would take at least that long to end the war. For me that meant that at the end of my service I would reap the benefit of five years' reserve pay. It also meant that I would be leaving the Army on Celtic New Year's Day in 1948.

If 25 March was ever a milestone in my life, it was certainly true in 1945. On the 24th my Airborne Division had dropped on the east side of the Rhine, and there I was at Hamminkeln railway station almost exactly four years after joining up. The 25th was to be an odd day for me, being not only the anniversary of my joining up but also the day that I was officially declared killed in action!

Once on the ground at Hamminkeln, the survivors still had many problems. The gliders had to land on open ground and the well-positioned German forces equipped with their tanks, artillery, mortars, heavy, medium and light machine guns, accompanied by well-positioned snipers, picked us off at will as we sought what little cover was available. The casualty figures testify to the advantage enjoyed by the defenders as we delivered our cargoes of thirty men at a time, gift-wrapped in plywood Horsas.

My own twenty-six-man platoon was relatively lucky and every one of us got clear of our glider and reached the station yard where we took refuge from the murderous German fire. The yard covered a considerable area, part of it being stacked with neat piles of timber, each approximately the size of a two-storey house.

Unfortunately it turned out that the Germans were using these stacks of timber to cover their approach as they advanced towards us. We spent the first few hours playing hide-and-seek among the wood-piles, dodging the German Mk IV tanks which trundled up and down the rows of stacked timber seeking us out.

We were not equipped to deal with German heavy tanks. Indeed, the anti-tank guns that we did possess, six-pounders which could dispose of even a Tiger at close range, were almost certainly still within the Hamilcar gliders used to transport our heavier equipment. The concentration of enemy fire over the landing zones would have made it virtually impossible for such weapons to be removed. Most men were just thankful if they were able to crawl away from their gliders and find some sort of shelter from the incoming German fire.

If German tanks dared to roam about in daylight they were quickly neutralized by RAF Tempest and Typhoon rocket-firing aircraft. The Luftwaffe was virtually out of action by this time, out of fuel if not quite out of aircraft, and these Allied aerial tank destroyers were unopposed. They could afford to loiter close by until called in whenever tanks posed a threat. It was a very one-sided match and in the open and in daylight the tank stood little chance. When moving about in close cover, however, such as the timber yard at Hamminkeln, or with smoke cover, or at night or in semi-darkness, then the German tanks became a problem – quite terrifying and lethally dangerous to lightly equipped infantry.

After our nerve-racking game of hide and seek with the German tanks, we were finally forced to vacate the yard. We withdrew to

'D' Company's arranged rendezvous point on the other side of the glider landing zone. We then moved up to take over the river bridge, defending it against repeated enemy attacks and probes with tanks and infantry.

It was some time later – I am unsure of the exact time for reasons that will become clear, but probably in the late afternoon or evening – that my section was sheltering below a high railway or river embankment when the enemy began a powerful bombardment of the area. A lot of heavy stuff was crashing in all around the place and, without well-dug trenches such as we had in Normandy, it was impossible to find anywhere that offered good protection.

There were several of us crouched in the lee of the embankment when apparently a large shell exploded on the top of the bank just above my head, killing many of those in the immediate area, as well as some others who were further away.[1] I neither remember the shellburst nor anything more for a period of thirty-six hours or so.

The next day, however, the 25th, the Rhine had been crossed and the battle around Hemminkeln was all but over. Some last-ditch German counter-attacks in the morning were repulsed and the attacking forces were annihilated. The airborne forces, including the remnants of 'D' Company, were then rested for a miserly four hours, starting the second phase of the operation on the morning of the 26th – the advance across northern Germany – acting as a spearhead for the land-based forces following in their wake.

At some time on the morning of the 26th 'D' Company had moved some distance beyond the railway station and was preparing to launch an attack on a large wood which, according to Intelligence reports, was heavily defended.

In the usual way, as a prelude to the attack, our artillery put down a heavy bombardment on the wood. Then the shelling ceased as our lads were preparing to attack, when a lone figure emerged from the wood, wandering through the early morning mist and greeting them with a wave of his hand. I was that lone figure and the lads all agreed later that I was very fortunate not to have been shot before I was recognized. When they saw me they

185

were convinced that they were seeing my ghost. In reply to their urgent questioning, I was able to assure them that there were no Germans in the wood, which was then occupied without a shot being fired.

When our Company Commander saw me his face turned white before changing to red as he bellowed, "Where the Hell have you come from?"

"I don't know Sir," I replied with complete honesty, "I was in that wood."

"Good God man," bellowed the Company Commander, "I've sent off a signal that you had been killed in action I saw your body lying on the embankment."

Others who were standing around nodded their agreement and also said that they too had seen me 'killed'.

No one was ever able to explain how I could have been wandering around alone in heavily occupied enemy territory for some thirty-six hours without being captured or shot. Nor could they understand how I had managed to survive our own massive shelling of the wood and emerge completely unscathed.

I have no definite answer to the mystery; the last thing that I could remember was diving for the shelter of the railway embankment when the shelling began, and then emerging from the wood a day and a half later. The period between is a complete blank.

I can only surmise that I must have been very severely concussed; the blast of the shell burst certainly killed several men all around me. I must have been completely unconscious when our Company Commander and the others saw the bodies, and I was presumed to be dead and was left with the others to await a burial party. On regaining consciousness, in the midst of a pile of broken and bloody corpses, I would have been the only living person in the area. I suppose that I would have hurried off in search of my Company, driven by instinct and fear of being left alone, this latter condition probably aggravated by having been temporarily deafened by the effect of the shell blast. The direction in which I chose to wander could only have been determined by chance, and it was our own shelling of the wood that caused me to leave it and thereby to encounter my own Company advancing to attack it. But this is only to surmise and to offer an explanation that is at least logical.

186

The reality is that I really remember nothing whatsoever of the period until the time I emerged from the wood. Although I was spared from any physical injury, I have no doubt that I underwent a hellish and terrifying experience and, mercifully, it was erased from my memory.

When the Company Commander had told me that he had sent off a signal that I had been killed, I immediately scribbled a hurried note to my mother to tell her to ignore any messages concerning my demise as I was still very much alive. Some time after she received my hurried note she got a flow of official communications telling her that I was 'Missing in Action'. I still have those official telegrams and I can only presume that when the burial party visited the embankment and discovered that I was not among the dead a revised signal went to the War Office in London rescinding the report of my being killed in action and posting me as 'missing'.

Despite the fact that I was obviously not in tip-top condition after this experience, and almost certainly unfit by any objective medical standard, I simply went back to my usual daily routine as though nothing had happened. The shortage of men after the mauling we took at the landing site was such that nobody was in a hurry to report me sick or as being in need of medical attention.

From this point in my narrative I rely on the regimental records for dates and locations, because after Normandy I never again kept a diary.

On 26 March we were briefly in the village of Brunen, about five kilometres east of Hamminkeln, continuing eastwards on the 27th to Rhade, where we stayed the night. The next day, 28 March, we marched twenty-five kilometres to Coesfeld without seeing any action, and we stayed there until the evening of 30 March when we were moved out by trucks which took us to Greven on the River Ems. The river crossing was a precarious exercise, as our only way across was by means of the badly damaged river bridge.

Once across the river we encountered an enemy anti-aircraft unit, who attacked with what they had – 20mm and 88mm anti-aircraft guns – and we took several casualties.

187

Our progress was ever eastwards, sometimes by truck, sometimes on foot. Our task was to penetrate deeply into northern Germany, clearing our path of enemy forces wherever possible. Larger enemy troop concentrations, such as the force defending Osnabrück, did not justify being confronted by our spearhead force and would doubtless be dealt with by the artillery and other units who were moving into the areas we had cleared.

Towards the end of the first week of April we had reached the banks of the River Weser, of Pied Piper fame, arriving soon afterwards at Kutenhausen where we were attacked by enemy tanks. We destroyed two of the tanks before moving on in preparation for crossing the wide river in assault boats. This was to take place at Weitersheim, but we had to overcome the enemy force holding the town before we could carry out the crossing. At the crossing point the river was 200 yards wide, with a swift current which made life interesting, but all was completed by 1600 hours on 5 April.

On the east bank of the Weser the first village we came to was Frille, held by a determined enemy force, which resulted in house-to-house fighting before we overwhelmed the defenders and took the village at around 2000 hours that evening.

We spent the night in Frille, and at first light we moved out, heading south-east, clearing the east bank of the river as we went.

By 9 April we were a mere twenty miles or so to the west of Hannover and on the 10th, intending to take the small town of Heitlingen, we discovered that American forces had already occupied it. This fact was a great morale-booster – the noose around the Nazi armies was tightening and the concentration of Allied forces was increasing as we advanced. It was as well to remember, however, that the concentration of Nazi forces was also increasing as they retreated, and for the most part they were neither demoralized nor yet unwilling to show resistance.

The next day we received reinforcements, sixty-seven trained replacements for those we had lost in the landings and subsequently.

For two days we stayed put, reorganizing with the reinforcements and integrating them. On the 14th we moved out, transported by trucks to a point north-east of Celle, then spending the night in some woods, before being transported to Nettelkemp, where we arrived at dusk on the 15th.

From this time forwards I was occasionally tempted to think it was all over and that Jerry wouldn't have much stomach for more fighting, but then, just as life seemed to be becoming a little easier, we would have a really hard day. 16 April was just such a day, the entire day being spent in hard action. A couple of small villages were cleared before midday, but then, while advancing towards Khalstorf, we came under heavy fire from a relatively strong defensive force who meant business. Having sorted out that problem, there was a full regimental attack on Karlsdorf, after which, at the end of the day we retired half a mile or so south to a hamlet called Gross Pretzier. We took twenty-five casualties that day and it all seemed so pointless and futile.

The next morning, at first light, 'C' Company attacked again, while we stayed put at Gross Pretzier for the whole day, but orders came for an advance on the town of Uelzen at 0200hrs on 18 April.

By 0830hrs we had taken the village of Katzein, two miles to the north of Rosche, while the Devons were attacking Rosche itself. Having been busy thereafter clearing up scattered German forces to the south-west of Polav, we returned to Katzein on the 20th leaving the attack on Polav to 'C' Company. Katzein was where we stayed until the 22nd, when we received a visit from Major General Gale and Major General Bols,[2] who decided that we should move back to Ebsdorf for a rest period – welcome news indeed.

The move to Ebstorf was achieved by a sixteen-mile march on 23 April, via Uelzen where we had been a few days earlier. We arrived in mid-afternoon for a very welcome rest, which lasted until the 28th.

From now onwards our advance continued on foot and our Airborne Company took over as the spearhead of the rapid advance by the British forces across Northern Germany. Once again I was right at the very front of what was going on.

As an experienced sniper, with a reputation for being able to spot the enemy before he spotted us, I was given the task of scouting ahead to determine the lie of the land and to seek out any possible enemy ambush.

189

A few miles to the north of Ebsdorf I came across what at first sight appeared to be some kind of prison camp. I entered with great caution and proceeded to check whether there were any armed German guards around, but found none; they had obviously fled when we approached. What I did see was a long and quite deep trench, half-filled with naked bodies of men, women and children. Nearby was a pile of dead bodies, waiting to be dumped into the trench.

Checking out some nearby huts, I found multi-tiered crude bunk beds on which lay many starving and near-dead people. The stench inside those buildings was like an open sewer, forcing me to place a handkerchief over my nose and mouth as quickly as I could. I had the greatest difficulty in preventing myself from vomiting.

A frail old man was most anxious to hand me a small tablet of soap. Unfortunately, I spoke no German or any language other than English, and I have always wondered why he was trying to give me the soap. I came to the conclusion that he was trying to say that the soap was made within the camp and was of human origin.[3]

I suppose that my words were not understood by those of the pitiful inmates who were still more or less alive, but, after assuring them that I would get some help, I withdrew and reported what I had seen to my Company Commander. He immediately passed the information to our senior officers and we then pressed on with our advance.

This unpleasant experience was imprinted on my mind and was not one that I was likely to forget. Memories such as that do not fade quickly, as the horror reinforces itself on every occasion that it comes to mind. I was more than a little irritated therefore when, years later, I had occasion to hear someone claim, in effect, that my experience had never happened. It was in the 1970s when, as an active supporter of the Freedom Association, and at times an outspoken member of Worthing Borough Council, I was invited to a meeting of a local Debating Society. A late-running Committee at the Town Hall caused me to arrive after the meeting had begun. As I joined the well-attended evening gathering a man on the platform was saying that the so-called Nazi Concentration Camps were a complete myth. He claimed that the camps had never actually existed, but were simply the result of clever international

Jewish propaganda. It took a moment for this astonishing assertion to register, but as soon as I was quite sure that this was indeed what had been said, I spoke out. From the bar at the rear of the large room I said, as loudly and as forcefully as I could, "Sir, I don't know who you are, but I do know that you are talking complete rubbish!"

I did not wait for his reply, but continued speaking, giving the startled audience roughly the account that I have related once again here.

At the end of my impromptu dissertation there was a hushed and uncomfortable silence, broken only when the original speaker 'shot himself in the foot' in the most amusing manner when he said, "You could not possibly have been inside those camps. Only trained medical staff were allowed to enter".

He seemed to be very sure that only trained medical staff were permitted to enter a camp whose existence, he had just assured us, was completely mythical. I pointed this out to him and added the fact that when I came across this particular camp our medical staff would have almost certainly been several miles to our rear.

I later discovered that the speaker that I had interrupted had been a recent National Front candidate in a nearby parliamentary Election, and that the vast majority of the audience were National Front members, or fellow travellers. Needless to say I was not invited to any further meetings of that group.

When I stumbled upon that first Concentration Camp I had no knowledge of the existence of such places. The exposure of the full horror of the obscenities perpetrated by the Nazi régime did not take place until the Allies discovered such camps and made thorough investigations of them.

The pictures of Belsen published immediately after the war were so similar to what I had seen that for many years I assumed that the camp that I had found was in fact Belsen. However, not many years ago I learnt that another British unit had liberated Belsen, and so I wrote to my former Company Commander seeking clarification of this point. He informed me that the camp that we had liberated was in fact one of Belsen's many satellites.

On 28 April we learned that we were to move up to Suttorf on the River Elbe. This was about ten miles east of Lauenburg where the British forces had formed a bridgehead, and we marched there the following day with no major incidents.

Leaving Suttorf in the early evening of the 30th we marched to the crossing point on the River Elbe. The crossing was carried out at midnight, using a temporary bridge put across the river by our sappers. Moving off eastwards immediately, we swung north a little later to attack the hamlet of Nosdorf.

Before dawn on 1 May we took the village of Nosdorf, moving on five miles or so immediately afterwards to Schwartow soon after first light.

On 2 May we encountered a stream of liberated prisoners of war, and a little later substantial units of a German army, complete with long columns of tanks and artillery. This huge German force was travelling westwards along the same routes that we were using to advance to the east. They outnumbered us many times over but fortunately they were no longer interested in fighting. It caused a very considerable traffic jam as their long lines of fully equipped, heavy, medium and light tanks, troop carriers, heavy artillery, large lorries and an assortment of smaller vehicles blocked the narrow roads.

This fleeing army, intent only on escaping from the Russians, considerably impeded our progress towards our next objective, Gladebusch. We took advantage of the situation to rest at the roadside, watching the enemy drive past us in full battle order. It was a very odd state of affairs, but certainly a sign that serious German resistance was almost ended.

The Germans were virtually indifferent to our presence. One high-ranking German officer, however, immaculately dressed and with a stiffly arrogant Prussian manner, left his staff car and crossed over to where we were resting at the roadside. In perfect English he told us that the German and British people had a great deal in common, whereas the Russians were nothing but savage barbarians. He suggested that if we were wise we would join forces with the Germans, attack the Russians and drive them all the way back to Siberia. He said that the Russians were desperately short of food, supplies and ammunition. They could neither feed nor guard prisoners, he maintained, nor did they have the spare bullets to shoot them. What they did to anyone that they caught was to

192

hack off their hands, or sometimes their feet to prevent them from running away or taking up arms against Russia in the future.

With the liberated German Concentration Camp still fresh in our minds, and still with the nightmare memories of living skeletons and piles of dead bodies, we were not too impressed with his stories of Russian atrocities. We were also far from being persuaded by his suggestion that we should start a new war just as the present one was ending.

At that time we knew nothing about German Concentration Camps, or their purpose of systematic extermination, but we told him about the death camp that we had liberated a week earlier. It was quite obvious from his baffled expression that he simply did not know what we were talking about.

The next day we moved up to Lutterstorf village, and then on to Bad Kleinen. There, on 3 May, 1945, at Bad Kleinen, midway between Wismar and Schwerin, on the banks of a river that linked the Baltic Sea with the great inland lake of Schwerin, and not many days' march from the Polish border, the victorious British and Russian armies met.

For us it was the end of a 280-mile advance across northern Germany that had begun on 24 March with the Airborne landing at Hamminkeln. We had been marching almost flat out day and night for what seemed like an eternity. Now we were camped on the western bank of the river, looking across at our Russian comrades-in-arms camped on the opposite side. They crossed over a wide bridge in considerable numbers from their side of the river and invited us to drink vodka with them; whatever else may have been in short supply they appeared to have an almost unlimited amount of their favourite tipple.

They obviously used their visit to have a good look round our tented camp, for when darkness fell a large band of them paid us another visit, this time uninvited. They entered our main supply tent and, at gunpoint, tied up the Quartermaster and his staff and made off to their side of the river with most of our rations!

When the theft was discovered we immediately placed an armed guard at our end of the bridge and refused to allow any more Russians to cross to our side. They did likewise. This may well have been one of the first acts of what was to be called the 'cold war' and which was to endure for half a century thereafter.

The morning after their raid on our supplies one of the lads from the Quartermaster's staff thought that he recognized one of the Russians who had been in their raiding party. A group of us crossed the bridge and were met at the other side by a Russian officer. We assumed that he was an officer as he wore some kind of uniform, while most of the others, Mongol types from their appearance, were dressed like peasants in scruffy smocks.

As best we could, by sign language, we pointed out the man who we believed had been a member of the gang who had stolen our food. The Russian seemed to understand what we meant; he nodded, then turned and strode across to the suspect that we had indicated. We assumed that he was going to question him, or bring him over to us for positive identification. Instead, he drew a revolver from its holster, put the barrel against the man's mouth and fired, blowing off half of his head. We were horrified as he returned to us, grinning from ear to ear, and indicating that, while the man may have stolen our food, he would certainly not be eating any more of it!

No offer was made to return our rations and as we retraced our steps to our side of the river I remembered the words of the German officer who, only a few days earlier, had told us that the Russians were different! Certainly they appeared to have been severely brutalized, but warfare is always a brutalizing experience and the Soviets had suffered more than most, particularly because the Nazis did not even acknowledge their right to the benefit of the Geneva Convention.

I doubt if the German officer would have recognized or understood that the war which brought about such brutality was his war, not theirs. He would not have been able to understand that the savagery and brutality of his own people, although just as horrific, or worse, could not be excused as resulting from years of suffering and privation. It was in evidence from the beginning, as they sought to make themselves masters of Europe.

Now it was all over, and we were going home.

On 17 May we left Bad Kleine for Lüneburg airfield from where we flew home the next day, with the immediate prospect of fourteen days' leave.

I had signed on for seven years, so I still had some years of service to complete, but I had somehow survived a World War – and come out without a scratch.

"This man must have had the devil's own luck," someone commented upon reading about my experiences. I would be the last to disagree with him.

ENDNOTE

Of the original 181 men of 'D' Company, which included HQ and men from the Platoons which had to be left off the Coup de Main force due to lack of space in the gliders, but who arrived in Normandy on D-Day, only forty returned to Bulford Camp. I count myself very fortunate to have been one of them. Despite all the action I had seen in Normandy, which killed, maimed or wounded so many of my colleagues, I returned unscathed – fortunate indeed.

Several of the less severely wounded members of 'D' Company, however, were able to rejoin us prior to our being sent into the Ardennes on Christmas Eve, three months later.

The Ardennes operation was also one in which I came very close to being killed a number of times, but my luck held. And it carried on holding throughout the campaign in Germany, even though I was at one point presumed dead by my colleagues.

Perhaps I come from a lucky family; my sister Prue joined the WAAF, my stepbrother Mick the RASC and saw service in the Middle East. My brother Ian joined the Tank Regiment, while my other brother, Terry, chose the Navy. All of us survived the war.

In Normandy, on seeing comrades dying and being mutilated and blown to bits by artillery shells, men with whom I had shared a barrack room, men I had trained with, socialized with – to the extent that we had become a very close band of brothers-in-arms – there was only one way of ensuring a degree of sanity and not becoming a nervous wreck.

We had to accept, with total conviction, that each and every one

196

of us had a time to be born, a time to live and a time to die. When one of our close mates was killed we just had to believe that his time was up, and then to get on with the job for which we had been so rigorously trained. Our job was simply to fight an enemy who threatened our homeland, and, hopefully, to avenge the deaths of our comrades, by killing a few more of the enemy before our own time was up and it was our turn to die!

Although at that time I never thought this simple mind-saving philosophy through to its logical conclusion; if one accepts such a conviction, one also has to assume that our individual lives are in some way programmed at birth, and that, thereafter, we are being guided along a predetermined course.

During the post-war years many have read my amplified diary notes. Many have been curious to know how I felt as I lined my rifle sights on a 'target', knowing that as I fired I was probably killing another human being. My answer has always been that as a highly trained Airborne sniper fighting in a war where you killed – and could just as easily be killed – I could not afford to regard the enemy as human beings. To me they were not boys with mothers and homes where people loved them, they were simply 'targets' to be hit as accurately as possible and they were no different from targets on the rifle range, except that they had the ability to fire back. I took a pride in making sure that very few were in a position to do so after I had fired at them!

Appendix I

BOB AMBROSE'S ACCOUNT OF CAPTIVITY, FROM THE
TIME OF CAPTURE AT ESCOVILLE.

Prefacing Note by Denis Edwards.

It is now several years since Bob Ambrose gave me this written
account of his experiences after his capture in Normandy.
Personally, having witnessed the disaster that led to his capture at
Escoville, and from which I so narrowly escaped, I was glad to
know that he had survived and delighted to see him return.

Because of his leg wound, which at first prevented him from
taking part in the POW working parties, Bob was able at times to
keep a daily record of his experiences. At other times when he was
not able to keep such a record, he still managed sometimes to write
retrospective accounts of what had been going on. He was particularly attentive always to keep track of where he was as his captors
marched him and his fellow prisoners on a gruelling but rather
circuitous route, while attempting to avoid being captured, first by
the Russians, and then by the Allies.

His daily records were written as a diary, in the present tense,
while his summaries and general notes, written when opportunity
arose, were in a mixture of present and past tenses. Where appropriate, and for ease of reading, I have transposed most passages
into the past tense.

With publication of this account in prospect, a number of questions spring to mind, questions which I should have asked Bob

before. At this time, however, it is not possible to check any of the detail, as Bob is now too frail to recall the events clearly. There are a few personal details – concern for his family, names of family friends and so on, people who were obviously important to him. There are also the more mundane details and concerns which loom large to a POW – keeping warm, getting enough to eat and keeping body and clothing clean and presentable. As he faced up to his fate as a prisoner, he undoubtedly worried about how the war was going, how long his captivity would last and what his captors might do with him.

On the whole however, it appears that he was treated fairly humanely by his German captors. As a matter of historical interest, it would seem from his account that, with the possibility of being overrun by the Russians, the Russian POWs to whom Bob refers were also being treated more or less correctly. In the early stages of the war, of course, with Nazi expectations of an easy victory, literally millions of Russian prisoners were starved or worked to death.

Survivors from our Airlanding Brigade underwent a diversity of experiences, but as fas as I know only two of us among the other ranks managed to keep any sort of written record of what was happening at the time. Bob's account, already well known to me and to some other surviving members of the Regiment, certainly deserves to be more widely seen.

PRISONER OF WAR – 7 JUNE 1944 TO 12 APRIL 1945

by

EX-CORPORAL BOB AMBROSE
No. 22 Platoon, 'D' Company, 2nd Battalion Oxfordshire and Buckinghamshire Light Infantry Glider-borne Infantry of 6th Air Landing Brigade, 6th Airborne Division.

I was a member of the Coup de Main glider force due to land between the Caen Canal and River Orne in Normandy soon after midnight on 5/6 June, 1944. The first Allied unit to go into action.

Unfortunately our Horsa glider (No.4), which should have been the first to arrive by the Orne River bridge, was pulled off course by its tug plane and landed near a bridge over the River Dives some eight miles to the east of our intended target. Soon after landing we ran into enemy units. Private Hedges was killed and Privates John Lathbury and Alf Whitford were captured (See Notes). Captain Priday (Company Second in Command) and Lieutenant Hooper (Platoon Commander) realized that we had landed in the wrong place and decided that we must rejoin our Company as soon as possible.

The area between where we landed and the Caen Canal/Orne River had been flooded by the Germans as an anti-invasion measure. This meant that as we were on the far side of the flooded Dives valley it was necessary to travel westwards through flooded and enemy occupied territory. It took us almost twenty-four hours before we were able to rejoin our Battalion at Ranville. *[Eddie*

Edwards notes that eight miles is a very long way for a body of men in uniform to travel through heavily defended enemy territory, especially when the enemy is alert to the fact that an invasion is in progress. It was a minor miracle that the platoon arrived at Hérouvillette at all.]

Having arrived at our objective and made our rendezvous with the Battalion, on 7 June we had the task of capturing the villages of Hérouvillette and Escoville. We took the first against modest defences and were surprised that we were then able to enter Escoville with little opposition. We had been told that it was heavily defended.

My Platoon was deployed along the road on the eastern outskirts of the village. About an hour after we arrived the Germans launched a massive counter-attack in which the Battalion suffered heavy casualties and became divided as the enemy thrust through the centre of the village. Our Platoon was overrun by enemy heavy tanks. We had no weapons that could stop them. Platoon Sergeant Barwick and several others were killed and eight survivors, myself among them, were taken prisoner. I had been hit in the leg by a sniper's bullet. Private Les Chamberlain was also wounded. Our Platoon Medical Orderly (Private Allwood) dressed my wound.

June/July, 1944 – Summary

I was separated from the others and taken to a hospital at Bagnolles where I remained until 12 June and was then transferred to a POW Hospital at Rennes where I remained until 24 July when I was discharged and entered Stalag 223 at Rennes.

25 July.   We were taken to Stalag 133 at Chartres, where we stayed until 5 August.

August, 1944

5 August.   We were loaded onto a train to begin a long journey to Stalag X11A (Limburg).

6–10 August.   These were nightmare days that I shall never

forget. We were transported in rail-trucks which, at this time of the year, were like furnaces. Although only one lad passed out in our wagon, in some of them there were many taken ill. There was no great shortage of food but water was in short supply. On 7 August we got nothing to drink until 2200 hours. French Red Cross supplied us with half a loaf of bread and a small cup of milk on 8 August. Stalag X11A (Limburg) proved to be only a transit camp. We arrived at 1600 hours on 10 August. It was such a relief to get out of those enclosed cattle trucks and breathe some fresh air. I also managed to get a wash – my first since 27 July! Accommodation was extremely poor. I felt ill following the long journey and was up through much of the night visiting the toilet.

11 August.　I met Private John Lathbury from our platoon. He had been taken prisoner soon after we landed by the River Dives, and so had been spared the experience of Escoville. Not knowing what had happened to him, I was very glad to find that he had survived. He told me that Alf Whitford was wounded in the leg and also taken prisoner but did not know where he had gone.

12 August.　I was deloused and had my clothes fumigated. I was also able to have a hot shower but had no towel so I dried by standing near a radiator. I was also formally registered as a Prisoner of War and given the Number 82932. Conditions were very bad and sleep almost impossible. It was very difficult to keep clean. I was told that I would be there for up to twenty-eight days. I just hoped to hell that it would not be that long. I was given a card to send home but couldn't let anyone know my address because I had not been allocated to a permanent camp.

In this temporary camp food was far from good. One-tenth of a loaf and some poor quality soup in the morning, and similar for lunch and tea. I had managed to keep back some of my Red Cross food but it wouldn't last long. Because of the heat I slept in the open air that first night.

13 August.	Another batch of prisoners arrived from another camp. Den Oakman from my home town was among them. It was a pleasant surprise. He said he had spent four days in solitary confinement. I was given a Canadian Red Cross parcel – one parcel to be shared between three men.
14/19 August.	Two more batches of prisoners arrived. The camp was getting very crowded.
20 August.	We were issued with American Red Cross parcels. One per man.
21 August.	Yet another batch of prisoners arrived. There was hardly room to stand.
22 August.	Mother's birthday. I felt so sorry that I couldn't be with her. Spent day as usual, with nothing to do.
23 August.	400 British and 1,000 Americans left for another camp. Lathbury was among them. I hope that it will soon be my turn.
24 August.	Usual routine. A rumour is going around that Romania is out of the war.
25 August.	1,000 British leave tomorrow. Thank God, Den Oakman and I will be going with them!
26 August.	At 1600 hrs we left that terrible camp on another train (fifty to each truck) to be transported to another camp.
27/29 August.	Three days spent travelling. Food and water fair. We expected to arrive at our destination the following morning.
30 August.	Arrived Stalag VIIIB (Teschen) in the morning. Due to my wounded leg I was confined to camp

and not treated too badly. We received Red Cross parcels on Tuesdays and Fridays (each shared between two men). I was surprised to find that I was in Czechoslovakia. I was certainly seeing Europe! Very good reception from existing prisoners. Some had been held for over four years but were looking far fitter than I had expected.

We were given food, coffee and tea. Later I was again deloused and allowed a hot shower – and I was given a towel! I was badly in need of a haircut and shave but since everyone was in the same position I guessed it would be some while before I could get a trim. Issued with Canadian Red Cross parcel (one between two) and twenty-five cigarettes per man. Sent mother a postcard now that I had a permanent address.

31 August. Didn't manage to get a haircut and shave, but was issued with a new shirt, pants and socks. It is good to get into some fresh clothes. As my trousers were in poor condition (with bullet hole, etc) I was given a reasonable pair by one of the prisoners who had been here a long time and knew his way around the camp!

September, 1944

1 September. Got a trim and shave. Greatly appreciated as I am feeling really scruffy. Washed my battle-dress blouse and a Russian repaired my torn trousers. Now I felt more like my old self. Good to be able to get a wash when you wanted one.

2 September. Given Red Cross parcel (one between two). Don Oakman and I mucked in together and, coming from the same town, we had plenty to talk about and got along fine. Wrote letter to mother. Letters and cards to family are so

204

	important when in enemy hands and far from home.
3 September.	Five years ago today war was declared. I didn't think that it could last much longer. News was good. With luck I could be back in "Blighty" for Christmas.
4/10 September.	Getting settled into the camp routine. Managed to get some more kit. I now had two suits of battledress, an overcoat, two shirts, two pairs of socks, two pants and also a toothbrush and razor. (I got the razor from a Russian in exchange for a bar of soap.) Sent postcard to mum. Den Oakman left for a Kommando on 4th I shall miss him.
11/30 September.	Same old routine day after day. Life was very monotonous but it could have been worse. Red Cross parcels cut down to half per week but we were told that they would resume with one each from 3 October. Sent letters and postcards to mother and other relatives.
30th September.	Wrote to mother again. May seem trivial but keeping in touch with home is really important.

October, 1944

1 October.	Sunday once again. It rained all day.
2 October.	Rained throughout the day. Sent postcard to Gladys Royffe. Issued with fifty French cigarettes.
3 October.	Rain ceased today thank goodness. They kept their promise and Red Cross parcels were now being issued on a weekly basis.
4 October.	I was issued with a vest, pair of pants and a pair of socks. My kit was gradually mounting up. I needed to find something to keep it in.
5 October.	Life continued as usual. I had now spent seventeen weeks in captivity. It seemed more like a lifetime. God knows what it must have been

205

like for those who had been cooped up for over four years. Perhaps they got used to it. I certainly had not.

6 October.	My leg wound was dressed again. It had not made much progress towards healing, but at least it kept me out of the coal mines!
7 October.	Red Cross parcel issued again. I now smoked very little so that I could use mine to do some swapping.
8 October.	I got a case with thirty cigarettes (twenty French and ten British Players). Swapped ten of them with a Russian in exchange for a ring. Wrote letters to mother and brother Jack and sent a postcard to Mr. & Mrs Brooks.
9 October.	Had my leg wound dressed again and paid a visit to the German Doctor for grading. This was the third time but so far no grading as my wound had not yet healed.
10 October to 7 November.	Life continues with the usual boring daily routine.

November, 1944

8 November.	I was pronounced fit by the German Doctor. This would cause a change in my lifestyle.
11 November.	Allocated to Working Party 902 and sent down the coal mines. Red Cross parcels had dried up and rations were poor.
19 November.	Received my first letter from home. It was certainly good to know that the family were all well. We worked down the coal mine in eight-hour shifts. We got very dirty but had no soap with which to wash.

December, 1944

7/12 December.	I had a very sore throat and was found to have diphtheria.

14 December.	I was placed in an Isolation Hospital at Kurnow (Poland) where I spent Christmas, remaining in the hospital until 18 January, 1945.

January, 1945 – summary

Having been out of hospital for only a day or two, I learned that because of the approaching Russians we had to be moved. We arrived at Stalag V111A (Gorlitz-Moyes) on Sunday, 21 January. We remained there until 10 February when we began a long march into the unknown.

February, 1945

10 February.	Brother Jack's birthday – eighteen today. He would probably be called up. I just hoped he would never become a prisoner. Issued with two days' rations (half a loaf bread and half a tin of Jerry meat). Parade at 0930 hrs but didn't move till 1230. Bitterly cold and darkness fell before we arrived at our resting place – an old barn. There were 3,000 British and 1,000 Russian prisoners. We were told before we left that anyone being difficult or trying to escape would be instantly shot. This announcement was greeted with cheers from all of us. I was given just one blanket to keep out the bitter cold.
11 February.	Hit the trail again at 0900, but only had to march twelve km today. During the night the lads stole eighty tins of meat from the guards. We also got a few chickens from the farm and milked some cows. The guards were furious and threatened reprisals.
12 February.	We marched twenty-two km and put up in

207

	large German barracks. Got a good issue of soup and coffee. This was my first drink in two days. Issued with two days' rations (half a loaf of bread, two small cheeses and half a tin of meat). The weather still very cold.
13 February.	My mate fell sick and I stayed with him so have now joined the 'slow column'. The Russians were getting nearer. Leignity has apparently been taken by them. Stay at Bautyen overnight but on the move again in the morning. Given some soup.
14 February.	(St. Valentine's Day). Got coffee at 0800 and although we were supposed to move off early we remained until 1030. We marched about twenty km to Koenigswartha. It was a nice surprise to find that there were beds for everyone. We got tea and, for a change, some good quality soup. Everyone was feeling much better. Morale was up 100% but I guessed it would not be long before we were on the move again.
15 February.	Got a good night's rest. Coffee at 0800, porridge at 1200 and soup at 1630. Also got one-sixth of a loaf, some margarine and five cigarettes per man. There were numerous air-raid alerts during the night. Generally the news was very good. Things were not going well for the Germans. Expecting to move again on Monday.

(I kept no further detailed notes of events, as writing while on the move proved too difficult, but I kept a log of our travels during the long march. This is my record of that march. Note that I cannot vouch for spelling of place names in all cases).

Feb 10th	Görlitz–Muyes–Reichenbach	20 km
Feb 11th	Reichenbach–Weigenberg	12 km
Feb 12th	Weigenberg – Bautzen	22 km

Feb 13th	Remained at Bautzen	
Feb 14th	Bautzen–Koenigswartha	20 km
Feb 15th/17th	At Koenigswartha	
Feb 18th	Koenigswartha–Kamenz	16 km
Feb 19th	Kamenz–Koenigsbruck	15 km
Feb 20th	Koenigsbruck–Radeberg	16 km
Feb 21st	Remained at Radeberg	
Feb 22nd	Radeberg–Meissen	20 km
Feb 23rd	Remained at Meissen	
Feb 24th	Meissen–Lommatzch (Cross River Elbe)	17 km
Feb 25th	Lommatzch–Dobeln	20 km
Feb 26th	Dobeln–Leisnig	20 km
Feb 27th	Remained at Leisnig	
Feb 28th	Leisnig–Bad Lausick	25 km
Mar 1st	Bad Lausick–Deutzen	19 km
Mar 2nd	Deutzen–Zeitz	31 km
Mar 3rd	Zeitz–Koenigshofen	18 km
Mar 4th	Remained at Koenigshofen	
Mar 5th	Koenigshofen–Steudnitz	20 km
Mar 6th	Steudnitz–Mellingun	30 km
Mar 7th	Mellingun–Azmansdorf	30 km
Mar 8th	Azmansdorf–Gotha	30 km
Mar 9th	Gotha–Strombedt	30 km
Mar 10th	Strombedt–Silgerhausen	32 km
Mar 11th	Silgerhausen–Bretenbach	14 km
Mar 12th/13th	Remained at Bretenbach	
Mar 14th	Bretenbach–Dudestadt	15 km
Mar 15th/Apr 2nd	Remained at Dudestadt	
Apr 3rd	Duderstadt–Osterhagen	25 km
Apr 4th	Osterhagen–Appenrude	22 km
Apr 5th	Appenrude–Hasselfelde	20 km
Apr 6th/7th	Remained at Hasselfelde	
Apr 8th	Hasselfelde–Wesserhausen	24 km
Apr 9th/10th	Remained at Wesserhausen	
Apr 11th	Wesserhausen–Ditfurt	10 km
	Total	**593 km**

Apr 12th	Liberated at Ditfurt by the Yanks
Apr 13th/16th	Remained at Ditfurt
Apr 17th	Ditfurt–Hildesheim (Airfield)
Apr 17th/23rd	Remained at Airfield
Apr 23rd	Left Hildesheim 1400 hrs and after a stop at Brussels we arrived back in good old 'Blighty', Dunsfold (Surrey), about 2030 hrs
Apr 24th	Got new rig-out, ration cards and cash and proceeded home on forty-two days' leave

So ended my long march and my captivity. There were some very frightening and dangerous times during my visit to continental Europe, but I was luckier than many and I am grateful to have survived the experience.

*To convert kilometres to miles, divide by eight and multiply by five – e.g. five miles is the same as eight kilometres. The total of 593 kilometres is equal to 370 miles.

Appendix II

THE SIX HORSA GLIDERS USED TO ATTACK AND CAPTURE THE BÉNOUVILLE BRIDGES.

A LIST OF THE 180 PERSONNEL OF THE COUP DE MAIN FORCE THAT CAPTURED THE BRIDGES OVER THE CAEN CANAL AND THE RIVER ORNE IN NORMANDY JUST AFTER MIDNIGHT JUNE 5/6, 1944.

Gliders were flown by 12 members of the Glider Pilot Regiment, who were trained to fight alongside the infantry after landing. Gliderborne infantry were supplied by the 2nd Battalion Oxfordshire and Buckinghamshire Light Infantry, from 6th Airlanding Brigade of the 6th Airborne Division. This comprised 4 platoons from 'D' Company and 2 platoons from 'B' Company, supported by a detachment of 30 men from the 2nd platoon, 249 Field Company, Royal Engineers (Airborne), 3 members of the Royal Army Medical Corps and a Liaison Officer from the 7th Battalion, the Parachute Regiment.

Glider Number 1 – Target: The Caen Canal Bridge

Rank	Name	Serving in ...	Coy/Platoon	Serving as ...
S/Sgt	Wallwork	Glider Pilot Rgmt		Horsa Pilot
S/Sgt	Ainsworth	Glider Pilot Rgmt		Horsa Co-Pilot
W/Cdr	Duder	RAF		Tug Pilot
Lt.	Brotheridge	2nd Oxf.Bucks	D 25	Platoon Cdr
Sgt	Ollis	2nd Oxf.Bucks	D 25	
Cpl	Caine	2nd Oxf.Bucks	D 25	
Cpl	Webb	2nd Oxf.Bucks	D 25	
Cpl	Bailey	2nd Oxf.Bucks	D 25	
L/C	Packwood	2nd Oxf.Bucks	D 25	
L/C	Minns	2nd Oxf.Bucks	D 25	
Pte	Baalam	2nd Oxf.Bucks	D 25	
Pte	Bates	2nd Oxf.Bucks	D 25	
Pte	Bourlet	2nd Oxf.Bucks	D 25	
Pte	Chamberlain	2nd Oxf.Bucks	D 25	
Pte	Edwards	2nd Oxf.Bucks	D 25	
Pte	Gray	2nd Oxf.Bucks	D 25	
Pte	O'Donnell	2nd Oxf.Bucks	D 25	
Pte	Parr	2nd Oxf.Bucks	D 25	
Pte	Tilbury	2nd Oxf.Bucks	D 25	
Pte	Watson	2nd Oxf.Bucks	D 25	
Pte	White	2nd Oxf.Bucks	D 25	
Pte	Windsor	2nd Oxf.Bucks	D 25	
Pte	Jackson 08	2nd Oxf.Bucks	D 25	
Major	Howard	2nd Oxf.Bucks	Officer Commanding Coup de Main Force	
Cpl	Tappenden	2nd Oxf.Bucks	Wireless Operator, Coy. HQ	
Cpl	Watson	Royal Engineers		
Spr	Danson	Royal Engineers		
Spr	Ramsey	Royal Engineers		
Spr	Wheeler	Royal Engineers		
Spr	Yates	Royal Engineers		

Glider Number 1, together with gliders 2 and 3, landed very close to its target, the Caen canal bridge, now named Pegasus Bridge. All three gliders landed within a few minutes of each other.

Glider Number 2 – Target: The Caen Canal Bridge.

Rank	Name	Serving in . . .	Coy/Platoon	Serving as . . .
S/Sgt	Boland	Glider Pilot Rgmt		Horsa Pilot
S/Sgt	Hobbs	Glider Pilot Rgmt		Horsa Co-Pilot
WO	Berry	RAF		Tug Pilot
Lt.	Wood	2nd Oxf.Bucks	D 24	Platoon Cdr
Sgt	Leather	2nd Oxf.Bucks	D 24	
Cpl	Godbold	2nd Oxf.Bucks	D 24	
Cpl	Cowperthwaite	2nd Oxf.Bucks	D 24	
Cpl	Ilsley	2nd Oxf.Bucks	D 24	
L/C	Roberts	2nd Oxf.Bucks	D 24	
L/C	Drew	2nd Oxf.Bucks	D 24	
Pte	Chatfield	2nd Oxf.Bucks	D 24	
Pte	Lewis	2nd Oxf.Bucks	D 24	
Pte	Cheesley	2nd Oxf.Bucks	D 24	
Pte	Waters	2nd Oxf.Bucks	D 24	
Pte	Clarke 33	2nd Oxf.Bucks	D 24	
Pte	Musty	2nd Oxf.Bucks	D 24	
Pte	Dancey	2nd Oxf.Bucks	D 24	
Pte	Harman	2nd Oxf.Bucks	D 24	
Pte	Warmington	2nd Oxf.Bucks	D 24	
Pte	Leonard	2nd Oxf.Bucks	D 24	
Pte	Weaver	2nd Oxf.Bucks	D 24	
Pte	Radford	2nd Oxf.Bucks	D 24	
Pte	Clark 48	2nd Oxf.Bucks	D 24	
Pte	Pepperall	2nd Oxf.Bucks	D 24	
Pte	Malpas	2nd Oxf.Bucks	D 24	
L/C	Harris	RAMC		Medic
A/Capt	Neilson	Royal Engineers		
Spr	Conley	Royal Engineers		
Spr	Lockhart	Royal Engineers		
Spr	Shorey	Royal Engineers		
Spr	Haslett	Royal Engineers		

Glider Number 2, together with gliders 1 and 3, landed very close to its target, the Caen canal bridge, now named Pegasus Bridge. All three gliders landed within a few minutes of each other.

Glider Number 3 – Target: The Caen Canal Bridge

Rank	Name	Serving in . . .	Coy/Platoon	Serving as . . .
S/Sgt	Barkway	Glider Pilot Rgmt		Horsa Pilot
S/Sgt	Boyle	Glider Pilot Rgmt		Horsa Co-Pilot
WO	Herman	RAF		Tug Pilot
Lt.	Smith	2nd Oxf.Bucks	B 14	Platoon Cdr
Sgt	Harrison	2nd Oxf.Bucks	B 14	
Cpl	Higgs	2nd Oxf.Bucks	B 14	
Cpl	Evans	2nd Oxf.Bucks	B 14	
Cpl	Aris	2nd Oxf.Bucks	B 14	
L/C	Madge	2nd Oxf.Bucks	B 14	
L/C	Cohen	2nd Oxf.Bucks	B 14	
L/C	Greenhalgh	2nd Oxf.Bucks	B 14	
Pte	Wilson	2nd Oxf.Bucks	B 14	
Pte	Hook	2nd Oxf.Bucks	B 14	
Pte	Stewart	2nd Oxf.Bucks	B 14	
Pte	Keane	2nd Oxf.Bucks	B 14	
Pte	Noble	2nd Oxf.Bucks	B 14	
Pte	Crocker	2nd Oxf.Bucks	B 14	
Pte	Basham	2nd Oxf.Bucks	B 14	
Pte	Watts	2nd Oxf.Bucks	B 14	
Pte	Anton	2nd Oxf.Bucks	B 14	
Pte	Tibbs	2nd Oxf.Bucks	B 14	
Pte	Slade	2nd Oxf.Bucks	B 14	
Pte	Burns	2nd Oxf.Bucks	B 14	
Pte	Turner	2nd Oxf.Bucks	B 14	
Pte	Golden	2nd Oxf.Bucks	B 14	
Major	Jacob-Vaughan	RAMC		Medical Officer
L/C	Waring	Royal Engineers		
Spr	Clarke	Royal Engineers		
Spr	Fleming	Royal Engineers		
Spr	Green	Royal Engineers		
Spr	Preece	Royal Engineers		

Glider Number 4 – Target: The Orne River Bridge.

Rank	Name	Serving in ...	Coy/Platoon	Serving as ...
S/Sgt	Lawrence	Glider Pilot Rgmt		Horsa Pilot
S//Sgt	Shorter	Glider Pilot Rgmt		Horsa Co-Pilot
F/O	Clapperton	RAF		Tug Pilot
Lt	Hooper	2nd Oxf. Bucks	D 22	Platoon Cdr
Sgt	Barwick	2nd Oxf.Bucks	D 22	
Cpl	Goodsir	2nd Oxf.Bucks	D 22	
Cpl	Bateman	2nd Oxf.Bucks	D 22	
L/Sgt	Rayner	2nd Oxf.Bucks	D 22	
Cpl	Ambrose	2nd Oxf.Bucks	D 22	
Cpl	Hunt	2nd Oxf.Bucks	D 22	
Pte	Allwood	2nd Oxf.Bucks	D 22	
Pte	Wilson	2nd Oxf.Bucks	D 22	
Pte	Hedges	2nd Oxf.Bucks	D 22	
Pte	Everett	2nd Oxf.Bucks	D 22	
Pte	St. Clair	2nd Oxf.Bucks	D 22	
Pte	Waite	2nd Oxf.Bucks	D 22	
Pte	Clive.	2nd Oxf.Bucks	D 22	
Pte	Timms	2nd Oxf.Bucks	D 22	
Pte	Whitford	2nd Oxf.Bucks	D 22	
Pte	Johnson	2nd Oxf.Bucks	D 22	
Pte	Lathbury	2nd Oxf.Bucks	D 22	
Pte	Hammond	2nd Oxf.Bucks	D 22	
Pte	Gardner 08	2nd Oxf.Bucks	D 22	
Pte	Jeffrey	2nd Oxf.Bucks	D HQ	
Capt	Priday	2nd Oxf.Bucks	D HQ	Coy. 2nd in Command
L/C	Lambley	2nd Oxf.Bucks	D 22	Coy. Clerk
L/Sgt	Brown	Royal Engineers		
Spr	Deighton	Royal Engineers		
Spr	Guest	Royal Engineers		
Spr	Paget	Royal Engineers		
Spr	Roberts	Royal Engineers		

Glider Number 4 was scheduled to land first, but was pulled off course by its tug aircraft and landed by a bridge over the River Dives some 8 miles to the east. Although losing some men in skirmishes along the way, the crew and airborne infantry and engineers successfully fought their way through the flooded Dives valley and back to Hérouvillette, to rendezvous with the Regiment on 7 June.

Glider Number 5 – Target: The Orne River Bridge.

Rank	Name	Serving in ...	Coy/Platoon	Serving as ...
S/Sgt	Pearson	Glider Pilot Rgmt		Horsa Pilot
S/Sgt	Guthrie	Glider Pilot Rgmt		Horsa Co-Pilot
WO	Bain	RAF		Tug Pilot
Lt	Sweeney	2nd Oxf.Bucks	D 23	Platoon Cdr
Sgt	Gooch	2nd Oxf.Bucks	D 23	
Cpl	Murton	2nd Oxf.Bucks	D 23	
Cpl	Howard	2nd Oxf.Bucks	D 23	
Cpl	Jennings	2nd Oxf.Bucks	D 23	
L/C	Porter	2nd Oxf.Bucks	D 23	
Cpl	Stacey	2nd Oxf.Bucks	D 23	
Pte	Allen	2nd Oxf.Bucks	D 23	
Pte	Bowden	2nd Oxf.Bucks	D 23	
Pte	Buller	2nd Oxf.Bucks	D 23	
Pte	Bright	2nd Oxf.Bucks	D 23	
Pte	Bleach	2nd Oxf.Bucks	D 23	
Pte	Clark 46	2nd Oxf.Bucks	D 23	
Pte	Galbraith	2nd Oxf.Bucks	D 23	
Pte	Jackson 59	2nd Oxf.Bucks	D 23	
Pte	Roach	2nd Oxf.Bucks	D 23	
Pte	Roberts 94	2nd Oxf.Bucks	D 23	
Pte	Read	2nd Oxf.Bucks	D 23	
Pte	Tibbett	2nd Oxf.Bucks	D 23	
Pte	Wixon	2nd Oxf.Bucks	D 23	
Pte	Wood	2nd Oxf.Bucks	D 23	
Pte	Willcocks	2nd Oxf.Bucks	D 23	
Lt	Macdonald	7th Para		Liaison Officer
Cpl	Straw	Royal Engineers		
Spr	Bradford	Royal Engineers		
Spr	Carter	Royal Engineers		
Spr	Field	Royal Engineers		
Spr	Wilkinson	Royal Engineers		

Glider Number 5 landed in a field adjacent to the Orne River Bridge, not exactly where planned but very well positioned for the job that was to be done.

Glider Number 6 – Target, the Orne River Bridge.

Rank	Name	Serving in ...	Coy/Platoon	Serving as ...
S/Sgt	Howard	Glider Pilot Rgmt		Horsa Pilot
S/Sgt	Baacke	Glider Pilot Rgmt		Horsa Co-pilot
F/O	Archibald	RAF		Tug Pilot
Lt	Fox	2nd Oxf.Bucks	B 27	Platoon Cdr
Sgt	Thornton	2nd Oxf.Bucks	B 27	
Cpl	Lally	2nd Oxf.Bucks	B 27	
Cpl	Burns	2nd Oxf.Bucks	B 27	
Cpl	Reynolds	2nd Oxf.Bucks	B 27	
L/C	Loveday	2nd Oxf.Bucks	B 27	
Pte	Collett	2nd Oxf.Bucks	B 27	
Pte	Hubbert	2nd Oxf.Bucks	B 27	
Pte	Clare	2nd Oxf.Bucks	B 27	
Pte	Peverill	2nd Oxf.Bucks	B 27	
Pte	Pope	2nd Oxf.Bucks	B 27	
Pte	Whitehouse	2nd Oxf.Bucks	B 27	
Pte	Whitbread	2nd Oxf.Bucks	B 27	
Pte	Lawton	2nd Oxf.Bucks	B 27	
Pte	Rudge	2nd Oxf.Bucks	B 27	
Pte	O'Shaughnessy	2nd Oxf.Bucks	B 27	
Pte	Annetts	2nd Oxf.Bucks	B 27	
Pte	Summersby	2nd Oxf.Bucks	B 27	
Pte	Woods	2nd Oxf.Bucks	B 27	
Pte	Wyatt	2nd Oxf.Bucks	B 27	
Pte	Ward	2nd Oxf.Bucks	B 27	
Pte	Storr	2nd Oxf.Bucks	B 27	
L/C	Lawson	RAMC		Medic
WS Lt	Bence	Royal Engineers		
Spr	Burns	Royal Engineers		
Spr	C.W.Larkin	Royal Engineers		
Spr	C.H.Larkin	Royal Engineers		
Spr	Maxted	Royal Engineers		

Glider Number 6 landed on schedule, close to the river bridge.

Appendix III

HARRY CLARK'S ACCOUNT OF THE AIRBORNE
LANDING AT HAMMINKELN AND SOME OF THE
SUBSEQUENT EVENTS.

Prefacing Note by Denis Edwards

There is a period of about thirty-six hours in my wartime experiences about which I have no recollection, as I have recounted in my record of the battle for the Hamminkeln railway station and neighbouring roads and bridges.

Harry Clark was in the same platoon as I was, No 25, and therefore we were transported to Hamminkeln in the same glider. He has recently supplied me with an account of what went on during those few hours that I was concussed, unconscious and presumed dead. While I was wandering aimlessly around the Rhine valley countryside oblivious to the fact that a war was taking place around me. Clark was keeping very busy.

This is how Harry W. Clark remembers that fraught and frightening experience. I have added notes in italics to relate the recorded events to my own recollections.

OPERATION 'VARSITY', MARCH 1945
BY
EX. PTE. 'NOBBY' CLARK
HARRY W. CLARK
No. 25 Platoon, 'D' Company
2nd Battalion Oxfordshire and Buckinghamshire Light Infantry
6th Airlanding Brigade of the 6th Airborne Division
Platoon Commander: Lt. DC Shaw. Platoon Sgt.: 'Bob' Ollis

Operation Varsity began on 24 March, 1945. On the way in to
Hamminkeln I was seated at the tail-end of our glider, when the
starboard wing tip and its aileron were shot away while we were
still up at around 1000 feet. Naturally, this gave Sgt. Stan Jarvis,
our young RAF Glider Pilot, and his RAF Co-Pilot, Sgt. Peter
Geddes, exceptionally difficult flying conditions. The tail section
was also shot away just as we came in to land close to a line of
trees bordering the Hamminkeln railway line.

Miraculously, during this nightmare landing, we were exceptionally fortunate in sustaining no casualties at all. Once on the
ground, the Platoon got out of the Horsa smartly and took up an
all-round defensive position.

The area at the time of landing was covered by a dense cloud of
smoke created partly by our 'softening up' artillery barrage and
partly by the smoke-screens drifting in from our ground forces
crossing the Rhine at this time. As we took up our positions, two
Horsa gliders appeared out of the cloud passing low overhead, and
within a few seconds there came a fearful noise as they crashed.
One of them hit the railway station and disintegrated. There were

no survivors. The second passed further over and crashed between the railway and the road.

[I also recall a glider coming in just above us. It was aflame from end to end and, while still some way above, men, without parachutes and with their clothing alight, were jumping from the stricken craft. Although they were individually not recognizable, we knew that they were our mates, men we knew well and with whom we had shared barrack rooms. It was a truly terrible sight]

A large enemy tank suddenly appeared out of the smoke some seventy-five yards to the rear of our position and was followed by a soldier on a motor cycle. They were heading for the nearby road bridge over the river. Later I learned that they were stopped and destroyed by a battalion of the Royal Ulster Rifles, also part of our Airlanding forces.

Within minutes of landing, No. 25 Platoon moved to the cover of several open-sided tall timber stores adjacent to the railway line and station. These covered areas contained high and neat square stacks of timber railway sleepers. Enemy tanks were in the immediate area and were actively seeking us out.

While we were within the cover of the stacked timbers a lone figure suddenly appeared, hands above his head and repeating over and over the word "Lightning". He was an American War Correspondent, clearly in a state of shock, and whose aircraft had been shot down forcing him to parachute to safety. While in flight he had been busily typing out his story on a portable typewriter that he had borrowed from a friend. Regardless of the carnage and mayhem all around us he was mainly concerned about how he would have to tell his friend that his typewriter had been lost! As he was unarmed we gave him a liberated German P38 pistol, and told him to stay in hiding among the stacks of timber until the fighting was over. *[As mentioned earlier, I have been informed that it was I who donated the weapon, although I had forgotten the fact. The P38 was the one I had carried through the Normandy and Ardennes campaign.]*

The Platoon moved off in a westerly direction towards our 'D' Company rendezvous point. At this stage the Company was in reserve with no objectives to capture. Arriving at the rendezvous point we were given the grim news that many of the Company had

220

become casualties during the actual landing. Our Platoon was in fact one of the very few to be still completely intact.

Unfortunately, because of damage to radios during the rough landings we had no radio contact with our Battalion HQ, and I was handed a written message from our Company Commander Major Tillett. I was instructed to deliver it with all haste to our Battalion Commander, Lt. Col. Darrell-Brown, at his HQ at Hamminkeln railway station.

I began my return journey back towards the station by crossing the Glider Landing Zone, which was by now mainly clear of the smoke. With enemy snipers and tanks still around the area I dodged from one wrecked Horsa glider to another, while many of them were still burning.

I edged carefully towards my destination. The many dead, injured and seriously wounded in and around the gliders were a horrific sight. At the front of one burning aircraft was its glider pilot, still wearing his headphones, arms outstretched and forming the shape of a crucifix in the flames. Fifty-three years later that sight still haunts me.

There were also a number of bodies of paratroops, all close together and covered by white parachutes. They were Americans from the 17th U.S. Airborne Division who should have landed to our south but had been dropped into our area.

[I recall that several groups of lost American Paratroops were in the area at around that time and I remember directing some of them towards their own Divisional area.]

Arriving at Hamminkeln railway station I had no difficulty in locating our Battalion Commander. He was riding towards me on one of our small and flimsy folding Airborne pedal cycles. I passed my written message to him, which he read swiftly, and then told me that he had been in contact with 'D' Company. It seemed that my highly dangerous journey had probably been unnecessary!

[Major Tillett, – or Colonel Tillett as he became – has confirmed that communication had been established, so 'Nobby's' journey was in fact wasted. Lt. Col. Mark Darrell-Brown who had skilfully and successfully commanded our Battalion almost from the commencement of the Normandy campaign, through the Ardennes and now into Germany, was a big and hefty man by any

221

standards. He must have appeared a strange sight on that very small cycle. Presumably he had been unable to extract his Jeep from the wreckage of his glider and had been obliged to take up cycling.]

I learned from our Battalion Commander that 'C' Company was under considerable pressure at the railway-bridge and it had been decided that 'D' Company should be sent to reinforce them. I asked him what the casualty situation was within our Battalion and he told me that about sixty-two percent had been killed, wounded or were missing. That left about 250 men to capture and hold all of our predetermined objectives, compared to our original force of around 650. Telling me to hurry and rejoin 'D' Company, he wished me good luck, and to my complete surprise, he shook my hand!

Following the railway track along its western side was the quickest, but not necessarily the safest, route back to the Company; but I could not face the prospect of re-crossing the landing zone and seeing all that carnage again. Apart from that consideration, exploding ammunition, shells and mortar bombs were creating a deadly danger around the burning gliders.

As I hurried towards 'D' Company's positions I could see a number of enemy tanks cruising around and setting fire to those gliders that were not yet burning. They faced little opposition since most of our anti-tank guns and mortars were destroyed during the landings, and presumably the 'Tempest' and 'Typhoon' tank-busters were still busy supporting the land-based forces crossing the Rhine.

Arriving at the Company, I found most of them grouped around a deep bomb crater. Cpl. "Bill" Bailey, a Normandy veteran, came over to tell me that an enemy sniper had just killed Denny White, one of my best mates. I was then told that another of my close friends, Don Fogaty, had been killed in one of the other Horsas that had crashed. Both were long-standing mates of mine. There was certainly not a lot of good news to be had on that fateful day.

Our new position on the eastern (enemy side) of the River Issel was very exposed to German forces who were now grouping along the partly-built autobahn which ran along our front and was about 150 yards away. To our right front, and about half a mile distant, was the village of Ringenberg. We were told that around that area was a large enemy force with numerous tanks.

During the afternoon of the 24th some of No. 25 Platoon, including myself, moved into a small house close to where the railway bridge crossed the River Issel. Several counter-attacks were launched against us during the fading hours of daylight. Although we received considerable support from our own heavy artillery, which was some miles away on the other side of the River Rhine, to our dismay some of their shells were exploding around our own positions!

Every time that this occurred we were forced to wade across the river and take shelter under the railway bridge, and then rush back to our defensive positions when the shelling eased up. Much of the enemy counter-fire at that time was from mortars and machine guns.

[It now seems likely that it was one of these badly-ranged Allied shells that put me out of action for around thirty-six hours.]

During the late evening I was ordered by our Platoon Commander to accompany L/Cpl "Swill" Balaam to go forward on a two-man 'Standing Patrol'. Firstly we were to carry out a 'Recce' of the area around the autobahn, and then to lie up close to the road to detect possible enemy movements. We were both veterans of the Coup de Main force at Pegasus Bridge in Normandy and so were all too well aware of the danger of the mission upon which we were now about to embark.

Fortunately the area was well covered by trees and bushes. Just before midnight we moved out into no-man's-land carrying only our small arms in order to avoid noise. We reached a point some twenty-five yards or so from the road and settled down behind a clump of bushes to listen and observe. Almost immediately we became aware of movement beyond the autobahn. The rattling of equipment and low-pitched voices warned us that an enemy group was on the move and coming our way.

Throwing caution to the wind, we hurried back to our Platoon, calling out the night's Password as we approached our defensive positions. We gave our information to Lt. Shaw immediately, but before he was able to act upon it, an attack was launched against one of our other Companies over to our right.

223

One of our defensive positions was overrun and several men were taken prisoner, but the enemy attack was repulsed and a counter-attack drove them off.

Shortly after dawn on 25 March enemy infantry were observed moving towards our area, supported by several tanks. Now with fully effective radio communication we were able to call for support, so that within a very short time our heavy artillery shells, now re-ranged, began exploding among the advancing enemy.

This was quickly followed by several rocket-firing Typhoon aircraft – in what the pilots called a 'cab-rank' formation – swooping in low, in line one behind another. They seemed to take no time at all to destroy all the tanks, an awesome demonstration of the decisive power of this very effective weapon.

From an upstairs window in our small house I saw the enemy force virtually annihilated as I watched. It was with some awe that I saw a lone enemy medic moving around his dead and wounded comrades. The courage and devotion to duty of this very brave man, under that hellish fire, held my attention for many minutes.

By the end of that day we were in sore need of a rest and we slept in some houses on the outskirts of Hamminkeln until the morning of 26 March.

During those two days of fighting, No. 25 Platoon suffered a number of casualties. Several were killed and some died later of wounds, but some of the wounded recovered and survived the War. Among these was our Platoon Commander Lt. Shaw, and Sergeant 'Bob' Ollis, who had also been injured in the crash-landing of glider No 1 at Pegasus Bridge in Normandy, but recovered and again took over as our Platoon Sergeant. Sniper Corporal Wally Parr, another Coup de Main veteran (also wounded in Normandy the previous summer and who had said, 'Don't worry lads, I'll be back,' as he was carried off on a stretcher) was also wounded again but recovered and later rejoined us.

Later on 26 March we began the long advance across northern Germany and ten days later we carried out an assault crossing of the River Weser. At 2000 hours on the evening of 5 April, 1945, I was hit by four bullets and lost my right hand.

Having taken part in the D-Day capture of Pegasus Bridge on the night of 5/6 June, 1944, and survived the Ardennes campaign, then fought my way across much of northern Germany, now, with victory within sight, my war and military service was ended.

Appendix IV

THE CHÂTEAU ST COME MYSTERY
(SPECULATION ABOUT A CURIOUS ASPECT OF THE
AUTHOR'S EXPERIENCES)

Prefacing note by Denis Edwards

I have received considerable assistance in preparing the manuscript for this book, notably from Sid Green, as acknowledged in the initial pages. While he was reading through my original Normandy Diary record, he commented on the matter of the unmarked, and apparently uninjured, dead bodies that I saw at Château St Come. He asked me how an enormous detonation at close range could leave men dead but unmarked, without even disturbing a fanned-out hand of playing cards, when lesser explosions visibly tore them to pieces in a grisly and horrible manner. I have no answer; we were told that this odd effect resulted from concussion after a massive detonation of shells close by. We all accepted this explanation, but more than half a century later it seems that there may be a case for seeking a more logical reason.

Anyone who saw the lifelike attitudes of some of the dead at St Come would be shocked that a man could die so suddenly that he literally had almost no time to blink. I stress *some* of the dead, because of course most of the corpses were not like that at all. The majority were gruesomely dismembered and mutilated as a result of the bombardment by the heavy artillery of both sides, and by the Allied naval guns.

I have asked Sid Green to express his thoughts in this Appendix, with whatever alternative rationale he can offer to explain the mystery. The words are his own, and his conclusions are not necessarily shared by me or by those of my colleagues who also saw this amazing phenomenon.

He has asked me for any supplementary recollections that I may have, but I have been unable to help, except to say that in September, 1993, I saw on Channel 4 television, a documentary called *The Liberators*. It concerned coloured American soldiers and their experiences in the European theatre of the Second World War. Channel 4 were kind enough later to send me a tape of the programme, in which a coloured American soldier recalled how three of his tank-crew colleagues were killed. He found them dead inside their tank. The tank had not been hit, and they were apparently uninjured and unmarked, very much like the strange corpses I saw at St Come. The following is what Sid Green has offered as an alternative possibility – speculation to be sure, but food for thought perhaps?

Eddie Edwards's account of the dead soldier at St Come, holding a hand of fanned-out playing cards will surely arouse the curiosity of many people. The official explanation was that these men died as a result of concussion, a massive detonation had killed them instantly, and it may be possible, even if difficult for ordinary folk to understand or accept, that this explanation is completely accurate.

Despite this possibility, it is unlikely that men would decide to play cards during a massive bombardment, or while two Germans were reloading their machine gun close by. These people must have been killed at different stages in the battle, and to that extent the shell-blast theory holds good. It is still very difficult, however, to accept that a massive shell blast could kill a man instantly, while leaving him unmarked and his playing cards undisturbed. There is another account of the same battle, in which is described a further case of playing cards being held in the hands of such corpses[1]. This case was not the single Scot in a shallow scrape, as observed by Eddie, but involved two Highlanders in a trench, both holding playing cards.

One must surely question how a massive shell-blast could achieve this effect, while lesser explosions evidently would rip a man apart and scatter the pieces over a wide area. There is circumstantial evidence to suggest, but not to prove beyond doubt, that some weapon other than conventional artillery caused these deaths. Nerve gases – and there are many different types – are reputed to act by paralysing the whole nervous system, perhaps not instantaneously, but incredibly quickly. To cite examples is difficult since fortunately, real-life authentic accounts of death from nerve gas are hard to find, because, as we all know, it has never been used in warfare, or has it?

The Allies had no nerve-gas technology during WWII, but were stockpiling the old WWI gasses – mustard gas and phosgene – against the eventuality that Germany would make a first-strike using gas. This fact, along with a reaffirmation of the official claim that none of the combatants in WWII tried to use gas, was released

[1] *Pegasus Bridge*, Stephen Ambrose, Allen and Unwin, 1984

officially in 1997, and reported in the *Independent* newspaper of 28 May that year.

As for German capability to wage gas warfare, who better to know what they produced than Albert Speer, Hitler's minister of production?

Much has been written about Speer, most recently *The Good Nazi*[2] by Dan van der Vat, who exposes the skilful way in which Speer disingenuously affected ignorance of Nazi crimes, and contrition, so avoiding the hangman's noose.

The interrogation of Speer at the end of WWII was a marathon affair, resulting in literally tons of archived evidence and notes, all enormously useful to the Allies. Much later, in prison, Speer wrote his own memoirs – published later as *Inside the Third Reich*[3] about which Dan van der Vat has the following comment:

"His draft memoirs, written in prison without access to archives, differed from them hardly at all, a testament to a memory which seems to have been of photographic quality in the short term, and capable of total recall (*except for certain sensitive subjects*)"[4].

In his memoirs Speer records the fact that Germany possessed a new and deadly gas called Tabun, against which no defence was possible. He states that production of this gas had for some time been running at no less than 1000 tons per month. His description of the materials used for its manufacture, methanol and cyanide, suggests that it was designed to get cyanide into the bloodstream through respiration or skin contact, certainly a recipe for a quick death.

However, Gitta Sereny's biography of Speer[5] draws also on material from his immediate post-war de-briefings, and interrogations before and during his trial. She notes that he testified that another nerve gas, Sarin, was also in production, and that he had personally halted the production of both Sarin and Tabun by diverting the component chemical production to other sectors of

---

[2] *The Good Nazi*, Dan van der, Vat, Weidenfeld and Nicolson, 1979
[3] *Inside the Third Reich*, Albert Speer, Weidenfeld & Nicolson, 1970
[4] Dan van der Vat's parentheses, Sid Green's italics.

the economy. He claimed not to have believed Hitler's avowal that the nerve gases would be used only against the Soviets on the Eastern Front, and so he decided to take an action that amounted to sabotage. A 'sensitive issue' no doubt, because in his memoirs Speer makes no mention of Hitler's readiness to use Tabun against the Soviets or anyone else; on the contrary, he says that Hitler was generally opposed to the use of gas. To lend even more weight to the selective memory process of which Dan van der Vat accuses him, Speer had evidently also forgotten all about Sarin by the time he wrote his memoirs.

Speer does record however that the existence of Tabun gas, and other secret weapons, was known to Robert Ley, head of the Labour Front, who begged Speer to persuade Hitler to allow the gas to be used. Speer says that this occurred in the autumn of 1944, but he is silent as to what was actually done and leaves the result of Ley's request unrecorded.

It is very likely that neither side knew what the other possessed in the way of gas technology – although it is now clear that Germany in fact had a decisive advantage. One way to find out would be to make a tentative and limited first use of the weapon, then to hold one's breath and wait to see how the other side would respond.

(A strange coincidence occurs at the time of writing these words. On the second day of November, 1998, I notice that in this day's issue of the *Guardian* newspaper Churchill's readiness to use mustard gas against Germany is reported, the fact being released to the public for the first time – after more than fifty years. He was, it is stated, quite upset that his desire to 'drench German cities in gas' was rejected by the War Cabinet.)

Speer notes that on 5 August, 1944, Winston Churchill called for a full report on Britain's capacity to wage gas warfare against Germany, although how he knew this is a mystery if the information was only released in 1998. It also needs to be said that with the war in its fourth year, the timing of Churchill's request seems curious. What could have prompted this interest in gas warfare just

---

[5] *Albert Speer: His Battle with Truth*, Gitta Sereny, Macmillan, 1995.

a few days after the battle around Bréville and Château St Come? Also documented in Speer's memoirs is the fact that late in 1944 Hitler demanded a mass production and distribution of gasmasks, appointing his personal physician, Karl Brandt, to oversee the project. Brandt told Speer that he believed that this was an insurance against a war with gas that was to be initiated by Germany, not by the Allies. Gasmasks were of no effect against nerve agents, as Speer knew very well, which may imply that Nazi intelligence knew roughly what the British might use in retaliation; perhaps that they had knowledge of Churchill's fulminations about the need to drench German cities with gas.

At that time the Normandy bridgehead was threatening to break open, unleashing an uncontrollable advance by the Western Allies on a second front. Nothing could have been more perilous for the Nazis, nothing more certain to put a premature end to the thousand year Reich. If ever there was a 'make or break' time, this was it. Hitler, on the point of losing the biggest gamble in history, a gamble that he had so nearly won, must have been desperate to try anything to turn the tide. His other actions were certainly no less desperate. Deprived of air power, Germany was throwing explosive at Britain, a ton at a time, with no precision at all, by means of the enormously expensive and elaborate V2 rocket. However effective this may have been at knocking down a few buildings in Greater London, it stood no chance at all of eliminating the Normandy bridgehead and was an extravagant and absurdly expensive gesture of extreme desperation. If reprisals could be avoided, Tabun and Sarin would be an infinitely safer, cheaper and more effective way of annihilating the second front.

Hitler was obviously far from being squeamish, and was never scrupulous about the Geneva Protocol on warfare unless it suited him to be so. With the prospect of winning the war fast disappearing, why would he not use this secret weapon? Churchill, it seems, would have used it given the chance – so why not Hitler?

If a tentative first use of nerve gas at St Come is in fact something like what actually happened, it raises further questions, two of which seem to demand some attempt at answers:

Firstly, why did the use of the gas stop there?

Secondly, why did the Allies steadfastly refuse to acknowledge

231

that it had been used by the enemy, or by any of the combatants?

As to the first of these questions, the Channel Four documentary with the account of the unmarked tank crew corpses may well indicate an example of such further use of nerve gas at roughly the same time. If so, then the probability is that there were yet more examples, perhaps unrecognized. There must exist the possibility that the Germans became alarmed that their victims at St Come, and maybe elsewhere, comprised Germans as well as British. In WWI it was often the case that gas attacks were uncontrollable and a shift in the wind could result in spectacular 'own goals'. It is possible that here too German gas killed friend and foe alike.

A more likely reason for a halt to gassing would be that its use by the Germans resulted in an immediate Allied threat to dump their stocks of mustard gas on German cities. They could deliver it by bomber aircraft on a massive scale, something the Germans could not hope to match. It is also most odd that many years ago, in prison and forbidden any access to outside sources, Speer wrote of Churchill's call for an enquiry into gas warfare, when officially the fact was released into the public domain only in 1998. German intelligence may have reported Churchill's reaction and subsequent intentions to the Nazi hierarchy soon after an experimental use of nerve gas by the Germans, and so caused plans to employ it on a wider scale to be abandoned.

Perhaps even the atomic bomb was used as a counter-threat, since the Germans were far behind in nuclear technology, even though Speer records in his memoirs that he, and Hitler too, understood very well the implications of the bomb. They might well have developed a German bomb were it not for the fact that the necessary technology depended upon "Jewish Physics", as Speer concedes.

The second question is more complex and a satisfactory answer is more difficult to find. Secrecy about gas may have been intended to avoid panic, but it may even have had a connection with the rivalry between the Allies themselves. Not only were the western partners in the alliance afraid of the Soviet steamroller, but the British and the Americans too were in competition for technological advantage when the war would be over. As an example, in the last weeks of the war the V2 rocket plans and documentation had been dumped in a mineshaft in what became the British sector of Germany. The mine was then dynamited by the Nazis. It has been alleged[6] that United States personnel posed as geologists to investigate the mineshaft where the secret papers were located. They crated up everything to do with the V2 and calmly drove a convoy of loaded lorries into the American sector so ensuring US postwar supremacy in rocketry and missile development.

The article in the *Independent* newspaper already referred to reports that the British retrieved a stockpile of Nazi nerve gases. Such gasses were manufactured for many years thereafter at Nancekuke, a site in Cornwall. The Nancekuke facilities were apparently hired out to, or used by the United States as late as 1964 to help them develop their own arsenal of gases, and so it would seem that Britain did indeed achieve an advantage in nerve gas technology immediately after the war. Interestingly, Sarin is still a major chemical warfare agent, apparently not yet obsolete.

The most difficult factor to ignore in any hypothesis about the matter must be the nature of Adolf Hitler himself. We know that as he saw victory slipping away from him, he became increasingly besotted by the idea of victory being achieved through 'wonder weapons'. A man who would stop at nothing, who had no regard for ethics, or conventions, who was driven simply by a ruthless desire to win and to dominate, would hardly hesitate to use a weapon that might give him a decisive advantage. If Churchill had been champing at the bit to use old WWI gas technology against the Germans, why would Hitler be any less enthusiastic when he held a possibly winning hand? And why did Churchill's demand for an appraisal of the case for gas warfare originate within a day or two of the battle at the Château St Come?

We may never know the answers to all these questions, but we may eventually learn more than we have been told so far.

6 Brian Johnson, *The Secret War*, Arrow Books 1979

NOTES

Chapter 3

1 The term 'coup de main' is rather ambiguous in the French of today and may have been so in 1944, but I have not been able to verify this. Nowadays, a 'coup de main' can be a blow struck with the hand – something like a punch or a slap, or it can mean 'a helping hand'. Our task force, therefore, can be thought of as the force that was to give a helping hand to the beach landings, or as one that would give the Germans an unwelcome and unexpected 'smack in the eye'. I don't suppose it matters too much, as both meanings seem to work quite well.

Chapter 4

1 Lieutenant Denholm Brotheridge is officially recognized as the first Allied casualty to be killed directly by enemy action on 'D' Day, although Lance Corporal Greenhalgh was the first casualty – drowned accidentally after being trapped in the flooded wreckage of Glider No. 3. He was later buried some miles away near Sword Beach, his death recorded in the official roll as having occurred on 7 June, 1944, but that is clearly an official error.

Den Brotheridge was cut down by machine-gun fire as he led the charge across the canal bridge. In one account of his death which I have heard, he died following a wounding by a grenade fragment. However, Major Jacob-Vaughan, has been able to give first-hand evidence. 'Doc' Jacob-Vaughan volunteered to fly in with us as our MO, despite the paratroopers' distrust of gliders, which he shared. Doc set up a medical post about halfway between the two bridges, soon after the gliders landed. Brotheridge, mortally wounded, was brought to him and 'Doc' remembers very clearly that he had a bullet hole through the neck.

Den is buried in Ranville churchyard rather than in the adjacent war cemetery. Ranville war cemetery is the resting place for the majority of our Airborne casualties killed in action in those the first few days, as well as for over a thousand others of numerous regiments who died in the area during the three months that the Germans managed to contain our bridgehead.

2 After the War I heard that one of the Paras on board had, by some miracle, escaped that dreadful crash. Although seriously injured, he was somehow found and helped by French locals actually within the German-controlled outskirts of Caen. They looked after him and concealed him from the Germans until Caen was liberated some weeks later.

3 I did not witness the attack myself, as I was busy at Le Port, but I recently received a letter from Captain N.R.K. 'Jock' Neilson who was in charge of the thirty Royal Engineers. He recalls how he decided to check that the impact of the bomb had not damaged the bridge mechanism, and so raised and lowered it a couple of times, to the ironic pleas from our lads begging not to be left stranded.

4 In 1995 I revisited Le Port and at last I could see quite readily why we had not been fired upon. The church tower had been replaced of course, and it was evident that a sniper in the tower would not have been able to see us, given the positions we were in at the time, and the route of our comings and goings between the field and the churchyard. At the time, naturally enough, we didn't have the freedom of movement to establish the sniper's line of sight, knowing only that he was uncomfortably close to us and very dangerous.

5 In his autobiography *Caught in the Act*, published by Hutchinson in 1986, Richard Todd devotes some seventy pages to his time with the Airborne Forces and includes a graphic account of the period prior to, during and following D-Day. He mentions that, in the battle for Le Port, 'B' Company of the 7th Parachute Battalion was being troubled by a sniper located in the ancient church and that early in the day a Corporal Killeen had attacked the building with a PIAT and put paid to the sniper. I can only assume that this was a different event, and that at some later time our German machine-gunner was able to gain access to the church.

6 Gus Gardner was a quiet, modest and gentle character. Caring for his sick wife for many years after the War prevented him from revisiting Normandy, but when she died, shortly before the fiftieth anniversary, he was able at last to go and to take part in the reunion there. Later he visited me at the D-Day Museum at Shoreham Airport and gave me a magnificent set of photographs that he had taken of the simulated glider landings, despite the fact that he was almost blind. We had a long chat, after which I took him to the station and made sure he got on the right train. It was typical of him to give no hint of the fact that he was dying. Just a few weeks later I learned with great sorrow that he had died of cancer.

235

Chapter 5

1 Alf Whitford, who died in January, 1998, was one of those in Glider No. 4 who didn't get away and make it to Hérouvillette. Soon after landing he was hit in the leg and, unable to move, he was taken prisoner. His wounded leg troubled him for the rest of his life.

2 During my visit to Escoville in 1995 I noticed that the low wall behind which we had sheltered is now a higher wall, and the track down which the German infantry were advancing, until they were held up by Minns, is now a main road. Much of the wooded land to the immediate south, where the German SPs were located, has been cleared and is now the site of an estate of new houses.

3 Bob Ambrose, a survivor of 22 Platoon who was captured outside Escoville, gives an account of his life as a POW in Appendix 2.
John Lathbury, also of 22 Platoon, never got as far as Hérouvillette or Escoville. He was captured soon after Glider No. 4 landed off course near the River Dives. In captivity, John was forced to work in a German mine for the rest of the war, digging out a light-coloured powdery substance. His captors never told him what it was. At the end of 1997 I was informed that he had died from asbestosis.

4 Frank Minns, from Ashford in Middlesex, was, at thirty years old, a little older than most of us. He was one of the most unassuming and modest men you could meet, with the astonishing and unusual habit of saying 'please' when he told us to do anything. As well as liking him very much, I had reason to be grateful to Minns for his heroic action at Escoville which enabled our Section to escape the enemy infantry assault on the château. The bullet which was deflected by his bayonet scabbard and pierced his heart may have been a stray shot, or it may possibly have been fired by a sniper using the din of the bombardment to fire into our positions without giving away his position. We used the shorter type of bayonet known as "pig stickers", and the scabbard for this, together with an ammunition pouch, was carried on a web strap which went over the left shoulder. It was the scabbard that cost poor Minns his life.

5 Some of the naval guns of those times were much heavier than most field guns, and could throw shells weighing several tons. The Germans were so fearful of the devastating power of the big British naval guns that Rommel recommended to Hitler that the Panzers be pulled out of the line to allow the Allied bridgehead to expand. The Panzers would then be used in a decisive battle after an Allied advance from their bridgehead, when the naval guns would no longer be within range. Permission was refused. (ref. William Shires, *The Rise and Fall of the Third Reich*)

Chapter 6

1 As the reader will discern from what I have written, I have no love of fanatics of any description, and the Hitler Jugend youngsters were as fanatical as any of the German forces I came up against. However, it could be said in mitigation that membership of the movement was compulsory, and that draconian penalties were in force in Germany from 1939 onwards against parents who tried to find ways to avoid the indoctrination of their sons and daughters. If the kids became fanatics, and in many cases swaggering bullies as well, it is perhaps not so surprising.

2 The weapon we called a "Schmeisser" was properly an "MP-38", and the term Schmeisser is now said to have been applied in error, but as the name was used universally, it served to identify it well enough and I am happy to stick to it. Before Operation 'Paddle', the advance to the Seine, we received orders to hand in all captured enemy equipment. I handed in the Schmeisser, but was reluctant to part with the P38 pistol which was good insurance for me if I should ever be in a tight spot when out on patrol or sniping, and so I hung onto it, along with the Helios watch. These two items went back to England with me in September. See the chapter about the airborne landings in Germany for details of how I "lost" my P38.

3 This is an oddity for which the official explanation leaves some questions unanswered. Appendix 4 is an attempt to look at the matter a little more critically – and to speculate a little – about the cause of these oddities.

4 I did not record the name of the owner of the cider barrel trench at the time, but I remembered it later as being that of Private 'Col' Gardner. 'Col' was an eccentric upper class character, with a public school speaking voice, but who was without any wish or ambition to be identified with the officer class, or even to accept promotion. He preferred to serve as a private soldier, which he did until his death in Germany in March, 1945. He was nicknamed 'the Colonel', or 'Col' for short, because of his upper class background. 'The Colonel' and I later shared an interesting experience near the end of our Normandy expedition, which is mentioned in Chapter 9.

5 Wally was, and still is, a real London character. He was frequently reduced in rank from corporal to private when not in action, since he was always getting into scrapes of one sort or another. He was never cut out to be a 'spit and polish' conformist, but excelled as a fighting soldier. The pattern followed by his military career was to be promoted in battle and then reduced in rank at home.

6 It wasn't appreciated by us at the time, but is now usually understood that the battle for Caen was taking pressure off the Americans over on the western side of the Normandy bridgehead. This allowed them to take the port of Cherbourg by 3 July, a much-needed facility for supporting and enlarging the bridgehead. The Germans seemed more afraid of a breakout towards Falaise by the British, but when the German High Command realized that the

Americans were about to break out on the western side of the bridgehead, the two German divisions diverted from the Caen area were too little and too late.

7   One of my Perspex souvenirs is now displayed in the D-Day museum at Shoreham Airport, near Brighton in Sussex.

8   We had no idea what was happening at the time, but the enormous force of bombers which went over our positions flattened a huge area south of Caen, across which the British then attacked towards Falaise, with three armoured divisions. Unfortunately, the Germans had expected the attack, although they were surprised at the ferocity of the bombing. While the British were charging across the area devastated by the bombers, the Germans put down a heavy artillery barrage on top of them. The big German tanks, Tigers and Panthers, brought about a massacre of the British armour, knocking out at least 200 British tanks in a virtual turkey shoot. The British Shermans were very exposed and completely out-gunned, presenting easy targets for the Nazi tanks who wreaked havoc with deadly accurate long-range gunnery.

A week later a Canadian attacking force in the same area suffered a similar fate to that of the British, but despite these setbacks the pressure towards Falaise persisted and eventually paid off.

9   I can find no words to convey to the reader the sheer misery of being wet and cold in a waterlogged hole in the ground, soaked to the skin and with no immediate prospect of doing anything about it. The summer of 1944 was a poor one and the only consolation we had, and it wasn't much, was the knowledge that Jerry was probably as miserable as we were.

Chapter 7

1   Once the Germans had recovered from the initial shock of the invasion they did very well at delaying a breakout of the flood of Allied men and armour that came pouring in.

Away from the beaches, a large part of the Normandy bridgehead area was composed of hedgerows, small fields, lanes and villages. Snipers had no problem with such terrain – the ditches and hedgerows were virtually made-to-measure for them. Armour, however, was severely impeded, especially in the American-held areas and the Cherbourg peninsula. Although this was not good terrain for what the Germans did best – fast-moving armoured warfare – ironically their newer armoured vehicles, designed for 'Blitzkrieg' offensive warfare, proved to be perfect defensive weapons in this kind of country. They were impervious to much of the Allied anti-tank weaponry, and yet armed with very heavy and effective guns particularly the 88 mm weapon. The terrain did mean that they were often encountered at very close range, however, which made them vulnerable to infantry weapons such as the 'Bazooka'. This American weapon got the better of quite a number of Nazi tanks, but our roughly equivalent PIAT, as I have noted, was not effective against heavy tanks.

238

As any Allied advance was bound to be led by armour, it is not surprising that the Allied breakout was so long delayed, and that we Airborne forces were obliged to dig in and wait so long. The Nazi armour was eventually mastered only with considerable assistance from Allied tank-busting aircraft, such as the rocket-firing Typhoon.

2 It is strange, even to me, when I read what I noted at the time, that, given a short spell of inactivity, I thought life had become a bit humdrum. I do remember how awful it was to be continually bombarded while crouching in a wet trench, and I cannot imagine why I was complaining about boredom when the shelling stopped for a while!

3 Our airborne forces having helped secure a bridgehead, our continuing task was always simply to protect the left flank of the British forces and we were not expected to play a role in breaking out of the bridgehead, nor were we equipped to do so.

With the fall of Caen the Germans had moved some of their Panzer forces from the Caen area to oppose the American forces in and around the Cherbourg peninsula, but this could not prevent the German line being split by the Americans on 25 July. The British and Canadian forces were able to take advantage of the weakened defences around Caen and pushed south towards Falaise, as noted elsewhere in this narrative. As the Americans moved forward they became free to wheel eastwards or westwards or both. A thrust to the east threatened to come up and around to encircle the more easterly German static positions. This did in fact almost happen, at Falaise, where a British and Canadian thrust from the Caen area formed a pincer with American forces advancing northwards from Le Mans. This just missed catching a large German force, but it managed to extricate itself just in time by withdrawing eastwards through the 'Falaise gap'.

Nonetheless, the German position was now inevitably one of strategic withdrawal to regain a defensible position beyond the Seine, which meant that we could at last leave our trenches and start moving forward.

Chapter 9

1 Until his accident, Major John Howard had enjoyed a brilliantly successful army career and is rightfully credited with being a key factor in the successful capture of the bridges in Normandy. In my opinion, this accident cost the Army a brilliant future general.

2 Why this name should have been applied to this particular battle is an oddity, since the term was used by Winston Churchill to describe a battle which never really occurred, but which he had expected to occur in the Ardennes in 1940, just before the fall of France. Simply because the location was identical to that of the 1940 event, and not because of any protrusion in the Allied lines as is popularly thought, the name was re-applied.

3 In the American film *The Battle of the Bulge* there appeared to be little snow

on the ground for most of the time. My memory is that we were perpetually knee-deep in the stuff. It was the coldest winter that I could ever remember.

Chapter 10

1 I believed for years that it was a German shell that exploded over my head and put me out of action. 'Nobby' Clark's account of this period (See Appendix 3) suggests that it was a badly ranged Allied shell, not German, which brought about my concussion and the ensuing events.
2 Our Airborne generals were always in the thick of the action and they would always conduct their battles from the front line. They carried Sten guns and were ready for instant action – just like the rest of us.
3 Of course, for those pitiful people, a bar of coarse soap may have been a prized possession, and the gesture of offering it to me may have been a gesture of gratitude. The soap has been passed to a friend who is researching the Holocaust. Hopefully, with the progress of modern technology, it may be possible to establish whether it is of human origin.

INDEX

244